What Others Have Said About
Sound the Trumpet: How to Blow Your Own Horn

"I have played the trumpet, as an enthusiastic, largely self-taught amateur, for many years and own a whole variety of trumpet tutor books; most are incredibly daunting, immediately too demanding and are, all-in-all, not much fun!

"This book is quite different—it has a very attractive, friendly approach, is extremely well presented, deals with all the basics and more and has plenty of tips and simple, attractive 'how to do,' and 'how to approach' ideas. The book is thorough and covers all the basic techniques of playing and the usual pitfalls and problems, but in an attractive, friendly way. There are also further sources of study and music, suggested practice routines and charts etc. and even instructions on how to correctly clean and maintain the instrument!

"This book will be useful to both the beginner and the more experienced player, is excellent value, and I give it my highest recommendation, but do so wish that it had been in print 30 years ago!!"

— David Hutchins, Sevenoaks, Kent, UK

"This book is the most thorough treatment of the various aspects of trumpet playing that I have seen. Very informative and helpful. Even my current teacher, who has played with the Metropolitan Opera (NYC), was impressed.

— Don Young, Cranford, NJ

This is an absolutely fantastic book. I just started to learn to play the trumpet, and this book is part of the fun. You can learn about tricks, what music to get in order to listen, techniques, notes, etc. I use it when I am not playing and it keeps me interested. Every trumpet should be sold with this book. This is like a user's manual. You will also learn about troubleshooting, maintenance and cleaning. With this book you will not feel lost and will be prepared for your 1st classes.

— J. R. Torres, Rhode Island

"My sincere thanks and heartfelt admiration for what you have done in *Sound the Trumpet: How to Blow Your Own Horn*. Truly a marvel. I've never before seen so much good musical knowledge in one place. Wow!"

— Kent Larabee, Silverdale, WA

No question about it, this book is everything it's cracked up to be! I highly recommend the book for any player, young or old, beginner or in my case, a 35 year comeback player.

— Joe Kaye, Philadelphia, PA

"The book contains a wide range of useful information for the aspiring trumpet player, and the visuals are especially attractive and helpful. I look forward to buying a copy when they come available."

— Professor Chris Schmaltz, Southwestern College

"I have found your books to be very helpful. I recently started to play the trumpet and your books along with lessons are exactly what I was looking for. Thank you very much."

— David Hoover

Jonathan Harnum has played trumpet for over 25 years in various genres, has taught music at all levels both privately and in public schools for over 15 years and is currently a Ph.D. candidate in music education at Northwestern University. He is the author of *Basic Music Theory: How to Read, Write, and Understand Written Music; Basic Jazz Theory;* and *All About Trumpet.* Harnum is currently focused on research in music practice in preparation for his degree and his next book, *The Practice of Practice.* He and his wife Michelle live in the Chicago area with their dog Skwirl.

Sound the Trumpet

How to Blow Your Own Horn

This book is dedicated to my teachers and
to my students, who are also my teachers.
Thank You!

And Special Thanks to: My wonderful Michelle, Doris and Russ Riemann, my students and
their parents, and Hank and Ana Hartman at Matanuska Music in Wasilla, Alaska. Also a
thank you to Prad who helped proofread the early version of this book.

Sound the Trumpet: *How to Blow Your Own Horn, 2nd edition*

Published by Sol-Ut Press
www.sol-ut.com

Sol-Ut and the Sol-Ut logo are trademarks of Sol-Ut Press. Send E-mails regarding this book to sol.ut.press@gmail.com

ISBN: 1450590187

EAN13: 9781450590181

For general information about this book including supplemental materials, or to learn more about Sol-Ut Press, visit our web site at www.sol-ut.com.

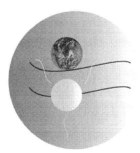

SolŪt Press

Musician-friendly Resources.
www.Sol-Ut.com

Sound The Trumpet

How to Blow Your Own Horn

Table of Contents

Chapter 0: The Chapter Everyone Skips 1

Welcome to *Sound the Trumpet*! 1
Why *Sound the Trumpet?* 1
Overview of *Sound the Trumpet* 2
Sound the Trumpet: Overview 3
Up Next 8

Part I

Chapter 1: War and Worship: A Brief History of the Trumpet 11

Just the Facts 12
Trumpets of Now and the Future 14
Innovations and Expectations 15
Up Next 16

Chapter 2: Listen! 17

Why Listen? 17
Some Listening Tips 17
Classical Trumpet Music 18
Jazz 21
Notes From the Edge: Avant Garde 28
Watch and Learn: Trumpeters on Video 29
Listen to other Artists 30
Up Next 30

Chapter 3: How to Create a Buzz 31

What's an Embouchure? 31
Dry Embouchure vs. Wet Embouchure 32
What The Buzz is About 32
But First, a Word From Your Sponsor: Air 34
Buzz with the Mouthpiece 34
Buzzing Exercises for Strong Lips 36
Sources for Further Study 39
Up Next 39
Mouthpiece Anatomy 101 40
Of Throats and Cups and Shoulders 40
What to Look for in a Mouthpiece 41
7C, 3D, B2? What Does it Mean!? 42

Chapter 4: Doin' the Mess Around 43

Forget the Details and Just Go For It! 43
The Details 43
Hold It! 44
Posture 45
The Alexander Technique 47
Go For It! 47
Exercises to Get You On Your Way 48
Up Next 48

Chapter 5: Fast Fingers 49

Finger Technique? 49
The Right Hand 49
The Left Hand 50
Exercises For Accuracy and Speed 51
What's Up Next 52

Chapter 6: Avoiding Bad Breath 53

Why Learn to Breathe? 53
The Physiology of Breathing 53
The Correct Breath 54
The Breathing Tube 56
Some Breathing Exercises 56
When to Breathe 57
When You Have Too Much Air 58
Using Gadgetry to Help You Breathe 58
An Encouraging Word 59
Resources for Further Study 60
Up Next 60

Interlude: The Practice of Practice 61

Don't Say the P Word 61
Come on Baby, Light my Desire 63
How to Get Better 63
Start a New Habit 64
Where to Do It 65
How to Do It 66
The Ideal Practice Session 67
Other Ways to Play 70
Trumpet is Just the Beginning 71
The Practice Session Details 71
Mistakes and How to Deal With Them 74
Practice Awareness 74
Sources for Further Study 75
More Better Practice Advice 75
Up Next 75

Part II

Chapter 7: Taking Notes 79

Warning! Take Your Time 79
An Ultra-Brief Intro to Written Music 79
You Got Rhythm! 81
The Rests of the Story 81
C and G: Your First Notes 82
More Notes: D, E and F 83
Reading the Music 85
Simple Duets 87
More Notes! 88
Playing Higher: Notes Above G 88
Up Next 89

Chapter 8: Tongue Tips for Trumpet 91

Use My Tongue for What? 91
Basic Tonguing 91
The Tongue's Role in Playing High and Low . . . 94
Tongue Placement: Low, Middle, High 95
Tongue Use in Lip Slurs 95
The Oral Cavity's Role in Your Tone Quality . . . 95
Double and Triple Tonguing 95
Multiple Tonguing While Changing Notes 99

Sources for Further Study 100
Listening Examples of Multiple Tonguing 100
Up Next 100

Chapter 9: Lip Slurs & the Oral Cavity 101

What is a Lip Slur?. 101
Lip Slurs and Physics: Downhill is Easier 102
Lip Slurs: Going Up!. 104
Large Interval Lip Slurs 105
Further Study 106
Up Next 106

Chapter 10: Simple Tunes 107

Some Simple Songs 107
Eighth Notes. 109
Duets 111
Just a Taste 112
More Notes! Eb and Ab 112
Some Minor Ditties 114
A Challenge 115
Up Next 116

Chapter 11: Trumpet Tuning Tips 117

What's Tuning All About?. 117
Basic Trumpet Tuning. 117
Tuning The Whole Trumpet 118
Out of Tune Notes on Trumpet 120
Changing the Pitch Without a Slide. 122
Tuning Without a Tuner 122
Up Next 124

Chapter 12: How Low Can You Go? Pedal Tones 125

Put the Pedal to the Metal 125
Pedal Tone Exercises. 126
Lower Your Standard: Double Pedal Tones 127
Sources for Further Study 128
Up Next 128

Chapter 13: Home on the High Range 129

What is the High Range? 129
Don't Get Hung Up on High Range 130
Beware of Lip Injury!. 130
A Brief Word on Special Range Techniques. . . . 131

The Loose-Lip Flap 131
Can You Say "Oo-Ee?" 131
The Lip Buzz 131
The Pencil Exercise 133
Lip Failure Study 134
Pianissimo Playing for Range 136
Three Pianissimo Exercises 138
The 2 Octave Scale Exercise 139
Scheduling Your Range Workout 140
A Final Word on High Range 141
Resources for Further Study 141
Up Next 141

Chapter 14: Endurance 143

How to Endure 143
Why Resting and Endurance Are Best Friends . . 143
Memorize 144
Long Tones 144
Ways to Save Your Chops 148
Sources for Further Study 150
A Final Word About Endurance 150
Up Next 150

Interlude: Clean up Your Axe 151

Why Clean My Trumpet? 151
Routine Cleaning 152
Trouble-Shooting 154
The Monthly Overhaul 154
Cleaning Supplies 156
Up Next 157
Clean Trumpet Jokes 158

Part III

Chapter 15: Trumpet Sound Effects 161

Make Your Trumpet Talk 161
The Vibrato 161
Alternate Fingerings 165
Scoops, Doits, Falls, and the Horse Whinny 167
The Growl and Flutter-Tonguing 170
Ornaments Aren't Just for Christmas 171
The Best Sources for Learning Cool Sounds 173
Up Next 173

Chapter 16: Mutes & Dampfers & Plungers, Oh My! 175

What is a Mute? 175
The Practice Mute or the Whisper Mute 176
The Straight Mute 177
The Wah-wah, or Harmon Mute 177
The Cup Mute 178
The Plunger 178
The Bucket Mute 179
Other Mutes 180
Mute Holders 180
Up Next 180

Chapter 17: So Many Trumpets, So Little Time 181

A Trumpet for Every Occasion 181
Cornet 181
Flügelhorn 182
The C Trumpet 182
The Eb/D Trumpets 183
The Piccolo Trumpet 183
The Pocket Trumpet 183
Rotary Valve Trumpet 183
Heraldic Trumpets 184
A Trumpet You Can't Have: The Firebird 184
If It's Got Valves, You Can (probably) Play It . . . 185
Natural Trumpets 186
Up Next 186

Chapter 18: The Transposing Trumpeter 187

Trumpet is a Bb Instrument 187
The C Transposition 188
The Other Transpositions (Eb, F, Ab, etc.) 190
The Order of Flats 191
The Order of Sharps 191
Transposing in Foreign Languages 196
How to Practice Transpositions 196
Sources for Further Study 196
What's Up Next 196

Chapter 19: Trumpet Music 197

Un-Boggling Your Mind 197
Essential Method Books 198
Essential Etude Books 200
Essential Jazz Standards 200
Jazz Trumpet Solo Transcriptions 202
Classical Solo and Small Group Repertoire 204
Symphony Excerpts 207
Books! 209
Up Next 210

Chapter 20: Gear to Grind Through 211

Why Do I Need More Stuff? 211
Metronome: Your Rhythmic Best Friend 211
Tuners for In-tune Tunes 213
Microphones 214
Recording Devices 215
Cases 216
Electronic Effects 217
Up Next 218

Chapter 21: The Practice of Performance 219

Why Perform? 219
Performance Anxiety 220
There is No Such Thing as a Wrong Note 223
How to Prepare for a Performance 224
Stage Craft 101 224
Find Performance Venues 226
Sources for Further Study 227
Up Next 229

Chapter 22: Trumpet All-Stars 229

The Best of the Best 229
The Cornet Masters of Band Music 229
Orchestral Trumpet Masters 230
Classical Soloists 232
Jazz Trumpet Masters 233
Just a Few of the Best 237
Up Next 237

Postlude: How Do You Didgeridoo? 239

How Do You Do, Didgeridoo? 239
Play Didj to Enhance Your Trumpet Skills 240
How to Do Didgeridoo 241
Circular Breathing 242
Harmonics 244
Vocalizations 245
Inventing Rhythms 245
Finding a Didgeridoo 245
Sources for Further Study 246
Up Next 246

Codicil

Supplement: How to Find a Trumpet for Your Very Own 249

Consider Renting or Leasing 249
Where to Look 249
What to Look For 250
The Last Word 251

Index 253

Trumpet Fingering Charts 259

Standard Fingering Chart 259
Alternate Fingering Chart 260

Piano Keyboard 261

Piano Keyboard (in concert pitch) 261
Piano Keyboard (with trumpet pitches) 262

THE CHAPTER EVERYONE SKIPS

Say all you have to say in the fewest possible words, or your reader will be sure to skip them; and in the plainest possible words or you will certainly be misunderstood.

~ John Ruskin (1819-1900)

In This Chapter

- Why *Sound the Trumpet*?
- Book Overview
- Chapter Overview
- How to use the book

Terms to Know

This section: There aren't any special terms to know in this section, but in the following chapters, any tricky terms or weird words will be explained here first.

Welcome to Sound the Trumpet!

Hi, and welcome to the fun-filled world of playing trumpet! If you're new to trumpet playing, this book will get you started and instill good learning habits. If you already play or are a teacher, this book may give you new insight and information. The goal of this book is to help you along in your journey toward mastery of the trumpet and to give you the necessary resources to achieve your goals. Once you've absorbed this book, you'll have a great foundation from which to build a lifetime of playing music on your trumpet.

Why Sound the Trumpet?

Starting anything new can be difficult, confusing, and sometimes even a little scary. When that something new is learning an instrument, you can throw in bewildering and frustrating as well. But if you're armed with the right attitude and some knowledge, new things are also exciting, challenging and rewarding. *Sound the Trumpet* aims to help you find the right attitude and contains the information you need to have a great time and succeed.

This book will help ease you into the world of playing trumpet with the knowledge and tricks I've learned from over 25 years of playing and 15 years of teaching. You'll start with the most basic ideas and build on them until you've learned about the trumpet from end-to-end, inside and out.

If you're already a player, this book is a great resource for things you already know, and maybe some things you don't. Use it as a reference to review your skills, to beef up your CD collection, to study for an audition, or to practice your scales.

All that being said, you still should use this book in conjunction with all other trumpet books you can lay your hands on. Get information from any source you can find and don't limit yourself to one source. Though this book is pretty comprehensive, it doesn't cover *everything*, and even if it did, you'll benefit from getting the same information from a different source using a different approach. Be a learning sponge.

Overview of Sound the Trumpet

General Information

Sound the Trumpet will take you through all the basics of trumpet, from its history, to recorded trumpet music, and of course, how to actually play the thing. All this information is shown to you in small doses so you won't feel overwhelmed by all that needs to be learned. Chapters are short and easy to get through, though mastering the information they contain will usually continue long after the chapter has been read.

That's a good thing. This book is meant to be a reference, which means you *will* come back to it again and again on your journey towards trumpet Mastery. Reading the book one time through will certainly increase your understanding, but you'll have to spend some serious time with these concepts to make them truly stick and become a part of your musicianship. Come back to the book from time to time for a review.

Sound the Trumpet deals with specific aspects of playing the trumpet and not much time is spent on the skills of reading music. Basic concepts will be explained, but for more specific information on reading music, check out *Basic Music Theory: How to Read, Write, and Understand Written Music*. You can find it at http://www.QuestionsInk.com (including free samples of the book), ask for it at your local music or book store, or find it at Barnes & Noble or Borders Books and Music.

The Structure of the Book

The Parts

Sound the Trumpet is divided into large sections called Parts. Within each Part are several chapters of related information.

The Chapters

Chapters contain information on one technique and they're short enough to take in without feeling overwhelmed. There are anywhere from six to eight chapters per Part. At the beginning of each chapter you'll see a brief overview of the chapter and a list of terms the chapter covers.

The Interludes

Interludes come between Parts and cover information that isn't directly related to playing trumpet, but is essential to becoming a well-rounded player. The first Interlude is about how to practice and the other is about cleaning your horn. Fun and necessary stuff!

The Icons

Icons in this book will alert you to things you should know as a trumpet player. Here they are:

Memory Tip

This icon is placed near methods used to improve your memory of terms, notes, and other fun stuff. These little memory tricks will save you some brain strain.

Notice!

This icon is placed near information that is particularly useful to know. Heed this information and you'll avoid common mistakes.

Theory Geek

This icon has two functions: it tells you things about reading music which are helpful, and is also next to information which isn't absolutely necessary but which you might find interesting.

The Appendix

This is an appendix that will never need to be removed surgically. In the back of the book you'll find fingering charts, scales of many types, a glossary of musical terms, lists of great trumpet and related web sites, an index to find things easily in this book, blank staff paper, blank practice journals and practice sheets, a piano keyboard to help you understand some music theory concepts like intervals and transposing, and information about how to find a trumpet for your very own.

Sound the Trumpet: Overview

Part I: The Bare Necessities

Chapter 0: The Chapter Everyone Skips

You're reading it. Information of a general sort to get you started on the right foot; or the left foot, if you're goofy-footed.

Chapter 1: A Brief History of Trumpet

From ancient Egypt and Australia, to middle ages Krakow, to the Himalayan mountains, to Europe, all in a few short pages. In this chapter you'll hear about the origins of the trumpet and the evolution of its physical form.

Chapter 2: Listen!

This chapter is before any information about exactly how to play the trumpet because you don't need any special skills to push *play* on your CD player, MP3 player, radio, or whatever you use to listen to music. And it's important that you start listening to trumpet music as early as possible because it will help you understand how the horn can sound. This is a large and incomplete list of many of the best recordings around.

Chapter 3: Creating a Buzz

In this chapter you'll learn a bit about the parts of a trumpet, then get started making sounds to use with the horn. You'll learn about the embouchure (how to form your lips for playing), the mouthpiece, the lip buzz, lip buzz drills, and mouthpiece buzz drills. Also included is important information about mouthpieces.

Chapter 4: Doin' the Mess Around

Finally we get down to actually playing the trumpet. This chapter gets you started and shows you how to hold it, what the valves do, and some basic exercises to get you on your way. Fun stuff!

Chapter 5: Fast Fingers

It's time to start training the three fingers of your right hand. In this chapter you'll find the details about fingering and how to make it cleaner, faster and more rhythmic. Also in the chapter are exercises to help you get your fingers limber and coordinated.

Chapter 6: Avoiding Bad Breath

We're not talking halitosis here. One of the most important aspects of playing a wind instrument is breathing. Learn the basics of what taking a good breath is all about in this chapter as well as exercises to increase your awareness of breathing and to increase your lung capacity.

Interlude One: The Practice of Practice

It takes steady and persistent effort to get better at anything, and playing trumpet is no different. There are ways to make this progress more enjoyable and more rapid. In this chapter you'll find suggestions about how to practice which will help you become a better player as quickly as possible. Though there are as many ways to practice as there are players, there are certain things the best players do which will help you, too. Learn about them here.

Part II: Getting Into It

Chapter 7: Taking Notes

Once you've got a good solid tone on trumpet, you'll start to be more specific about what you're playing. This chapter introduces how trumpet notes look when written down. In this chapter you'll learn fingerings for five notes, complete with, of course, more exercises and some duets. Be sure to visit the web site companion to this book. You'll find sound clips of all the exercises and duet parts to play along with. If you'd like a CD with these exercises and duets, it's also available on the web site (www.sol-ut.com).

Chapter 8: Tongue Tips for Trumpet

The tongue is an essential part of playing every wind instrument. Tonguing separates notes, the tongue can help you play higher, and different uses of the tongue can give your sound new textures. Start learning how to use your tongue correctly in this chapter.

Chapter 9: Lip Slurs and the Oral Cavity

No, this oral cavity won't require a visit to the dentist. When you change from one note to another without tonguing and each note has the same fingering, you're playing a lip slur. Lips slurs increase your flexibility and dexterity on the horn. The size and shape of the space inside your mouth (oral cavity) can make this challenging skill much easier. Learn how to do it and get some exercises to practice.

Chapter 10: Simple Tunes

Now that you've got a handle (Handel?) on the basics of playing trumpet, you can get started with some simple songs. These are tunes most of us know and are low in the trumpet range. Fun stuff! Also included are some duets to play with another trumpet player or other B♭ instrument, and a very cool Gypsy jazz tune, Dark Eyes.

Chapter 11: Tuning Tips for Trumpet

Because of how trumpets are made, certain notes are out of tune. When at extremes of your range, either high or low, the horn will also tend to go out of tune. Temperature and how warm your horn is will also affect the pitch of the horn as will how loud you play and any mutes you stick in the bell. Learn about all the things that make trumpet go out of tune and, most importantly, how to prevent and correct these problems.

Chapter 12: How Low Can You Go? Pedal Tones

The trumpet can make sounds way below the actual lowest note on the horn (a low F#). These ultra-low notes are called pedal tones and are great to do as a warm-up. Pedal tones are useful because they get your chops loose and relaxed, they require a lot of air and they train your ears because notes way down there don't "lock in" like notes within the normal range of trumpet. Learn all about pedal tones in this chapter.

Chapter 13: Home on the High Range

Playing a brass instrument, and especially trumpet, is a physically demanding endeavor. Good breath support is the prime source of high range, but it also takes strength in lip and other muscles, and correct posture. There are specific exercises and attitudes that will help you develop high notes on the trumpet, and these will allow you to play with more presence, more loudly and of course, higher. If that wasn't enough, these exercises will also allow you to play more quietly.

Chapter 14: Endurance

Playing a long performance can be a grueling affair both for your chops and your brain. Training for such a thing is important and your strength and endurance can be increased by paying attention to certain exercises in your practice schedule and by using specific techniques while playing. Learn how to increase your endurance in this chapter.

Interlude Two: Clean Up Your Axe

Many strange things can and will grow inside your trumpet if you don't clean it. Learn how to scrub it out without hurting the horn in this chapter. Included are a list of supplies you'll need and a blow-by-blow description of taking your instrument apart and putting it back together the right way without damaging the instrument.

Part III:

Chapter 15: Trumpet Sound Effects

The trumpet is capable of a whole range of sounds in addition to regular notes. You can make the trumpet speak by incorporating these techniques into your playing. In addition to the items listed in the chapter title, learn about vibrato, lip trills, flutter tonguing, doits, falls, turns, mordents, and the use of alternate fingerings.

Chapter 16: Mutes and Dampfers and Plungers, Oh My!

There is a bewildering array of things you can (and will) stick in the end of your trumpet to change its sound. In English they're called *mutes*, but are called *sordinos* in Italian, *dampfers* in German and *sourdines* in French. In this chapter you'll learn about all the mutes and why the plunger isn't just for bathrooms anymore.

Chapter 17: The Transposing Trumpeter

n a perfect world, all written notes would have the same relative pitch, but it just doesn't work that way. If you want to play orchestral trumpet music, you must be able to transpose. To transpose, you play a different note than what is written on the page. What must you do to read and play music to be transposed? If you don't know, this chapter will help you understand.

Chapter 18: Trumpet Repertoire

Repertoire is the music that is recognized as crucial to a player's vocabulary. There is so much material out there that it's nearly impossible for one person to get to all of it. Here's where you'll start making choices about what you want to play. Even if you know you want to play jazz or are sure that classical music is for you, or know that you will be the next big country music trumpet star, you should familiarize yourself with the standard repertoire for each style, because certain techniques will cross over into the other style. If you want to get paid to play trumpet, learning all styles is almost mandatory. Studio musicians do it. So can you.

Chapter 19: Gear to Grind Through

What is a condenser microphone and should I mic my trumpet with one? How *do* you mic a trumpet? How do you play with a mic when the mute is in? What is MIDI? What kind of stuff do I need if I want to play with a band that doesn't have extra sound equipment for me? What kind of options for recording equipment do I have so I can listen to myself? All these questions and more will be answered in this chapter.

Chapter 20: Performance Time!

This is the gravy, the frosting, the reward. It's the reason most of us buzz our lips into this brass tubing so often. Performing can be fun and frightening and incredibly rewarding all at the same time. Find out how to prepare for performances, what to expect when you perform, how to deal with performance anxiety, where to find opportunities to play and how to make opportunities to play.

Chapter 21: Trumpet All-Stars

In this chapter you will learn about some of the greatest trumpet players, both now and in the past and in many different styles. This list of trumpet greats is far from complete. I have included only players who have made some significant contribution to trumpet playing, to music in general, or to the betterment of our world.

Postlude: How Do You Didgeridoo

Want to learn how to play the oldest trumpet on the planet? Didgeridoo is an Australian instrument made from a termite-hollowed eucalyptus tree limb. If you think that's weird, wait till you hear it. The didgeridoo produces a bass drone and with the right rhythm, the sound can be truly hypnotic and primal-sounding. Playing didgeridoo will even help you to play trumpet better. In this chapter find out just what the didgeridoo is, how to play it, and how to develop the skill of circular breathing.

Codicils

Book Index

Look up a topic you're interested in. If it's in the book, the subject and page number will be listed here.

Fingering Chart

Find all the fingerings up to high E as well as alternate fingering.

Piano Keyboard

The piano is the best instrument there is for understanding many musical concepts from intervals to chords and beyond. That's why you'll find a paper piano keyboard in the back of the book. Included are the regular notes of the piano keyboard and also the names for trumpet notes.

Book Extras

To save paper and printing costs and to make the book more affordable, I've put many of the extra items from the first edition on the Sol Ut Press web site, where you can download them for free! In addition, there are *lots* of links to more information: videos, web sites, images, mp3s and more. Check out the books's site at www.AllAboutTrumpet.com/ST or go to www.sol-ut.com.

Up Next

Whew! Lots of information, but it's a great idea to have in mind what you're getting into. Hope you read the chapter and it wasn't too long-winded for you.

Next up is a chapter about the origins and history of the trumpet. You might be surprised how old the instrument is.

PART I
THE BARE NECESSITIES

WHAT YOU'LL LEARN IN THIS PART

- A Brief History of the Trumpet
- The Best Trumpet Recordings
- Making a Sound on Trumpet
- The Buzz
- Mouthpiece Information
- Beginning Exercises for Lips
- Finger Exercises
- How to Breathe
- Interlude: How to Practice

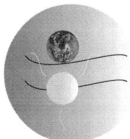

SolUt Press

Musician-friendly Resources.
www.Sol-Ut.com

CHAPTER 1

WAR AND WORSHIP: A BRIEF HISTORY OF THE TRUMPET

History doesn't repeat itself, but it does rhyme.

~ Mark Twain

In This Chapter

- Origins of the Trumpet
- Oldest Known Trumpet
- Uses of the Trumpet
- Trumpets Today
- Trumpets Tomorrow

Terms to Know

crook: a length of tubing used to change the pitch of a brass instrument lower or higher.

harmonic series: a series of notes which a valveless trumpet can play. Large distance between pitches in the low in the range, small distance between the high pitches.

natural trumpet: a valveless, keyless trumpet.

keyed trumpet: a trumpet with 1 to 12 keys like a saxophone.

In the mid 1300s in Krakow, Poland a man climbs a high church tower, its stone steps cold from the chill morning. He clutches a trumpet to his chest, keeping it warm. This morning he'll play the *Hejnal*, also known as the *Hymn to the Lady*, from the top of the high church tower. It is the only song he knows well. He's been practicing it for months.

Just over the hills to the east the Mongol horde rides toward Krakow, thirsty for pillage and plunder. The trumpeter climbs the stairs, oblivious, whistling the tune he is about to play.

He climbs to the top of the tower, steps to a tiny stone balcony, waits a few moments, then lifts his horn to his lips when the sun flares at the horizon. He brings the horn up, takes a deep breath, and plays. The *Hymn to the Lady* springs forth loud and powerful. The song is to be played four times, once to each of the four directions. He finishes the fourth repetition and is pleased with himself for not making any mistakes. He turns to go back down the dark stairwell. A glint on the eastern horizon catches his eye.

He turns eastward and shades his eyes as he peers into the bright sunrise. Are those riders? And so many? For a second, he can't believe what he is seeing. He's heard talk of some trouble southeast of his village, a long way off. Could these be the same raiders? Here, and so soon? He stands frozen, his horn dangles limply from his hand. He gives a quick shake of his head in disbelief, looks one more time at the cloud of dust on the horizon and lifts his horn to his lips again.

He hasn't yet learned the songs for alarm, fire, or attack. The *Hymn to the Virgin* is the only arrow in his musical quiver. He points the bell of his horn toward the center of Krackow and blasts as loud as he can. The fifth time he plays the song, it's faster, even louder, and with much urgency. It wasn't until the seventh or eighth repetition that people in the village suspect something is awry. On the fourteenth repetition the call suddenly stops mid-note.

Back at the tower, the young man's lips had begun to get sore after the seventh repetition, and now, after thirteen repetitions, his lips feel like ground mutton: pink, soft and painful. *But thirteen is an unlucky number*, he thinks. *Maybe one last repetition before I head for cover.* He lifts the horn and blows one last time.

Below him on the ground a small man on a large horse fits an arrow to his bow, draws back the feathers to his ear and lets the arrow fly. The warning trumpet blast cuts off abruptly and the young man falls into the dark stairwell. But the archer was too late. The brave trumpeter's calls had saved many lives and most of the city. Today, in honor of the trumpet player's sacrifice, the same Hymn to the Virgin is sounded from the same church tower and is stopped mid-song, just where it stopped that day over 700 years ago.

Just the Facts

Though I've taken some liberties with story above, the trumpet player of Krackow embodied two of the oldest uses for trumpet: war and worship. Because of their loud volume and the ability to carry messages over long distances, trumpets have been associated with war as far back as we can remember. And for perhaps the same reasons, trumpets also have been used in worship.

Ancient trumpets are simple elongated tubes of bone or metal often with a flared bell at the end. The didgeridoo, an ancient Australian trumpet still in use today, often has no bell (for more on didgeridoo, see "How Do You Do, didgeridoo?" on page 249). Some trumpets have gentle curves in them, like the Alp horn, cornettos, and the shofar, a trumpet made from a ram's horn that is one of the earliest instruments used in the Jewish faith, especially during Rosh Hashanah.

To the right is a picture of John Kenny playing the carnyx, an ancient Celtic trumpet made of bronze with a 5 octave range (that's a lot!). It has a boar's head at the top and was used from around 200 BCE. It could be heard when the Romans invaded the British Isles and the carnyx has been depicted in art as far away as India.

John Kenny playing the Carnyx. Find great links about this instrument and all these others, too, at www.sol-ut.com.

In Tibet a type of trumpet used for worship is the *dung*, a trumpet almost fifteen feet long. It's used in ceremonies and its sound is meant to scare off evil spirits. I don't know about you, but a 15 foot dung would probably scare me.

In the ancient Olympic Games there was a trumpet competition as well as the athletic competitions, and it's likely the competitors played naked, just like the athletes did. In Rome, Tibet and Israel, the trumpet was considered so sacred that only priests were allowed to play or touch them.

The oldest trumpet we know of that is still in existence was played in 1353 BC. It was found in King Tut's tomb. It's 120 cm long (about 2 feet) and is a conical tube which flares to a 26cm diameter bell (about 10 inches). If you want to hear how this ancient thing sounds, check out this chapter's links at www.sol-ut.com. As you can see, trumpets didn't always have valves. For thousands of years they were simple straight tubes with a bell at the end. The tube could be made from wood, metal, cane, anything tubular (radical and gnarly tubes were discovered later). Cornettos (also known as the *cornett*, or the *zink*) are trumpets made of wood and they have little similarity with the modern cornet as the name suggests. You can find examples of cornetto instruments and links to videos on the Sol Ut Pres web site (www.sol-ut.com).

The *serpent* in the following example is the bass (not the fish, but the lowest voiced) instrument in the cornetto family. Invented in 1590 by Frenchman Edme Guillaume, the serpent is one of the oldest instruments still in use today. For a *fantastic* example of the instrument being played in the Michele Godard Trio, check out the video at http://bit.ly/ayVZCG.

It wasn't until the 1300s that someone thought to bend the straight trumpet into loops. The result was a trumpet about twice as long as the modern one, which we now call *natural trumpets*. They were easier to hold than the long cumbersome straight trumpets which they quickly replaced. Natural trumpets are similar to the modern bugle, being just a simple length of tubing wrapped around itself a few times with a mouthpiece at one end and a bell at the other.

symphony trombonist Doug Yeo with a serpent. Hear Mr. Yeo play at *http://www.yeodoug.com/articles/serpent/serpent.html*

Example 1.1 Parts of the natural trumpet.

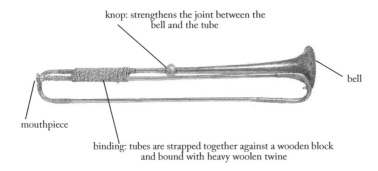

knop: strengthens the joint between the bell and the tube

bell

mouthpiece

binding: tubes are strapped together against a wooden block and bound with heavy woolen twine

Around the middle of the 1700s holes were added at critical points in the tubing. These holes allowed the performer to tune out-of-tune notes. Trumpets without valves of some kind are limited to certain notes in the harmonic series, also known as the overtone series. The harmonic series is a naturally occurring phenomenon in music. The same ratios of the harmonic series can be seen in the physical world. It is another expression of the Golden Mean, a fascinating subject worthy of a book all its own. The harmonic series is a fairly complicated idea. All you need to know about the harmonic series for our purposes is that between low notes, there are big differences in pitch. For instance, the first two notes of the harmonic series are an octave (8 diatonic notes) apart. As you go higher in pitch in the harmonic series, the pitches are closer together. You can see this in the musical notation of the harmonic series above. See the big gap between the first two notes? A natural trumpet can't play the notes within the gaps at the low end of the harmonic series.

The first three octaves of the harmonic series.

Keyed trumpets solved that problem a little bit. Keyed trumpets appeared in the late 1700s, though their creation is somehow credited to Anton Weidinger of Vienna, in 1801. Keyed trumpets had anywhere from 4 to 6 keys much like saxophones keys, though smaller. These keys allowed the instrument to play other notes in the harmonic series. Later, around 1810 the keyed bugle came into use, and it could have as many as 12 keys.

1845 Graves keyed bugle (with a crook by the mouthpiece) restored by Robb Stewart. See more of Robb's work at wwwvintagecornets.com

Natural trumpets and keyed trumpets are limited to one tone center because they are a fixed length. The length and diameter of tubing determines the pitch, so the only way to shorten or lengthen your instrument was to insert longer or shorter piece of tubing (a *crook*) to get a different starting note, or tonal center.

The valve changed all that. Invented in the early 1800s, the valve was a revolution in trumpet design. It was a system that improved upon the crook idea without doing away with crooks. All the crooks were on the horn already, and the valve simply directed the air into the crook of the right length.

Take a look at your horn and/or the diagram on the next page. Trace the direction of air flow with your finger for these valve combinations. Open (no valves pressed): the air goes directly through the valves and out the bell. Second valve: the air takes a detour through the shortest slide on the trumpet, the second valve slide, then out the bell. First valve: the air takes a detour through the second longest slide on trumpet, the first valve slide, then out the bell. Third valve: sends the air through the longest slide on the trumpet, the third valve slide, then out the bell. Combinations of two or three valves will send the air through two or three slides, then out the bell. Pretty ingenious, no? There are seven valve combinations. Can you figure them all out?

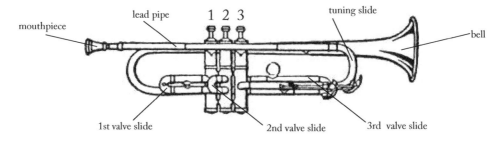

If you can get a good tone on your horn, experiment with your valves to find the relationship between the valve and the sound. For more information about getting a good sound on trumpet, see "What The Buzz is About" on page 38.

Trumpets of Now and the Future

Basic trumpet design has changed little since 1815, but improvements have been made not only in quality, but in production, too. There are many more trumpets in the world now than there were in 1815, that's for sure. And despite what is said by a few people who live with beginners, that's a great and beautiful thing.

Innovations continue. Dave Monette, a trumpet maker in Portland, Oregon has made the most significant contribution to changes in modern trumpet design. His horns range from tried and true to revolutionary, and are capturing the eyes and ears of trumpet players and musicians the world over.

Wynton Marsalis and Terence Blanchard play a Monette horn, as does Charlie Schlueter of the Boston Symphony, and these are only three of thousands. They are great trumpets. See gorgeous pix and learn more at the Monette web site: **www.monette.net**.

Example 1.2 Three of Dave Monette's horns. Can you find the mouthpiece on the decorated trumpet? It's built in.

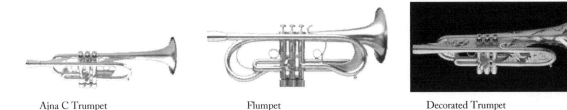

| Ajna C Trumpet | Flumpet | Decorated Trumpet |

Innovations and Expectations

It's human nature to tinker and invent, to mess around with things. This leads to different musical styles, different art, different technology, and of course different instruments, in this case trumpets.

Bobby Shew, a player and teacher of phenomenal talent sometimes uses an instrument called the Shew Horn. It's a trumpet with two bells. A fourth valve changes which bell the sound comes from. With a mute in one bell, Shew delivers some amazing solos that sound like a tight two-player duet. You can't buy a Shew Horn any more, but there is hope.

The folks at Harrelson Trumpets have invented a horn with a similar idea. It's called *The Medusa*, seen to the right. It's got two bells of different weights. To see vids and more pictures of this interesting horn, check out the "extras" page for *Sound the Trumpet* at www.sol-ut.com, go to the Harrelson Trumpets web page, or friend them on Facebook. They have a whole bunch of videos explaining some of their horns, as well as some of the other experimental gear, like a harness that takes *all* the weight of the horn while you play. This has important applications for those who might have trouble holding the horn. There are other innovative horn designs coming from these folks. Go visit them online to see and *hear* for yourself.

Don Ellis, a trumpet player active in the 60s and 70s used a quarter-tone trumpet. The smallest interval between notes in Western music is called a half step. Ellis' trumpet used intervals of a quarter step. The sound is strange and even a little unsettling, but still very cool. Even thirty years later, the sound of the quarter tone trumpet is still out there on the edge. To find the info about this recording, see "Notes From the Edge: Avant Garde" on page 34.

The Medusa, by Harrelson Trumpets
Find the valve that switches the sound
from one bell to the other.

Expect more inventions and improvements in time. Who knows? Maybe you'll be the new inventor of a horn that will become wildly popular. You don't have to be a whiz inventor or someone with a metal shop to make your own trumpet. Experiment with an old piece of garden hose. Chop it off at about 3 feet, stick a mouthpiece in one end, and blow. For a higher sound, cut the hose shorter. Twirl it around your head as you play. If you live near the ocean, bull kelp will also make a fun trumpet and if dried correctly it can last years.

Throughout the book I'll reference extra information that can be found at the Sol Ut Press web site (www.sol-ut.com). Check in to the *Sound the Trumpet* pages to find all the extra resources for the book, including videos, links to more information, music, games, and other useful stuff.

Up Next

One of the very best things you can do to enhance your abilities on trumpet is also the easiest and most fun! It's listening. In the next chapter you'll get lists of some of the best recordings of trumpet ever made. It's vital that you get the trumpet sound in your head and in your soul. If you know what a trumpet can and should sound like, it will be easier to pull those sounds out of the horn when you play it yourself. The next chapter is meant as a reference, so if you're antsy to get started playing, skip it and get on with Chapter 3, but don't neglect your music library.

CHAPTER 2
LISTEN!

Those who do not hear the music think the dancers mad.

~ African Proverb

In This Chapter

- Why Listen?
- What to Listen To
- Symphonies
- Small Group Jazz
- Brass Ensembles

Terms to Know

brass quintet: Two trumpets, trombone, French horn, Tuba.
brass quartet: Usually two trumpets, two trombones.
early music: Western European art music style before the 1600s.
Baroque: Western European art music style from ~1600-1750.
Classical: Western European art music style from ~1730-1825.
Romantic: Western European art music style from ~1825-1900
Contemporary: Western European art music after 1900.

Why Listen?

The reason this chapter is early in the book is that listening to music requires you only to have a pair of working ears. You don't need the special skills required to actually *play* trumpet, you only need the skills required to play your radio, CD player, MP3 player, cassette player, or turntable. Or for those of you retro-rebels, your 8-track, reel-to-reel machines, or Victrolas.

Recordings are the easiest and least expensive way to experience great music made by the Masters. However, it's not the *best* way to experience music. The best way is to hear music *live* being created by a warm body (or bodies) in the same room with you. There is no other experience like it and after your first good experience, you'll be hooked. After your first exposure to a live performance by a Master musician, you'll be flabbergasted, astounded, amazed and inspired. There is no substitute for live music. Listen to live musicians every chance you get.

Listening is far and away the *very* best thing you can do for your trumpet playing and your musicianship skills. There is no substitute for it. Listening to music is food for your own music. If you don't listen to other players, your road to trumpet mastery will be long and lonely. That would be sad. Consider the words of the famous philosopher Nietzsche: *Life without music would be a mistake.*

Some Listening Tips

Listening tips? Am I serious? Oh, yes, very serious. If you haven't listened to a lot of music yet, you're in for a challenge with all this unfamiliar music to listen to. If something is unfamiliar, our reaction is often one of dislike or disdain. When you first listen to a piece, try to suspend all judgement until you've listened to it several times and your ears have begun to learn it.

When I was a freshman in high school in Sitka, a small town on an island in Southeast Alaska, I began to explore recorded music. At the time I wanted to find out what this whole *jazz* thing was about. I knew a few trumpeters' names and little else. I had heard of Miles Davis and figured I should get one of his albums. I chose *Bitches Brew*. Those of you who know this album are probably laughing right now. It's a highly successful jazz fusion album that was way out there to my poor untrained ears. My first reaction was, *This is jazz? I don't think I like jazz.....* Fortunately, I persisted in my search and now that I have a lot more listening experience, I enjoy the album much more and I have more knowledge of all the other flavors jazz has to offer.

I hope to help you avoid any misunderstandings like I experienced back then through these lists of recordings. But even more than that, I'd like to challenge you to open up your ears and your mind to different sounds and different genres of music. Something that you may react to unfavorably on first hearing might become an old and dear friend if you keep trying to understand it. Often we dislike what we don't understand.

Then again, dislike is dislike. If you give a recording a good honest try and after several listenings it still doesn't do anything for you, forget about it and move on to something else. There is so much music in the world that you're *almost* guaranteed to find something that really moves you if you keep searching. The beautiful thing is that if you *don't* find what truly moves you, you can just go ahead and create it yourself!

After a couple years, come back to an album you didn't like in the past and you may be surprised to find your tastes have changed. Or not. Okay. Let's get to the recordings.

Classical Trumpet Music

What a huge repertoire to choose from! Classical music covers a wide span of years and the earlier stuff, like Bach's music, was written before the valve, for natural trumpets. This broad genre includes arrangements of medieval music from composers like Galliard, Bird, Gibbons, and Bull, Baroque composers like Bach, classical composers like Mozart, romantic composers like Beethoven, and everything up to today which also includes Stravinsky, Wagner, Tchaikovsky and many, many more. Distilling 400 years of compositions is no easy task but I'll give it a shot.

We'll break this very large category into orchestral, small ensemble, and solo categories. In each category the music is arranged by artist and also included are Title, composer and album information. Here you go. Go to www.sol-ut.com for a hyperlinked version of this list.

Orchestral Trumpet

Because much of this music has been around for a long time, there are many recordings of one piece. I'll provide you with what I (and many others) consider to be the best recordings. If you really enjoy a particular piece of music, search out other recordings. It's interesting to hear how a piece can be interpreted by a different conductor using a different symphony.

Album Title	Composer	Conductor/Orchestra	Recording Info
Symphony No. 9 in E Minor, Op. 95	Antonín Dvořák	István Kertész/ London Symphony	Penguin Classics 460604
Shastakovich	Dmitri Shostakovich	Leonard Bernstein/ New York Philharmonic	Sony: SMK 61841

Album Title	Composer	Conductor/Orchestra	Recording Info
Handel	George Frederic Handel	Georg Solti Chicago Symphony	London: D 235413
Mahler	Gustav Mahler	Klaus Tennstedt/ London Philharmonic	EMI
Messiah	Handel	Sir John Eliot Gardiner/ English Baroque Soloists et al	Philips 434297 (2 cds)
The Planets	Holst	Sir John Eliot Gardiner/ Philharmonia Orch.	Deutsche Grammophon 445 860-2
Le Chant du Rossignol L'Histoire du Soldat	Igor Stravinsky	Pierry Boulez/ Cleveland Orchestra & Chorus	Deutsche Grammophon ASIN: B00005M9HW
Bach	Johann Sebastian Bach	Leonard Bernstein/ NY Philharmonic	Sony: SM2K 60727
Mozart	Leopold Mozart	Herbert von Karajan/ Berlin Philharmonic	EMI Classics: 7243 5 6696 2 9
Symphony 5	Mahler	George Solti/ Chicago Symphony	Uni/London Classics 30443
Mussorgsky: Pictures 1-10, Night on Bald Mountain	Mussorgsky	Guiseppe Sinopoli/ NY Philharmonic	Deutsche Grammophon 429785
Pictures at an Exhibition	Mussorgsky	George Solti/ Chicago Symphony	Uni/London Classics 30446
Pictures at an Exhibition and Other Russian Showpieces	Mussorgsky, Tchaikovsky, et al	Fritz Reiner/ Chicago Symphony	RCA 61958
1812—Festival Overture, Swan Lake, Sym No. 6, et al	P. Tchaikovsky	George Solti/ Chicago Symphony	London/Decca Double Decker 455810
Capriccio Italien	P. Tchaikovsky	George Solti/ Chicago Symphony	
Tchaikovsky Symphony IV	P. Tchaikovsky	George Solti/ Chicago Symphony	London/Decca Jubilee 430745
Romeo & Juliet	Prokofiev	Lorin Maazel/Cleveland Orchestra	Decca 452970
Pines & Fountains of Rome	Respighi	De Waart/ San Francisco Symphony	Polygram Records ASIN: B00000E2PJ
Respighi: The Pines of Rome, Debussy: La Mer	Respighi, Debussy	Fritz Reiner/ Chicago Symphony	Sony 68079
Strauss	Richard Strauss	Michael Tilson Thomas/ London Symphony	CBS: MK44817
Rimsky-Korsakov: Scheherazade	Rimsky-Korsakov	Hervert von Karajan/ Berlin Philharmonic	DG The Originals 463614
Rimsky-Korsakov: Scheherazade Igor Stravinsky: Song of the Nightingale	Rimsky-Korsakov, Igor Stravinsky	Fritz Reiner/ Chicago Symphony	RCA 68168
Ein Heldenleben/Also Sprach Zarathustra	Strauss	Fritz Reiner/ Chicago Symphony	BMG/RCA Victor 61709

Album Title	Composer	Conductor/Orchestra	Recording Info
Stravinsky: Petrouchka	Stravinsky	Zubin Mehta/ NY Philharmonic	Sony 35823
Stravinsky: Petrouchka, Le Sacre du Printemps	Stravinsky	Pierre Boulez/ Cleveland Orchestra	Deutsche Grammophon 435769
Orchestral Excerpts	Various	Phillip Smith (NY Philharmonic principal)	Summit Records DCD 144

Solo Classical Trumpet

Album Title	Genre	Composer	Artist	Recording Info
Trumpet Concertos	Baroque	Bach, Handel, Haydn, Vivaldi, Albinoni, Telemann, Cimarosa, Torelli, et al	Maurice André	EMI Classics (USA) CDZB 7 69152 2
Baroque Trumpet Concertos	Baroque	Stolzel, Telemann, Vivaldi, Torelli, et al	Maurice André	Seraphim Classics CDR 72435 7342322
The Ultimate Trumpet Collection	Various	Handel, Bach, Hummel, et al	Maurice André	Erato 92861
Trumpet Rhapsody	Classical	Artunian, Hummel, Biber, et al	Timofei Dokshizer	RCA CD 74321-32045-2
David Hickman, Trumpet	Contemporary	Kennan, Stevens, Turrin, et al	David Hickman	Crystal 668
Phillip Smith, Principal Trumpet, NY Philharmonic	Various	Broughton, Turin, et al.	Phillip Smith	Cala Records 513
Thomas Stevens, Trumpet	Classical-Contemporary	Hindemith, Bozza, et al	Thomas Stevens	Crystal Records 761
Thomas Stevens, Trumpet	Various	Maxwell-Davies, Antheil, et al	Thomas Stevens	Crystal Records 665
Treasures for Trumpet	Various	Various	Robert Sullivan	Summit (classical) ASIN: B000066TXB
Trumpet Masterworks	Baroque-Contemporary	Inesco, et al	George Vosburgh	Four Winds ASIN: B00005UF3P
Trumpet in Our Time	Contemporary	Rouse, Korf, et al	Raymond Mase, Michael Powell, et al	Summit (Classical) 148
American Trumpet Sonatas	Contemporary	Dello Joio, Kennan, et al	Jouko Harjanne, Juhani Lagerspetz	Finlandia 17691
Cornet Favorites	Cornet Music	HL Clarke, Simon, JB Arban, et al	Gerard Schwarz, William Bolcom, et al	Nonesuch 79157
Clasic Wynton	Various	Purcell, Handel, Mouret, Bach, et al	Wynton Marsalis	Sony 60804

Brass Ensembles

Album Title	Genre	Composers	Artist	Recording Info
Greatest Hits (vol. 1 and 2)	Various	Various	Canadian Brass	
Bach: The Art of Fugue	Baroque	J.S. Bach	Canadian Brass	Columbia MK 44501
Plays Renaissance, Elizabethan and Baroque Music	Early Music	Various	American Brass Quintet	Delos D/CD 3003
The Antiphonal Music of Gabrieli	Early Music	Gabrieli, Frescobaldi, et al	Cleveland Brass Ensemble, Philadelphia B.E. etc	Sony 62353
A Brass and Organ Christmas	Various	Handel, Schutz, Holst, et al	Bay Brass, Fenstermaker, et al	Gothic Records ASIN: B00004Y6PX
Portrait of an Artist: Arnold Jacobs, Tuba				
Lollipops	Various	Mozart, Rimsky-Korsakov, et al	Phillip Jones Brass Ensemble	Claves ASIN: B00063WCM
Phillip Jones Brass Ensemble: Greatest Hits	Various	Mussorgsky, Tchaikovsky, et al	Phillip Jones Brass Ensemble	London/Decca 80702
Sousa: Stars and Stripes Forever	Marches	J.P. Sousa	Phillip Jones Brass Ensemble	London/Decca 410290
The Lighter Side	Various	Bernstein, Saint-Säens, et al	Phillip Jones Brass Ensemble	London/Decca 473185
20th Century Album	Contemp.	Copland, Britten, et al	Phillip Jones Brass Ensemble	Decca ASIN: B00060OHU

Jazz

This style of music was born in New Orleans, experienced its heady adolescence in New York, Kansas City, and Chicago and after languishing for a while, interest in jazz has been reborn and it's approaching maturity now everywhere in the world. One of the United States' few original art forms.

Another huge category, this will be broken down into solo artist/small combo and big band. In the case of the solo artist, there are so many albums to choose from that I've highlighted albums which I think are particularly enjoyable. So, if you don't have a lot of cash to part with, you're likely to be quite happy with the titles in bold. Go to www.sol-ut.com for a hyperlinked version of this list!

Solo Jazz Trumpet

Artist	Album Title	Recording Info
Louis Armstrong		
	Louis Armstrong: A Portrait of the Artist as a Young Man, 1923-1934	Columbia/Legacy,
	West End Blues (w/ King Oliver)	CBS
	The Hot Fives & Hot Sevens (3 albums)	Columbia
	Satch Plays Fats	Columbia
	Louis Armstrong and His All Stars Play WC Handy	Columbia

Artist	Album Title	Recording Info
(Armstrong cont'd.)	The Louis Armstrong Story (4 albums)	Columbia
	The Essential Louis Armstrong (2 albums)	Vanguard
	Ambassador Satch	Columbia
	What a Wonderful World	MCA
	The Definitive Louis Armstrong	Columbia/Legacy
	The Majestic Years	Avid Records AVC 541
Roy Eldridge		
	Little Jazz	Inner City
	Little Jazz & the Jimmy Ryan All Stars	Fantasy
	Roy Eldridge and His Litle Jazz (3 albums)	BMG
	The Big Sound of Little Jazz	Topaz
	Art Tatum & Roy Eldridge	Pablo
	Happy Time	Original Jazz/Pablo
	The Nifty Cat	New World
	After You've Gone	GRP
Dizzy Gillespie		
	Sonny Side Up (w/ Sonny Stitt & Sonny Rollins)	Verve
	Diz & Getz	Verve
	Bird & Diz	Verve
	In the Beginning	Fantasy
	The Greatest of Dizzy Gillespie	RCA Victor
	The Champ	Savoy
	Diz & Roy	Verve
	Jambo Caribe	Verve
	Dizzy's Diamonds (3 disc set)	Verve
	Jazz at Massey Hall	Fantasy
	Concert in Paris	Roost
	Dizzy on the Riviera	PHS
Clifford Brown		
	The Beginning and the End	Columbia/Legacy
	Clifford Brown and Max Roach at Basin Street	Verve
	Study in Brown	EmArcy/Verve
	More Study in Brown	EmArcy
	Live at the Beehive	Columbia
	A Night at Birdland (vol. 1 and 2)	Blue Note
	Clifford Brown in Paris	Prestige
	Daahoud	Mainstream

Artist	Album Title	Recording Info
(Brown cont'd.)	At Basin Street	EmArcy
	Jordu	EmArcy
	The Best of Max Roach / Clifford Brown in Concert	GNP
	Brown & Roach, Inc.	EmArcy
	Clifford Brown Memorial Album	Blue Note
Fats Navarro		
	Fats Blows	Past Perfect
	The Fabulous Fats Navarro (vol. 1 & 2)	Blue Note
	Boppin' a Riff	BYG
	Good Bait	Roost
Miles Davis		
	Kind of Blue	Columbia
	Birth of the Cool	
	Somethin' Else	Blue Note
	Miles Davis (vol. 1 & 2)	Blue Note
	Workin'	Prestige
	Cookin'	Prestige
	'Round Midnight	Columbia
	My Funny Valentine	Columbia
	Milestones	Columbia
	Seven Steps to Heaven	Columbia
	Miles Smiles	Columbia
	E.S.P.	Columbia
	Cookin' at the Plugged Nickel	Columbia
	Filles de Kilimanjaro	Columbia
	Nefertiti	Columbia
	Bitches Brew	Columbia
	Live/Evil	Columbia
	Tutu	Warner Brothers
Lee Morgan		
	Moanin'	Blue Note
	The Best of Lee Morgan: The Blue Note Years	Blue Note
	The Sidewinder	Blue Note
	Search for the New Land	Blue Note
	Cornbread	Blue Note
	Meet You at the Jaz Corner of the World (vol. 1 & 2)	Blue Note

Artist	Album Title	Recording Info
(Morgan cont'd.)	Like Someone in Love	Blue Note
	Live at the Lighthouse	Blue Note
	The Cooker	Blue Note
	Lee Morgan	Blue Note
Kenny Dorham		
	Horace Silver & the Jazz Messengers	Blue Note
	The Jazz Messengers at the Cafe Bohemia (vol. 1 & 2)	Blue Note
	Kenny Dorham 1959	Prestige
	Whistle Stop	Blue Note
	Coltrane Time	Solid State
	Trompete Toccata	Blue Note
	In 'n Out	Blue Note
	Una Mas	Blue Note
	Blue Spring	Fantasy
Clark Terry		
	Swahili	Trip
	Oscar Peterson Trio plus 1	Mercury
	Serenade to a Bus Beat	Riverside
	Out of the Storm	Verve
	Tonight	Mainstream
	Clark Terry Live at the Village Gate	Chesky
	Gingerbread Men	Mainstream
	Portraits	Chesky
	Take Double	EmArcy
	The Happy Horns of Clark Terry	Impulse
Freddie Hubbard		
	Maiden Voyage	Blue Note
	Open Sesame	Blue Note
	Ugetsu	Riverside
	Free for All	Blue Note
	Caravan	Riverside
	Empyrean Isles	Blue Note
	Speak No Evil	Blue Note
	Black Angel	Atlantic
	Keystone Bop	Fantasy
	Red Clay	Sony
	Ready for Freddie	Blue Note

Artist	Album Title	Recording Info
(Hubbard cont.'d)	The All Seeing Eye	Blue Note
	Super Blue	Columbia
	Hub Tones	Blue Note
	This is Jazz	Epic Legacy
Chet Baker		
	Carnegie Hall Concert	CTI
	The Most Important Jazz Album of 1964/65	Colpix
	Mulligan Meets Konitz	World Pacific Jazz
	Smokin' With the Chet Baker Quintet	Roulette
	I Remember You	Inja
	The Touch of Your Lips	Steeplechase
	Star Eyes	Marshmallow
	Chet	Riverside
Maynard Ferguson		
	This is Jazz	Sony
	Chameleon	Sony
	Conquistador	Sony
	Master of the Stratosphere	Sony Special Product
	These Cats Can Swing	Concord Records
	New Vintage	Wounded Bird Records
	Verve Jazz Masters '52: Maynard Ferguson	Polygram Records
Woody Shaw		
	Cape Verdean Blues	Blue Note
	If You're Not Part of the Solution, You're Part of the Problem	Milestone
	Love Dance	Muse
	Little Red's Fantasy	Muse
	Unity	Blue Note
	The Homecoming	Columbia
	The Moontrane	Muse
	Rosewood	Columbia
Blue Mitchell		
	Blowin' the Blues Away	Blue Note
	Silvers Serenade	Blue Note
	Horace-Scope	Blue Note
	A Blue Time	Milestone/Fantasy
	Soul Time	Riverside
	Heads Up	Blue Note

Artist	Album Title	Recording Info
(Mitchell cont'd.)	Fraffitie Blues	Mainstream
	Vital Blue	Mainstream
	Blue Mitchell	Mainstream
	Boss Horn	Blue Note
Tom Harrell		
	Silver and Brass	Blue Note
	Silver and Voices	Blue Note
	Silver and Wood	Blue Note
	Sail Away	Contemporary
	Play of Light	Blackhawk
	Aurora	Adamo
	Moon Alley	Criss Cross
	The Art of Rhythm	RCA
	Tall Stories	Contemporary
	Look to the Sky	Steeplechase
	Playing With Fire	Mama
	Real Book	BMG/ECM
Art Farmer		
	Modern Art	United Artists
	Art	Argo
	Homecoming	Mainstream
	To Duke With Love	Inner City
	The Summer Knows	Inner City
	Silk Road	Arabesque Recordings
Doc Cheatham		
	Good For What Ails Ya'	Classic Jazz
	Doc Cheatham & Nicholas Payton	Verve
	The Fabulous Doc Cheatham	Parkwood
	Butch Thompson & Doc Cheatham	Daring
	Doc Cheatham & Sammy Price (vol. 1 & 2)	Sackville
	New Tango '90	Muze/MTS
	At the Bern Jazz Festival	Sackville
Nicholas Payton		
	Payton's Place	Verve
	From This Moment On	Verve
	Dear Louis	Verve

Artist	Album Title	Recording Info
(Payton cont'd.)	Gumbo Nouveau	Verve
	Nick at Night	Verve
Wynton Marsalis		
	Think of One	Columbia
	Black Codes from the Underground	Columbia
	Wynton Marsalis	Columbia
	Hot House Flowers	Columbia
	The Majesty of the Blues	Columbia
	Marsalis Standard Time, vol. 1	Columbia
	Blood on the Fields	Sony
	Joe Cool's Blues	
Roy Hargrove		
	Parker's Mood	Verve
	Habana	Verve
	With the Tenors of Our Time	Verve
	Approaching Standards	Novus

More Jazz Trumpet Players

The above list is, believe it or not, only a start. Here are some other artists you should check out: Terell Stafford, Nat Adderly, Bix Beiderbecke, Arturo Sandoval, Terence Blanchard, Lester Bowie, Fabrizzio Bosso, Randy Brecker, Donald Byrd, Bill Chase, Don Cherry, Johny Coles, Conte Candoli, Dave Douglas, Jon Faddis, Greg Gisbert, Tim Hagans, Wilbur Harden, Eddie Henderson, Ingrid Jensen, Thad Jones, Booker Little, Brian Lynch, John McNeil, Claudio Roditi, Red Rodney, Wallace Roney, Doc Severinson, Jack Sheldon, Bobby Shew, Marvin Stamm, Ira Sullivan, Buddy Childers, Al Porcino, Snooky Young, Dave Stahl, Bernie Glow, Conrad Gozo, Johnny Frosk, George Graham, Lew Soloff, Jimmy Maxwell, Laurie Frink, Peter Olstad, Roger Ingram, Dave Trigg, and Cootie Williams.

Big Bands With Great Trumpet Sections

Album Title	Big Band Leader	Featured Instrument	Recording Info (ASIN)
Chameleon	Maynard Ferguson	trumpet	Sony Legacy 46112
Tonight Show Band vol 1 & 2	Doc Severinsen	trumpet	Amherst
Long Yellow Road	Toshiko Akiyoshi	tenor sax	BMG/RCA (B00000GAYU)
Opening Night: Thad Jones/Mel Lewis Big Band at the Village Vanguard	Thad Jones & Mel Lewis	all	Alan Grand Productions #1939 (B0000640MK)
Ken Burns Jazz Collection: Count Basie	Count Basie	piano, all	Polygram Records #549090
Ken Burns Jazz Collection: Duke Ellington	Duke Ellington	piano, all	Sony #61444

Album Title	Big Band Leader	Featured Instrument	Recording Info (ASIN)
The Essential Glen Miller	Glen Miller	trombone	RCA #66520 (B000002WRM)
Carnegie Hall Jazz Concert	Benny Goodman	clar., tpt, sax	Sony #65143 (B00002MZ2L)
This is Tommy Dorsey & His Orchestra	Tommy Dorsey	trombone	Collectables #2815 (B00005B51I)
The Best of Harry James	Harry James	trumpet	Curb Records #77391 (B000000CXI)
Lunceford Special: 1949-1950	Jimmy Lunceford	ensemble playing	Sony #65647 (B00005LNAX)
Dream Band Vols. (1-5)	Terry Gibbs	all	Contemporary #7654 (B000000X99)
Serendipity 18	Bob Florence	all	Mama Foundation #1025 (B00000I4ZS)
Coming About	Maria Schneider	all	Enja #9069 (B000005CC5)
Latin From Manhattan	Bob Mintzer	all	DMP #523 (B0000064UG)
Vavoom!	Brian Setzer Orchestra	guitar, vocals	Interscope Records #490733 (B00004U8KD)

Other Great Recordings with Trumpet

Album Title	Artist	Style	Recording Info
The Best of Irakere	Arturo Sandoval	Latin	Columbia CK 57719
The Very Best of Tito Puente	Tito Puente, et al	Latin	BMG 74465 99001 2
Chase	Bill Chase et, al	Rock/Jazz fusion	One Way Records #26660
Blood, Sweat and Tears' Greatest Hits	BST	Rock/Jazz fusion	Sony #65729
What is Hip: Anthology	Tower of Power	Funk	Rhino Records #75788
Earth, Wind and Fire: Greatest Hits	Various	Rock/Jazz fusion	Sony #65779
Jump, Jive and Wail	Brian Setzer Orchestra	neo-swing/ rockabilly	Interscope Records
Hot	Squirrel Nut Zippers	neo-swing	Mammoth/PGD #980137
Big Bad Voodoo Daddy	Big Bad Voodoo Daddy	neo-swing	Interscope Records

Notes From the Edge: Avant Garde

We crafty humans are always striving for the different, the new; things as yet unheard, unspoken, or unseen. It's the explorer that lurks in the blood of most humans. Music also benefits from this curious trait of ours because it is the ability to explore and experiment and innovate that brings us new styles of music.

Below are some examples of the more risky and daring endeavors involving trumpet. This includes the use of a quarter-tone trumpet (a trumpet that plays and extra note between the normal half step we currently use) in the recording by Don Ellis. Out on the edge is where Life can be most real.

Album Title	Artist	Info	Recording Info
Electric Bath	Don Ellis	electrified 1/4-tone trumpet	GNP Crescendo GNPD 2223
Ethnomusicology, Vol. 1	Russell Gunn	Jazz meets Hip-Hop	Atlantic 83165-2
Constellations	Dave Douglas	eclectic from jazz to Eastern European to classical	Hat Art CD 7165
A Tribute to Jack Johnson	Miles Davis	Jazz/Rock Fusion	Columbia CK 47036
Americans Swinging in Paris	Art Ensemble of Chicago	free jazz masters	EMI International (B000065BS0)
This is Our Music	Don Cherry	free jazz	Atlantic

Watch and Learn: Trumpeters on Video

As if you didn't have enough to go through already, right? Well, if you can't see Master trumpet players live, video is the next best thing. When we actually *see* someone playing some mad trumpet music, it somehow makes the experience more real. Instead of getting just the sound, with video, you can actually see these Masters showing their soul. It's amazing! Plus, it's a lot easier to transcribe a musical idea when you can see which valves to push.

Video Title (Artist)	Length (if available)	Produced By
Satchmo: Louis Armstrong	86 min.	CMV Enterprises
Let's Get Lost (Chet Baker)		Columbia Video
Bix: Ain't None of Them Play Like Him Yet		Playboy Home Video
Miles Ahead: the Music of Miles Davis	60 min.	WNET/13 in assoc. w/ Obenhaus Films, Inc., Toby/ Byron Multiprises
The Miles Davis Story	125 min.	Columbia Music Video, 2001
Miles Electric: A Different Kind of Blue	123 min.	Eagle Eye Media, 2004
A Night in Tunisia: A Musical Portrait of Dizzy Gillespie	28 min.	View Video Educational Video Network, 1990
Things to Come: Dizzy Gillespie and Billy Eckstine	55 min.	Vintage Jazz Classics, 1993
Dizzy Gillespie and the United Nations Orchestra	90 min.	Eagle Eye Video,
Jazz then—Dixieland, 1 & 2 (Al Hirt)	60 min.	Century Home Video, 1983
Blues & Swing (Wynton Marsalis)	79 min.	Clearvue/eav, 1988
Tackling the Monster: Marsalis on Practice (Wynton Marsalis)	53 min.	Sony Classical Film & Video, 1995
Listening for Clues: Marsalis on Form	53 min.	Sony Classical Film & Video, 1995
A Unique Approach to Improvising on Chords & Scales (John McNeil et al)	53 min.	International Production Group, Inc., 2000

Video Title (Artist)	Length (if available)	Produced By
Becoming an Improviser: Creative Practice with Chords & Scales (John McNeil, Rufus Reid, et al)	56 min.	International Production Group, Inc., 2000
Spera on Jazz (Dominic Spera)	160 min.	University of Wisconsin, Madison, 1986
Trumpet Course: Beginning to Intermediate (Clark Terry)	50 min.	Kultur International Films, 1981, 1990
Steps to Excellence: A Trumpet Clinic (Allen Vizzutti)		Yamaha Musical Products, 1984
One Night With Blue Note		Blue Note Records, 2003

Listen to other Artists

Here is a list of other jazz musicians to listen to: **saxophonists** Charlie Parker, Sonny Rollins, Stan Getz, Sonny Stitt, Phil Woods, Ornette Coleman, Joe Henderson, David Murray, Frank Morgan, Bobby Watson, Tim Berne, John Zorn, Chico Freeman, Courtney Pine, Joe Lovano, Bob Berg, and Jerry Bergonzi; **clarinetists** Benny Goodman, Artie Shaw, Don Byron and Eddie Daniels; **trombonists** Bill Watrous, Steve Turre, Robin Eubanks and Ray Anderson; **pianists** Duke Ellington, Count Basie, Oscar Peterson, Thelonius Monk, Dave Brubeck, Herbie Hancock, Cecil Taylor, Geri Allen, Mulgrew Miller, Kenny Barron, Gonzalo Rubalcaba, Eduard Simon, Renee Rosnes, and Marilyn Crispell; **guitarists** Charlie Christian, Django Reinhardt, Joe Pass, Wes Montgomery, John Scofield, Bill Frisell, and Kevin Eubanks; **vibraphonist** Lionel Hampton, Steve Nelson and Gary Burton; **bassists** Ray Brown, Christian McBride, John Clayton, Charlie Haden, Dave Holland, Niels-Henning Oersted Pedersen and Lonnie Plaxico; **drummers** Chick Webb, Max Roach, Art Blakey, Buddy Rich, and Tony Williams, and **vocalists** Ella Fitzgerald, Billie Holliday, Sarah Vaughan, Frank Sinatra, Nina Simone, Bobby McFerrin and Cassandra Wilson.

Here are a few classical musicians to listen to: **pianists** Glen Gould (esp. the *Goldberg Variations*), Emil Gilels (esp. Beethoven piano sonatas 21, 23, 26), Murray Perahia (also the *Goldberg Variations*), Arthur Rubinstein (Chopin ballades and scherzi), Paul Jacobs (Debusy piano preludes), Vladimir Horowitz (Carnegie Hall Concert 1965), Stephen Hough (Liszt Piano Sonata in B minor), and Van Cliburn (Tchaikovsky Piano Concerto No. 1); **string players** Yo Yo Ma (cello, esp. the *Bach Cello Suites*), Mstislav Rostropovich (cello, Dvoràk Cello Concerto in B minor), John Williams (guitar, any recording), Andres Segovia (guitar, any recording), Christopher Parkening (guitar, any recording), and the Emerson String Quartet (Beethoven string quartets); **flutists** Jean Pierre Rampal and James Galway; and keep an ear out for **conductors** Sir Georg Solti, Fritz Reiner, Kurt Masur, Michael Tilson Thomas, Leonard Bernstein, Herbert von Karajan, Lorin Maazel, and Daniel Barenboim.

Of course neither of these lists is complete, or even close. These are just a smattering of artists who come to mind immediately. You should listen to as many musicians as you can. Listening will increase your awareness and appreciation for different styles of music.

Up Next

That's a lot of recordings, so chip away at it when you can. Radio on the Internet is a great way to get access to music without paying for an entire album. Run some searches and you'll probably find what you're looking for.

Next we finally get you started buzzing your lips. The lip buzz is the foundation of all sound that will come out of your horn. It's very important, and practicing the buzz is the best thing you can do for your trumpet sound. Read on.

CHAPTER 3
How to Create a Buzz

A man thinks that by mouthing hard words he understands hard things.

~ Herman Melville

In This Chapter

- Forming the Embouchure
- Buzzing
- Mouthpiece Buzzing
- Buzzing Exercises
- Mouthpiece Information

Terms to Know

embouchure (AHM-ba-sher): The position and use of lips, tongue, and teeth when playing a wind instrument.

buzz: The sound made when air is forced through a brass player's embouchure.

mouthpiece: On a brass or woodwind instrument, the part responsible for receiving the embouchure's vibrations. Placed on the lips for trumpet players.

aperture: The opening in your lips where the air escapes and the buzz happens. Aperture should not be too wide or too open.

chops: A cool word for "embouchure." Can also refer to one's ability on an instrument.

What's an Embouchure?

All wind instrument players have an embouchure. Embouchure (AHM-ba-sher) is a French word meaning "the mouth of the river." In our case, the river is your air stream and the mouth of the river is *your* mouth. Embouchure in the trumpet world means the shape of your lips, tongue and teeth when you play trumpet.

Learning how to form your embouchure is a crucial step in playing trumpet and you want to get it exactly right or you may have problems later that will be hard to fix. When practicing your embouchure at first, do it with a mirror so you know you've got it right.

The cool word for embouchure is *chops*. After a long session of playing, you could say, "Man, my chops are sore!" In addition to referring to your mouth, chops also mean your ability on an instrument. You could say, "Wow! Max Roach and Clifford Brown have some great chops!"

The Face is the Place

The face is a unique place in the human body, especially the muscles that control it and allow you to grin, frown, scowl, raise an eyebrow, and of course, buzz your lips. Most muscles are connected to bones on each end, but not the facial muscles. These muscles are connected to your head bones on one end, but the other end is connected to soft tissue like the lips.

And just in case you're wondering, there are several nerves that allow you to feel your face, but there is only one that is important to us for playing the trumpet, and that is the seventh cranial nerve. The seventh cranial nerve controls most of the muscles in the embouchure.

The Muscles of the Embouchure

The lips aren't muscle. They're soft tissue. You can see this best in the diagram on the right. The lips don't do the work when playing trumpet. The surrounding muscles allow you to buzz your lips correctly and the most important ones are those at the corners of your mouth. Here's what they look like and their Latin names which you are allowed to promptly forget:

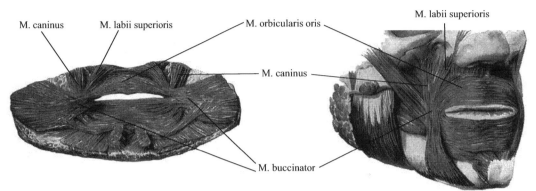

Why am I showing you this in such detail? Will it help you? Well, yes and no. It's not especially important to know that M. buccinator is the muscle at the corners of your mouth responsible for the "heavy lifting" in trumpet playing. I'm showing you the chop muscles so that you understand it's the muscle doing the work and not the lip. As with any kind of muscle-building, it takes a *lot* of time, effort and practice to teach the muscles to work efficiently. Think about how long it takes a body-builder to get their body to look like it does. If you consistently practice the exercises for building up your chops you'll get some dramatic results immediately. To get truly strong however, you'll slowly build your chop strength and efficiency day by day, over the course of a few years.

Dry Embouchure vs. Wet Embouchure

The large majority of trumpet players wet their lips with their tongue before playing. This is called a "wet embouchure." Some players don't wet their lips before playing, and this is known as a "dry embouchure."

Why one or the other? With a wet embouchure, the lips will buzz more easily and it's easier to slide the mouthpiece to the best location. Those who use a dry embouchure say that it's easier to play higher and there isn't a lot of moisture interfering with the tone. Though most players use and recommend a wet embouchure, try both and see which one you prefer.

What The Buzz is About

All sound is vibration. With trumpet, the vibration is provided by the lips and the air column. The buzz is the sound your lips make which is amplified by the trumpet into a gorgeous sound (with practice). Experience is worth a million words.

Take a deep breath. Lick your lips (or not, if you're using a dry embouchure), place them together as though you're saying "mmmm". Tighten the corners of your mouth and blow air through the middle of your lips. Use a LOT of air! From the middle of your lips you should get a funny buzzing sound caused by your lips vibrating together quickly. It's a lot like when you pinch the neck of a full balloon and let the air out. Same principle. Your mouth should look something like the following picture.

How to Create a Buzz

The *aperture* is the spot where the air escapes and the buzz happens. The aperture should be oval-shaped and not too long across the lips or too open. Ideally, the aperture should be right in the middle of your chops, so strive for that. However, there are players who have an aperture somewhere other than right in the middle. If you can't get the aperture in the middle, check with a teacher to be sure your particular embouchure will work. It's tough to make changes once you have habits set in place.

Example 3.1 Buzzing lips. Use a mirror to check the shape of your embouchure.

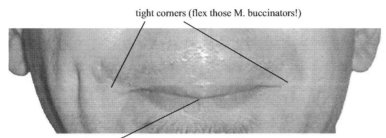

tight corners (flex those M. buccinators!)

the aperture: air escapes here, causing the "buzz"

Be careful to keep the soft, squishy, inner part of your lips from blowing outward like you're giving someone a raspberry. Strive for that "mmmm" type of lip formation. Some players find it helpful to keep the lips *slightly* rolled in.

When you practice the buzz, be sure to take deep breaths. For more information about breathing, see "The Correct Breath" on page 54. Your stomach will be quite firm when buzzing because you're using those muscles to push all the air in your lungs through the very small opening in your lips. It is a mistake however, to tighten your stomach muscles on purpose. Just blow and let your stomach muscles do what they do when you blow.

If you can't get a buzz at first, blow harder and try holding your lips more tightly together using the *corners* of your mouth. If you look at the muscle diagram shown on page 38, you'll see that the muscles just above and below the lip stretch parallel with the lip. Those muscles are meant to contract your lips together purse-string style, *not* to press them together. Use the corner muscles and the purse-string muscles against each other to create the necessary tension. Purse your lips and smile at the same time, or try to whistle and smile at the same time.

When you do get a buzz going, your lips might itch and tickle because you aren't used to vibrating your lips like this. The sensation goes away quickly, so keep at it. Here are the steps for making a buzz:

1 Look in the mirror and smile at yourself.

2 Take a deep breath.

3 Place your wet/dry lips together as though saying "mmmm". Keep the corners of your mouth tight, like you just had a big bite of lemon.

4 Force the air in your lungs through your lips. Use your stomach muscles to help push the air out.

5 Hold the sound of the buzz steady for as long as you can. Strive for a big, fat sound.

6 Repeat for a few minutes.

Once you have a good buzz, do it for as long as you can in one breath. Strive for a clear, "fat" tone and a steady sound. Think "ten-pound bumblebee." Take another breath and do it again. Time yourself and keep a record of how long you can buzz before the muscles in your lips give out (see the *Tracking Sheet* in the Appendix). It's a good idea to do this sitting down and if you feel yourself getting dizzy and light-headed, stop for a minute or two until it goes away. *The buzz will strengthen your lips more than almost anything else you can do!*

The buzz is a very important aspect of playing trumpet and the better your buzz, the stronger your playing will be. I've heard *all* beginning players' tone improve with just a little buzzing.

Try to buzz high, low, and in between. Buzz continuously through your range from high to low. Try to buzz a simple song, like *Row, Row, Row Your Boat*, or *Mary Had a Little Lamb*. This will *not* be easy at first, but keep trying and it'll come. Try to increase your range both higher and lower. As simple songs get easier, try more difficult songs, like *Somewhere Over the Rainbow* from The Wizard of Oz.

Don't neglect your buzz! You can do it anywhere. Well, I suppose walking down the street practicing your buzz might get you some funny looks, but that can be fun, too. Do it in the shower, in the car, any place you happen to think of it. You'll notice a rapid improvement in your trumpet tone and lip strength if you practice buzzing regularly.

But First, a Word From Your Sponsor: Air

Playing a wind instrument takes a *lot* of air and your nose is just too small to do the job right. When you take a breath while playing trumpet, DON'T breath through your nose. Breathe from the corners of your mouth or drop your lower jaw and breathe through your mouth. Except in special circumstances (see "Lip Failure Study" on page 134), you'll *always* use your mouth to breathe. For more tips on proper breathing see "The Correct Breath" on page 54.

Buzz with the Mouthpiece

Take the mouthpiece in your right or left hand and with only your thumb and middle finger, hold the mouthpiece gently by the end of the shank (the long tubular part). Splay out your other fingers. Lick your lips (or not if you're using a dry embouchure), take a big breath, and place the mouthpiece directly over the buzz aperture. Ideally this should be close to the center of your lips, but it's not crucial. It's more important to center the mouthpiece over the aperture where your lips are buzzing. Blow just like you did when doing the buzz above. The sound of the buzz through the mouthpiece is usually more clear and higher than the buzz without the mouthpiece.

Don't press the mouthpiece into your lips very hard. Press just hard enough to make a seal so you aren't spraying air and spit out the corners of your mouth. As you start to play higher, you'll want to cram the mouthpiece into your face harder but *resist this*. The more relaxed you are, the better your sound will be. Playing without too much pressure is something most trumpet players struggle with at some point in their playing if they're serious about playing well. Get yourself into the good habit of using the least amount of pressure you can get away with.

How to Create a Buzz

Example 3.2 Left: Randi Bernier demonstrates how to hold the mouthpiece correctly: End of the shank with only two fingers (middle and thumb) to help avoid excessive pressure. Right: Place the mouthpiece carefully over your buzz. Placement should be where the 'piece is most comfortable and where you get the best tone. This may be in the center, like Randi, or it may be a little off-center. Practice with a mirror!

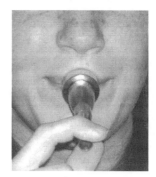

You'll find it's easier to produce a buzz with the mouthpiece. Buzzing with your mouthpiece can also be done almost anywhere, and a mouthpiece fits easily into a pocket. Do the same exercises with your mouthpiece as you do with the buzz alone: high, low, low to high and back to low, buzz simple songs, then harder ones.

The more you spend time on your buzz the better player you will be. A short time buzzing with the mouthpiece alone will dramatically improve your tone. If you buzz a lot, you'll get better *very* quickly. Trust me! Do it! At the end of this chapter are suggestions for buzzing exercises. Go through them once a day and you'll have a better trumpet tone and a stronger lip in a week or less.

Mouthpiece Placement

If you've been placing the mouthpiece in the center of the lips like the pictures show and not getting very good results, you may consider placing the mouthpiece elsewhere.

Remember that the ideal placement of the mouthpiece is where it sounds and feels the best. It's not crucial to place the mouthpiece in the center of the lips if this feels wrong to you. Some teachers insist on placing the mouthpiece in the center of the lips only, without regard to the shape of the student's face and teeth, and without regard to where the mouthpiece feels most comfortable to the student. Experiment with placement to hear where you get the best sound.

Cootie Williams, master of the plunger mute and trumpeter for Duke Ellington, played with an off center embouchure and it certainly didn't hurt his career at all. If that doesn't convince you, you should know that Maynard Ferguson, master of the stratosphere, also plays off-center.

The Chin

The chin should be flat, not bunched up. Check yourself in a mirror to be sure you're chin is flat. While playing a long tone on the trumpet or with your buzz, reach up and feel your chin. If it is bunched up, pull it down so that it's flat. A good way to practice this is to form an embouchure without the mouthpiece, and be aware of your chin. Use your hand to check its flatness. When you can get a buzz with a flat chin, this will transfer to when you have the horn or mouthpiece on your face. Use a mirror.

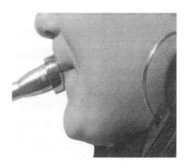

Buzzing Exercises for Strong Lips

Below is a short series of exercises to be done with the lip buzz alone *and* with the mouthpiece. The exercises take only 6 minutes (longer wouldn't hurt you) and are a great way to warm up and strengthen your lips before playing. At first, go through the whole series with just the lip buzz, then the whole thing with just the mouthpiece. Do one or the other every day. Both is better. After a week or so, mix and match. Make up your own.

If you're unfamiliar with reading notes, a note with an "x" as its head means the note has no specific pitch. If you'd like to learn more about reading music, check out *Basic Music Theory: How to Read, Write, and Understand Written Music.*

Each of these exercises has 3 or more variations of loudness: soft, medium, loud, and mixed. Try 'em all! In this book's appendix is a chart to keep track of several buzz exercises. Chart your progress with the buzz, and any other exercise. Post it in your case or practice room so you're reminded to do the exercises and improve.

Lip Buzz Exercises:

Do all of the following with the buzz alone. Do them daily and get ready to possess a much better tone and range almost immediately! Do them with steady volume throughout, then add the crescendo (gradually louder) or decrescendo (gradually softer) when you're ready.

1: Long Buzz (1min):

BREATHE as needed, keep the tone as clear, fat and warm as you can. Listen very carefully.

Do these in the low and middle register at both soft and medium loudness.

1   straight tone: no volume change

2   crescendo: get louder

3   decrescendo: get softer

2: Start and Stop (30 sec.):

Don't stop the sound with your tongue—stop your air instead. Go slowly, BREATHE as needed, keep the tone as constant, clear and fat as you can, listen very carefully.

Do these in the low and middle register at both soft and medium loudness.

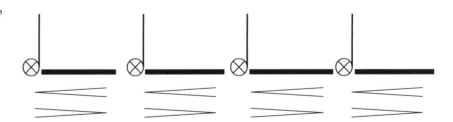

3: Hi to Low (30 sec.):

Start at a high but comfortable pitch and with
a continuous sound, move slowly from high
to as low as you can go.

BREATHE as needed, keep the tone as
constant, clear and fat as you can, listen
very carefully.

Do these at medium volume. You want a
buzz that is constant and has no gaps in the
sound. No gaps means your lips are
warmed up.

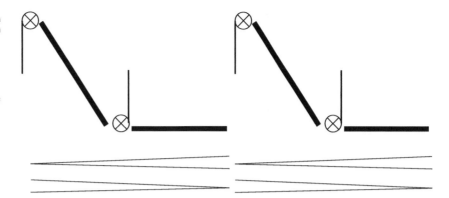

4: Hi-Lo-Mid (30 sec.):

Start at a high but comfortable pitch, keep
the sound constant and go as low as you can
with a good sound and hold the sound
steady. When you're about to run out of air,
go up to a mid-range pitch.

BREATHE as needed, keep the tone as
constant, clear and fat as you can, listen
very carefully.

(be aware that it is much more difficult to go
from low to high than it is to go from high
to low. Use those stomach and lip muscles,
and not mouthpiece pressure!)

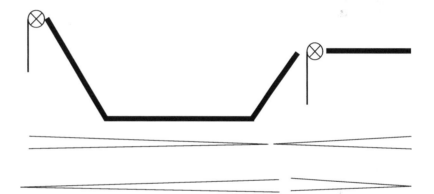

#5: The See-Saw (30 sec.):

Start at a high but comfortable pitch, keep
the sound constant and go as low as you can
and still maintain a pitch, go back up and
try to get as high as your original note, then
back down again. Repeat this until you run
out of air. Don't use pressure to play high.

BREATHE as needed, keep the tone as
constant, clear and fat as you can, listen
very carefully.

(be aware that it is much more difficult to go
from low to high than it is to go from high
to low. Use those stomach and lip muscles,
and not mouthpiece pressure!)

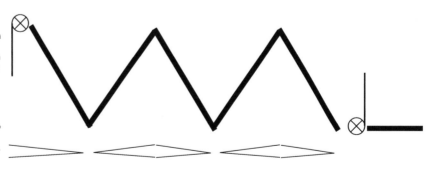

Mouthpiece Buzz Exercises

For mouthpiece buzz exercises, simply go back and repeat all that you did with the buzz alone, then add the following. Play the pitch on piano, then match the pitch with your buzz.

5: Pitch Matching (2 min.):

Match the pitches to the right (or choose your own) on piano or some other instrument. If you don't have access to an instrument, use the radio or CD to buzz along with a song. BREATHE as needed, keep the tone as constant, clear and fat as you can, listen very carefully.

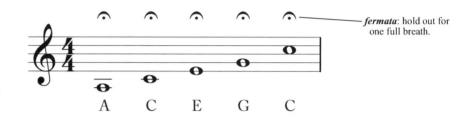

fermata: hold out for one full breath.

A   C   E   G   C

Here are the trumpet notes as you'll find them on a keyboard. Use the keys right in the middle of the keyboard. If you already know the notes on the keyboard, you'll notice these names are different than what you know. To learn more about this, see "Trumpet is a Bb Instrument" on page 187.

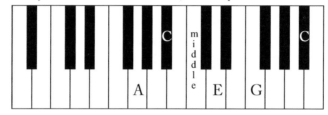

6: Descending/Ascending Chromatic Scale (1-2 min.):

Buzz this scale down and then up. Hold each note for one full breath. Pause between notes. As you become more familiar with the sound of these notes, buzz the upcoming pitch *before* you play it on the piano.

Here are the trumpet notes as you'll find them on a keyboard. Use the keys right in the middle of the keyboard. If you already know the notes on the keyboard, you'll notice these names are different than what you know. For more information on transposing, see "Trumpet is a Bb Instrument" on page 187.

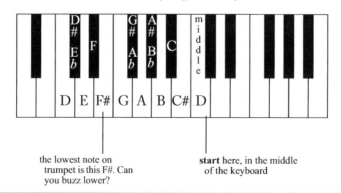

the lowest note on trumpet is this F#. Can you buzz lower?

start here, in the middle of the keyboard

How to Create a Buzz

Sources for Further Study

Here are some books and other sources which will help you continue your study of the buzz and its benefits. Links to all these resources can be found at www.sol-ut.com. Click on the *Sound the Trumpet* cover and choose the "Book Extras" button.

Title	Author (Publisher)
Bert's Basic Brass (interactive DVD)	Bert Truax (http://smartflix.com/store/video/807/Berts-Basic-Brass)
Brass Basics and the BERP (audio CD)	Mario Guarneri (http://www.berp.com/about.html)
Chops (pics of 480 top players' embouchures)	Bill Spilka. (Hard to find. Your best bet is to get it through an interlibrary loan.)
Embouchure Builder	Little & Lowell (Alfred)
The Buzzing Book	James Thompson (Editions BIM)
The Art of Brass Playing: A Treatise on the Formation and Use of the Brass Player's Embouchure	Philip Farkas (Wind Music, Inc.)

Up Next

At this point you might be saying, "But I wanna play trumpet, not mouthpiece!" All this buzzing business is great, and *very* important to you as a trumpet player, but it's not what you got into playing trumpet for, is it? You got into playing trumpet to play the trumpet, right? So let's get to it.

In the next chapter you'll learn about how to put the trumpet together, how to hold it, posture, and other related issues to get you started practicing the excellent habits used by the great players. Have fun!

On the following pages is information about mouthpieces you might find useful. If you're not interested at the moment, feel free to skip the pages and get right into playing trumpet, but be sure to come back for it later. Mouthpiece information is important.

Mouthpiece Anatomy 101

If there is any one thing which will seriously affect your playing, it's having the correct mouthpiece. If you're a beginner you don't have to worry much about mouthpieces at first, but as you get better, you may find that some mouthpieces work better than others. I've known players who had dozens of mouthpieces, though most players rely on a select few.

Mouthpieces come in a bewildering array of shapes and styles, cup depths and shank lengths, density and diameter. It's enough to drive anyone but a brass player loopy. Below you'll get a quick and basic education about what it all means.

Example 3.3 Left: Bach and Monette mouthpieces with parts labeled. Right: A mouthpiece in cross-section.

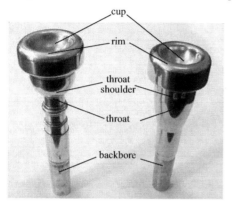
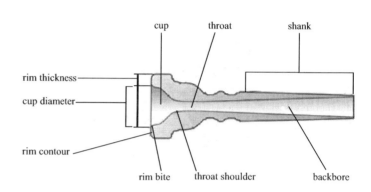

Of Throats and Cups and Shoulders

The Rim: This is where the mouthpiece meets your chops. A rounded rim gives a player more flexibility but tends to tire the lip more quickly. A flat rim allows for a sharper beginning to notes and adds brilliance to the sound but reduces flexibility. A wider rim provides better endurance, while a narrow rim provides more range. A sharp rim bite provides brilliance while a rounded rim bite is less brilliant but more comfortable.

The Cup: The cup is measured by diameter and depth. The larger both are, the more resonant your tone will be. However, the larger a mouthpiece is, the more difficult it is to control. Also, a deep cup and wide diameter can make higher notes more difficult to play. The general idea is to use the largest mouthpiece you can without sacrificing ability or range.

The Throat Shoulder: This is where the air passes from the cup to the throat. The shoulder influences tone quality and resistance. Rounded shoulders are more resonant than sharper shoulders.

The Throat: This is the narrowest part of the mouthpiece. It's where the air moves from throat shoulder to backbore. A throat that is too small will make a trumpet play sharp up high, and flat down low and will feel stuffy. The bigger the throat the fuller the tone, but too big and it becomes difficult to play softly and endurance suffers.

The Backbore: The backbore is where the air passes from the throat to the lead pipe of the trumpet. Intonation and tone quality are affected by the backbore. A small backbore will give the sound a brilliance but at the cost of a flat, stuffy upper register. A large backbore can give a better tone, but too large and notes lack definition and you'll tire easily.

How to Create a Buzz

What to Look for in a Mouthpiece

The most general rule is to find the mouthpiece that is the most comfortable. It's that easy. The first critical questions you should ask after finding a comfortable mouthpiece is, "Is it in tune?" If not, don't buy it. Be sure to take your tuner with you to the music store. (What? You don't have one? Better buy one at the music store. A tuner is a must. For more info, see "Tuners for In-tune Tunes" on page 213.

Here's what Dave Monette has to say about choosing a mouthpiece (from *Monette Mouthpiece Manual and User's Guide,* used with permission):

- When selecting a new mouthpiece, the size that feels most comfortable and that allows you to play with the most easy, natural embouchure and in the most resonant, centered way is usually the best size for you!

- If you are playing lead trumpet, use a lead mouthpiece! You would not run a marathon in wing tips, and you should probably not try and play the scream book in a big band on a B1-1 mouthpiece! [B1-1 is a very large mouthpiece—JH]

- If your sound shape is too narrow, you miss too many notes and you have difficulties playing "down into the center" of the equipment, try a wider inside-rim diameter with a comfortable cup depth.

- If your sound shape is too wide and you find yourself "swimming" in the equipment, try a narrower inside-rim diameter with a comfortable cup depth.

- Flatter rims, or rims with more "bite" on the inside edge may provide more control and security in articulation, but too much "bite" or "grip" can inhibit flexibility. If you often "splatter" articulations, try a sharper rim. If you feel the rim constricts you, try a wider inside-rim diameter, a rounder rim contour, or both.

- If a mouthpiece feels good, sounds good, provides better range and endurance, and plays more in-tune, you have found your new mouthpiece—even if it is not what you are used to!

And also from the same source (*Monette Mouthpiece Manual and User's Guide*):

Tips for the Very Confused

1 Does the mouthpiece you are trying feel too wide or too narrow?

2 Does the cup feel too shallow or too deep?

3 Does the rim contour feel too round or too sharp?

4 Do you need to take a break and come back to the process with a fresh perspective?

If after following these tips you still need help, find a teacher whose advice you trust, and purchase your mouthpiece. Then forget mouthpiece sizes and practice making music!

In the long run, players should always make a good mouthpiece selection based on what equipment helps them to sound better and make more music. If the process seems more complicated than that, you are making it more complicated than it needs to be.

7C, 3D, B2? What Does it Mean!?

Mouthpieces are usually stamped with a letter and a number and each manufacturer has a slightly different definition of what these numbers and letters mean. The information below may help clear up the confusion.

Generally, the number refers to the depth of the cup. A larger number *usually* means a shallower cup (see Laskey and Yamaha below for exceptions). For instance, a Bach 7C mouthpiece (a good depth for a beginner) will have a much shallower cup than a Bach 1C.

The letter often refers to the type of trumpet: B for B-flat trumpet, C for C trumpet, etcetera. Bach mouthpieces are an exception to this general rule. Experiment. Find what you like and what works for you. What works is a mouthpiece that gives you clarity, intonation and a free-blowing quality in all registers without sacrificing endurance.

Mouthpieces are not cheap, so most music stores will allow you to try out a mouthpiece before you buy. Be sure to bring your horn and tuner when shopping for a mouthpiece so you can try before you buy. Good luck!

Bach	Giardinelli	Laskey	Marcink- iewicz	Monette	Schilke	Stork	Warburton	Yamaha
1	1M	84D		B1-1	19	1	1M	18C4
1B		84B	1	B1-5M			2D	17C4
1C		85C		B1-5	18			
1.25C		80MC		B2	17		2M	
1.5B		75B		B4	16			
1.5C		68C	1	B3	16		3M	16C4
2C	3M	70C		B4S	15	2C		15C4/16
2.5C			3					14A4a
3			4	B5				14A4a
3B		70B						13A4a
3C		65MC		B6	15		4M	
5C	5C or 6M	60C			13C4	3C		14C4
6							5MD	
6C					12		5MC	9C4
7					11A		6MD	8C4
7C	7C or 7M	50C	5-6	B7F	11		6MC	11/11C4
8C		50B	7-8			5C		
9C			9-10				6M	6A4a
10.5C	10M	40C	11-12	B8	9C4	7C	7MC	8C4
11C	12M		13-15		8A4		8MC	
17					7B4			
20C					5A4			

CHAPTER 4

DOIN' THE MESS AROUND

Don't be too timid and squeamish about your actions. All life is an experiment. The more experiments you make the better.

~ Ralph Waldo Emerson (1803-1882)

In This Chapter

- Putting Your Trumpet Together
- How to Hold It
- Posture
- Valves 101
- Simple Exercises

Terms to Know

valve casing: The metal which surrounds and supports the valves. The fingers of your left hand wrap around the valve casing.

trigger: Found on the third- and first valve slide, these allow you to move the slides in and out for tuning.

valves: The piston-shaped devices that divert air into the first, second and third valve slides, changing the pitch of the trumpet.

long tones: Any single note held out for one large, complete breath. Long tones should be clear and unwavering with a full tone.

mouthpiece puller: Pulls out the mouthpiece when it gets stuck.

Forget the Details and Just Go For It!

There are basically two types of learners: those who like as much information as they can get before they try something new and those who jump right in regardless of what they do or don't know. There are benefits to each approach.

If you're the type who loves to leap before looking, then by all means, go for it. Open your case carefully so you don't dump your horn on the ground (the lettering on the case should be upright and the latches usually open upwards). Pick up the horn and see if you can figure out how to hold it correctly. Put the mouthpiece in and give it a little twist when it's snug. Now blow! Put your buzz to work.

If you'd like to know before you blow, or if you had trouble with the guessing approach, read on.

The Details

As long as your slides and valves are in place, a trumpet is one of the easiest instruments to put together. Simply put the mouthpiece into the lead pipe snugly, give it a little twist to the left or right to lock it into place and you're ready to go! If your slides and/or valves *aren't* in place, skip ahead to "All Together Now" on page 155 to take care of that problem.

It's pretty easy to jam the mouthpiece in so that it won't come out at all, so be careful when you put the mouthpiece in. Don't tap or pound it in with your palm, and try not to drop your trumpet on the mouthpiece! If either of these unfortunate things does happen and you're unable to get the mouthpiece out (don't worry, this happens to most of us at least once), take it down to your local music store and their repair person will take it out for you. Most band directors have a *mouthpiece puller*.

Hold It!

There are no hard and fast rules about how to hold the trumpet, but generally the trumpet is held around the *valve casing* by your left hand and the fingers of your right hand work the valves. Buddy Bolden, one of the great cornet players of New Orleans around 1900 (thought by many to be the first jazz musician) played left-handed. Most players stick to the standard because it's more comfortable. For various reasons, some people hold the trumpet other than the way I describe below. Do what's most comfortable and allows the horn to simply rest in your hand.

Put Your Left Hand In...

To hold your trumpet correctly, wrap the fingers of your left hand around the valve casing. If your trumpet has a *trigger* on the third valve slide, put your ring finger in the trigger, wrap your index and middle fingers around the valve casing and rest your pinky wherever you want. Some third valve triggers are adjustable. If yours is one of these you can loosen the set screw and change the finger ring to a comfortable distance. Some trumpets have a trigger on the first valve slide too, and this is where your thumb goes.

The picture below shows how I hold my trumpet. Some players put their pinky and ring finger under the third valve slide, wrapped around the valve casings. I played like this for many years, but switched my grip to allow my hand to be more relaxed. Your trumpet may be made differently than mine, and your hand may feel more comfortable in another position, so don't be afraid to experiment until you find what you like.

Example 4.1 The left hand position. Strive for a relaxed hand. Don't grip the horn, let it rest in your hand.

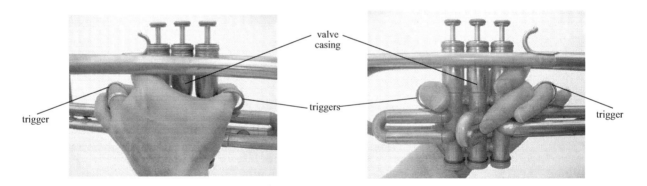

Put Your Right Hand On...

The first three fingers of the right hand go on the valves, slightly curved. Fingers are able to move much more quickly when they are slightly curved, like you're holding a tennis ball. Be sure to start this good habit right away. In addition, holding your fingers this way will help you avoid carpal tunnel syndrome, a painful and possibly long-lasting injury to the tendons that control the hand.

The pinky finger should rest on *top* of the finger ring, not hooked into it. This is very important. A common problem for trumpet players is using too much pressure against the mouth. With the pinky *inside* the finger ring, it's almost impossible not to yank the trumpet against your face, especially for high notes. This will cause problems! The finger ring is meant to be used to hold the trumpet with one hand while the other turns pages, works a plunger mute, picks your nose, or whatever. Don't use it as an octave key!

The right hand thumb should rest in the little valley between the first and second valve. This is also to ensure your hand stays loose and relaxed, allowing the fingers to move quickly and easily. If you keep your thumb here, you'll be less likely to grip the valves tightly which not only slows down your fingers but also affects the quality of your sound. Again, this might be a little uncomfortable at first, but stick with it and soon it'll feel natural. Here's a picture of the correct right hand position. Check the thumb and pinky in this picture.

Posture

Correct posture affects not only the body but the mind as well. You're more alert and able to concentrate when you sit or stand up straight. When playing a wind instrument, correct posture is even more crucial because it allows you to breathe correctly, and breathing is one of the most important aspects of playing trumpet. Whether sitting or standing, there are a few general ideas to keep in mind.

Be sure to bring the trumpet to your mouth and don't bring your mouth to the trumpet. If you bring your mouth to the trumpet, this will cause you to thrust your head forward slightly which will block your air flow. Check yourself in a mirror. Better yet, use two mirrors so you can see your profile, the angle of your trumpet and the straightness of your head and neck.

Whether you're sitting or standing, imagine there is a string coming out the top of your head and it's being pulled up, almost lifting you off your chair or off the ground. This will keep your spine lengthened which will allow your lungs to expand fully and will also help to open your airway, improving air flow.

Relax your shoulders and keep your chest up and out. Think about your elbows. They should be relaxed and slightly out from your side. Don't clamp them to your side. Stay relaxed as much as possible.

Seated Posture

Arnold Jacobs, the phenomenal tuba player and master teacher, has good advice about the seated posture. He advises that you should sit in such a way that you can stand up immediately. This sounds simple but will probably take some adjustment before you're able to do it. Try it once right now. If you need to lean forward before you stand, you don't have it quite right. Keep your back off the chair and sit on the front half of the chair. Don't cross your ankles and keep your feet flat on the floor, feet parallel and pointed forward.

Another helpful item that will help your posture is a small wedge-shaped cushion. This type of cushion is often used in Iyengar yoga classes as a prop and you should be able to find one online or at a store that sells yoga gear. The cushion will help flatten your lower spine and possibly alleviate or forestall any back pain that may be a result of poor posture. Try it out and see what you think.

A study of master trumpeters' seated posture was done recently and when sitting, all the players' legs were at a ninety degree angle. This allowed the abdomen to expand freely and allowed the player to take full advantage of the abdominal expansion necessary for a good breath. You should do this, too.

Standing Posture

When you stand up to play trumpet, a lot of posture problems are fixed automatically. It's easier to breathe deeply standing up and your sound will project through a room much better when you stand. If you're standing, be sure your hips are open and your feet are hip width apart, toes pointed forward and knees slightly bent. I can't stress enough how important all the things in the above sentence are. Do them! You will notice an immediate change in your sound, range and endurance. All the other advice also applies: chest up and out, elbows loose and relaxed, string pulling you up from the center of your head, and relax your shoulders. You may want to work with your teacher to be sure you've got the correct posture. Posture is that important.

Example 4.2 Left: Correct posture sitting. Be sure your back is off the chair. Middle: Correct posture standing.
Right: Don't be afraid to try something different.

The exact angle to hold the trumpet is slightly different for everybody because of how your teeth are formed and how your specific embouchure is shaped. As a general rule, the trumpet should be angled slightly downward almost parallel to the ground

When starting something new, it takes time to form the correct habits. Check your posture as often as you can and fix it when you notice you're sagging or lop-sided. Practice in front of a mirror. Have someone sneak a snapshot of you while playing. You might be surprised at your posture and will be more likely to correct it next time.

But again, posture isn't everything. If you look at Miles Davis, one of the best jazz trumpet players ever to live, you'll see that most times he pays little attention to correct posture, though he always looks relaxed. Shunryu Suzuki, a Zen master once said, "The secret of Zen is just two words: Not always so!" Try playing slouched over, play lying down on your back, standing on your head, under water, or any other way you can come up with. Simply stay relaxed, no matter what posture you're using. Be aware of how posture affects breathing. Always have fun!

The Alexander Technique

The Alexander Technique is a method used by actors, musicians, and athletes around the world to improve their performance. The Alexander Technique was developed by the Shakespearean actor F. M. Alexander in the late 1800s. Alexander experienced voice loss which threatened his acting career. He studied the reasons behind the loss of his voice and eventually discovered that a slight change of his head and neck position solved his problem. This discovery lead to even more study of head and neck position and its impact on performance, now known as the Alexander Technique.

I was first introduced to the Alexander Technique about fifteen years ago and it's made a big difference in my life, both as a musician and in daily life; things as simple as climbing a flight of stairs. If you're interested in the Alexander Technique, check out *The Alexander Technique: How to Use Your Body Without Stress* by Wilfred Barlow. You can probably find a teacher in your area. Look in the yellow pages or ask musicians, actors and athletes you know. Studying with an Alexander teacher is a great investment if you're serious about improving your playing.

Go For It!

By now, you're probably saying, "Enough with all the rules and suggestions! Just let me play the dern thing!" And that's just what you should do now and for the next week or two. Mess around with your horn and see what you remember from all your reading. It wouldn't hurt to review all this information mid-week to see if you've got it perfectly or if you picked up a bad habit. Find and eradicate any bad habits as soon as you can because the longer you practice a bad habit, the tougher it will be to change.

Some things to keep in mind or to try while messing around:

- **Stay relaxed**. Nothing will affect your sound more than the state of your body. A tense body will get tired more quickly and the sound produced by a tense body will also be tense and more difficult to control. Stay loose and relaxed. ***Remember to be patient with yourself!***

- **Mental checklist. Whenever you think of it, check these things**:
  1. Finger position - right hand pinky and thumb especially. Curve those three fingers. Relax.
  2. Posture - edge of your chair if sitting, open hips if standing, feet shoulder width, string pulling you up, chest out, elbows relaxed and away from your side.
  3. Pressure on your lips (the less the better—use just enough pressure to get a good seal)
  4. Don't puff out your cheeks.
  5. Breathing (from deep in your belly. See "The Correct Breath" on page 54)

- **Things to try while messing around**:
  1. Take lots of breaks. *Rest as much as you play*.
  2. Play one note as long as you can in one breath. Time yourself and try to better your record each practice session. (record your progress in the tracking chart in the Codicil)
  3. Make your sound go from loud to soft as smoothly as you can.
  4. Make your sound go from soft to loud as smoothly as you can.
  5. Play as low as you can.

1 Play as loudly as you can with a good sound. Play as loudly as you can until the sound gets distorted.

2 Play as softly as you can.

3 Play as high as you can. Be careful here! It's easy to jam the trumpet on your face to play high, but resist the temptation! Play as high as you can without excessive pressure.

4 Play from high to low with a continuous sound. This is called a glissando and is difficult for beginners, so use lots of air. Use half valves for a different sound.

5 Play from low to high with a continuous sound. This is even more difficult than number nine. Use half valves.

6 If you get frustrated or bored, STOP. Give it a rest and pick the horn up later in the day or tomorrow.

7 Congratulate yourself. You're playing trumpet!

Exercises to Get You On Your Way

Before we get into the details, there are several things you can begin to work on without knowing much else about the trumpet. Start perfecting these now and your sound and abilities will improve dramatically.

Long Tones: You started to do these when you were messing around (#2 above). A long tone is any note you hold for a full breath. Make the sound as clean and steady as you can. Project your deepest, richest, clearest tone to the edges of the room. Really listen! By keeping your air flow steady you'll keep the pitch of the note steady.

Start and Stop: Start a note and hold it for a second or two. Stop the note with your air. Start the same note again and see if you can get it to sound immediately without any kacks or sputters or clams. Try it again with a different note. Make the second note different from the first.

Trills: Play an open note (no valves down), then choose one valve to push up and down as fast as you can. Pay close attention to correct right hand position when doing this to get the most speed possible.

Listen: Have you listened to some good music today?

Finger Patterns: In the next Chapter are finger patterns you'll learn. Choose one or two easy ones and see if you can play them right now on the horn.

Up Next

The first three fingers of the right hand are the ones that do almost all the work. You can get all possible notes with just three fingers. Because you're using just three fingers, it's important that those fingers are nimble and quick. Music is all about patterns and in the next chapter you'll start learning some patterns to practice with your three fingers. Easy to do and great to practice.

CHAPTER 5

FAST FINGERS

Success is following the pattern of life one enjoys most.

~ Al Capp (1909-1979)

In This Chapter

- Finger Technique
- Hand Positions
- Changing Notes
- Finger Exercises

Terms to Know

dexterity: Skill and ease in using the hands.

metronome: Your best friend. It will keep your sense of timing sharp and precise. Buy one! Use it! To learn more, see "How to Use the Metronome" on page 69, and "Metronome: Your Rhythmic Best Friend" on page 211.

sixteenth notes (♫): Four notes per beat, foot tap, or metronome click. The count in $\frac{4}{4}$ time is "one-ee-and-uh, two-ee-and-uh, three-ee-and-uh, four-ee-and-uh."

Finger Technique?

Believe it or not, there are actually correct and beneficial ways to use your fingers on the trumpet. You already know how to hold the horn, so that part is already taken care of. What we'll be dealing with in this chapter is moving from one note to the next, finger patterns, and finger exercises to get your fingers moving faster.

As with every other aspect of the trumpet, the key to fast fingers is staying relaxed. The looser you are, the faster you'll be able to go. The practice of staying relaxed is something you'll monitor for as long as you play the trumpet. Always check in with your posture and level of relaxation to be sure you're staying upright and loose.

There are a few left hand techniques you should be aware of, but most of what we'll be dealing with happens in the right hand, so we'll start there. If you happen to be one of those rare individuals who works the valves with your left hand, then apply what follows to the correct hand.

The Right Hand

To refresh your memory, the right hand thumb should rest between the "valley" of the first and second valves, just under the lead pipe. The pinky finger rests on top of the finger ring, NOT in it. This is because that finger ring is very easy to pull on, and this will hamper finger speed, hurt your sound and probably your face, too. Fingers are curved like you're holding a tennis ball.

Changing Notes

The thing to remember is that you *must* practice these movements *very* slowly at first so your body learns them correctly. Start slowly and monitor your performance so you know each finger is perfect, then gradually speed up as fast as you can. Keep your fingering clean and correct at all tempos.

USE A METRONOME! This is *so* important. You want that rhythm in your fingers and the best way to do this is to practice finger patterns with a metronome. Whether you're just doing the patterns without the horn, playing scale patterns, or playing music, practice with the metronome so you know your rhythm is perfect. *This will help your finger accuracy more than anything else you could do!* To learn more, flip ahead to, "How to Use the Metronome" on page 69.

Two paragraphs ago I said practice slowly. This means slowly from one note to the next. However, the valve motion itself should be as fast as possible. Pound the valve down while you keep the air moving. This allows for a smooth transition from one note to another.

It's especially important to slam your valves when you're playing a slow song. Because the music is slow, you'll want to move your valves slowly too, but don't give in to the temptation. If you move your valves slowly, you won't get a clean change between notes. If your air is moving and you pound down the valves, your note changes will be clean and clear and beautiful. If you move your valves slowly you'll get another interesting effect we'll talk about in Chapter 15. When fingering notes which use more than one valve, be sure to press all the valves down at the same time. This will help you avoid chipped or missed notes (also known as *kacks* or *clams*).

Keep your finger tips on the valve buttons even when they're not pressing down on a valve. Look at the picture on the last page to see where your fingers should be all the time. This is a difficult technique to achieve when playing fast, and especially when using the first two valves. Keep that third finger down on the button if you can. The closer your fingers are to the valve, the quicker they can react. If your fingers are high above the valve buttons, it will take that much longer to push the valve down.

The Left Hand

The main thing to remember about your right hand is to keep it loose and relaxed. Try not to grip the valve casing tightly because eventually you'll need your ring finger and thumb to work the slides. We'll get to that later.

Example 5.2 The left hand. Keep it loose. You're not holding the horn so much as you are letting the trumpet rest in your hand. Don't squeeze.

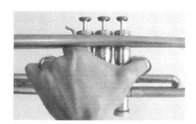
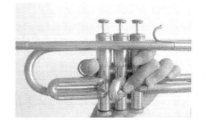

Exercises For Accuracy and Speed

These patterns can be done anywhere. Try tapping out finger patterns on the pad of your thumb. Curl your fingers and practice fingerings on a flat surface like a table top. Hold a pencil with your left hand, put your right thumb underneath and do fingerings on the top of the pencil. If you're really ambitious you can find a junker trumpet and use a hacksaw to cut off the valve casings so you have a portable set of valves to practice on. It's kind of fun to chop up a trumpet like that.

Otherwise, just practice on the horn itself. During your practice sessions you'll have the horn off your face about as much as you have it on your face. When the horn is off your face, don't just sit there and stare at the wall. Use the time to practice fingerings. There are also times during rehearsals when the director is occupied with another section and the horn isn't on your face. While you're waiting, actively practice by doing finger patterns. Every little bit of time you spend honing your skills will add up, so use that time wisely. You won't regret it.

To make things neater, the exercises below use numbers for valves instead of the graphic illustration which has been used up to now (0 = open, 1 = first valve, 2 = second valve, 3 = third valve).

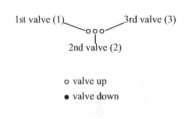

Practice these patterns until they're memorized and you know exactly how fast you're able to go. Start all exercises at a comfortably slow tempo (slow enough to do it exactly right) and progress from there. All exercises use the sixteenth note rhythm (4 notes per beat—the "+" symbol stands for "and", so the count is, "one-ee-and-uh, two-ee-and-uh, etc. For more information about counting and written music in general, get a copy of *Basic Music Theory: How to Read, Write, and Understand Written Music*. I'll show you the details of the exercise first and successive exercises will have only the fingering, but the rhythm is the same.

Always strive for perfection. START SLOWLY! Curve those fingers. Check your hand position. Dust off your metronome. It won't do you any good if it's in your case or, even worse, sitting in a music store somewhere waiting for you to buy it! If you don't have a metronome or don't use the one you have, ask yourself the question, "How good do I want to be?" Answer honestly.

A metronome will help you to track your progress. In the Codicil of this book is a chart used to monitor your exercises from day to day or week to week. It's important to know where you've been, where you are, and where you're going. Plus, it's more efficient to start practicing at the exact tempo you left off with instead of trying to find your fastest tempo all over again.

Example 5.3 Finger exercises. Repeat many times. Do these both with and without the horn, high, middle and low.

1. Single Finger

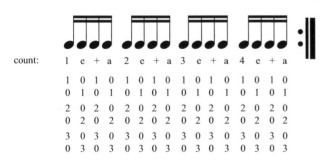

2. Two Fingers

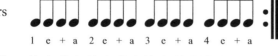

count: 1   e   +   a   2   e   +   a   3   e   +   a   4   e   +   a

fingering:

12   0   12   0   12   0   12   0   12   0   12   0   12   0   12   0
0   12   0   12   0   12   0   12   0   12   0   12   0   12   0   12

23   0   23   0   etc.
0   23   0   23

13   0   13   0   etc.
0   13   0   13

23   0   23   0   etc.
0   23   0   23

More Difficult Variations:

23   0   12   0   etc.
0   23   0   12

12   23   12   23   etc.
23   12   23   12

13   0   12   0   etc.
0   13   0   12

13   0   23   0   etc.
0   13   0   23

13   23   13   23   etc.
23   13   23   13

12   13   12   13   etc.
13   12   13   12

3. Combinations

count: 1   e   +   a   2   e   +   a   3   e   +   a   4   e   +   a

fingering:

0   13   12   13   0   13   12   13   0   13   12   13   0   13   12   13
1   0   12   0   1   0   12   0   1   0   12   0   1   0   12   0
1   0   13   0   1   0   13   0   1   0   13   0   1   0   13   0
23   1   0   1   23   1   0   1   23   1   0   1   23   1   0   1
12   2   23   2   etc.
13   12   2   12   etc.
0   12   2   12   etc.
0   13   23   13   etc.
1   0   23   1   etc.
23   1   2   1   etc.
2   23   12   23   etc.
12   2   0   2   etc.
0   12   1   12   etc.

more patterns:

0   13   23   13   etc.
1   0   23   0   etc.
1   0   123   0   etc.
23   1   2   1   etc.
2   123   13   123   etc.
1   0   23   0   etc.
1   0   123   0   etc.
23   1   2   1   etc.

difficult:

123   23   12   23   etc.
123   23   1   23   etc.
123   13   23   13   etc.
123   1   23   1   etc.
13   23   12   23   etc.

Try these fingerings "dry" (without sound) and also while blowing the horn. Once you've memorized a bunch, you can do them anywhere. For different variations when actually playing you can choose whether the pitch will go up or down from the starting note.

What's Up Next

Breathing is one of the most important skills that affect your sound and ability on trumpet. There are specific techniques that will help you get a great breath so your trumpet sound can be full and present and beautiful. Not only does correct breathing help your tone quality, but correct breathing will also help you play higher, softer, or faster. Learn all about proper breathing in the next chapter.

CHAPTER 6
AVOIDING BAD BREATH

Virtually any aspect of trumpet playing will improve in direct correlation with improved breathing.

~ Keith Johnson, *The Art of Trumpet Playing*

In This Chapter

- Why learn to breathe?
- Taking a Correct Breath
- The Breathing Tube
- Breathing Exercises
- Gadgets for Better Breathing

Terms to Know

breath mark: An apostrophe-shaped (') symbol placed above the staff to indicate a breath is to be taken.
diaphragm: The muscle that controls the inhalation and exhalation of the lungs.
breathing tube: A tube of PVC, cardboard or paper that help to open the throat for a good breath.
NB: No Breath. Don't breathe. Used as a reminder to avoid breaking a musical phrase with a breath.

Why Learn to Breathe?

The fact that trumpet is a wind instrument is the first clue that wind, or breath, is an inseparable part of the instrument. Without air the trumpet will make no sound at all. Your breath is as much a part of the instrument as the valves or mouthpiece is. If you start good breathing habits as soon as you begin playing, you'll make things much easier for yourself. The benefits of good breathing are a better sound, better intonation, higher range, and a more pleasing tone.

You might think breathing is such a natural thing that you don't really need to learn much more about it, but breathing for a wind instrument is special and needs to be done correctly if you want to be a good player. You can actually increase the amount of air you are able to take in, your *vital capacity*. Older players are especially encouraged to build their vital capacity with the exercises found in this chapter.

The Physiology of Breathing

Breathing is usually done without thought. Your body knows what it needs to do and does it. However, unlike digestion and most other automatic body functions, you can easily take control of your breath. It's easy to hold your breath or take a deep breath or expel all the air out of your lungs. Controlling the breath is important because taking a breath for trumpet playing is different from normal breathing. At first you'll need to be very conscious of what you're doing.

The following information may or may not be useful. It can be valuable to know exactly what is happening in your body when you breathe. However, it's not information that you *must* have in order to learn how to take a good trumpet breath. If you're bored by such details or feel you don't need to know, go ahead and skip forward. If you like such details and want to learn more, read on.

There is a rhythm generator in your brain which fires about 12 times a minute, on average, for your entire life. This happens for reasons not completely understood. This rhythm helps your brain know when it's time to breathe. When it *is* time to breathe your brain sends an electrical impulse down your phrenic nerve to your diaphragm.

The diaphragm is the main muscle of breathing. It stretches across the chest from side to side and front to back. When you inhale, the diaphragm contracts downward. This creates a vacuum in the lungs which draws air down into them. When the air enters the lungs, something has to be displaced to make room for it. That something is the rest of your innards: stomach, liver, intestines, etc. So when you take a deep breath, your stomach should push out. Here's a diagram to help with the visualization. Take a breath or three and try to feel what is going on inside.

Example 6.1 Cross-sections of the lungs and abdominal cavity showing diaphragm positions for inhale and exhale.

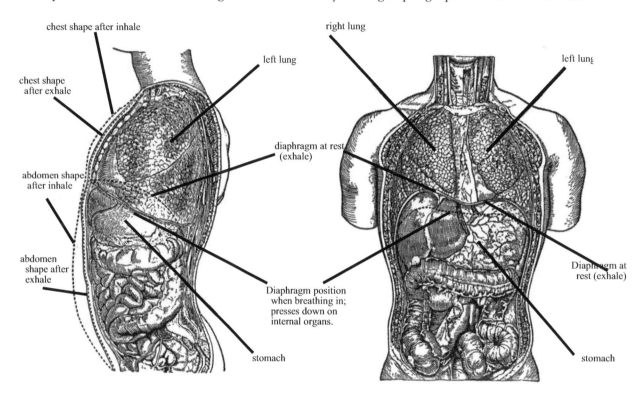

One of the reasons these diagrams (of the diaphragm) are helpful, especially the diagram on the left, is that they show what happens to your guts when you inhale. Stress and not wanting to look "fat" cause us to breathe shallowly, up high in our chests. As you can see, when you take a full, deep breath, your abdomen *has* to expand outward to make way for all the air you're taking in. If you want to play trumpet well, you're going to have to learn how to take a good breath. This will take some time and concentration, but keep at it! Work with your teacher.

The Correct Breath

A large breath can be thought of as a 3-step process, with the first step being the most difficult to learn. It's not really *that* difficult. It's more about awareness than anything else; awareness of what

Avoiding Bad Breath

your body is doing, awareness of what you want to accomplish, and awareness of whether you've accomplished it.

A very important aspect of the correct breath is posture. The less flesh that is in the way of the incoming air the better. If you're slouched over, this will cramp your lungs and they won't be able to expand to their full capacity. If your head is tilted left or right, up or down, your throat will be constricted and you won't be able to get the maximum amount of air through. Inhalation should be quiet. If you hear noise on your inhale, your throat is in the way. Sit or stand tall, jaw level with the floor, and chin slightly tucked in. You can also try thrusting your jaw forward a little to help open up the throat.

Proper Breath Step 1

When we are babies, we breathe like a trumpet player should. As we get older, the tensions of living in the world cause our breathing to becomes more shallow, up high in our chests. If you've watched a baby breathe, you've probably seen their little stomach push out with the inhale and go back in on the exhale. That's how it's supposed to be, and that's the first step of the 3-part full breath. It's the most important part, too, so be sure to practice until it's automatic. I've been playing trumpet for more than 25 years and I still try to remain conscious of this part of the deep breath.

The following preliminary exercises will help you feel what should happen during the first stage of a proper breath:

1. Lie on your back and relax; rest your hand on your stomach and take a deep breath. Your hand should rise up as your lungs fill and the air displaces the rest of your innards. If this doesn't happen, you're breathing shallowly up in your chest and your shoulders are probably moving.

2. Sit in a chair and lean over until your chest is resting on your lap. Take a deep breath. Stay in this position through several breaths and feel where your body is expanding. Place your hand on your lower back and take another breath. You should feel your body expanding even back there. You should feel the pressure around your midsection, from your belly to your back.

3. Now sit or stand and try to breathe in the same way. Can you do it? If not, keep practicing until you can.

4. This is the most important part of the breathing process. Practice breathing wherever you are, whenever you think of it until it becomes habit. This is one of the most important things to learn as a wind player!

Proper Breath Step 2

It's important to wait on Step 2 until you've got Step 1 down *very* well. This is because step 1 will give you much more air than any of the other steps. Also, step 2 is where we usually breathe, up higher in our chest, and it's easy to do only this part and neglect Step 1. Don't neglect Step 1!

After your abdomen pushes out and your lower lungs are filled as much as they can be, lift your chest up and out and you'll find you can continue to fill up with more air. Your upper chest will expand in this stage, but not nearly as much as your abdomen did in Step 1.

Proper Breath Step 3

There is some debate as to whether this part of the process is necessary. Some use it, some don't. Bobby Shew teaches it, so it certainly can work. Decide for yourself. The reason this step is debated is because it involves the shoulders rising, which is usually the sign of a shallow breath.

In the third step you're filling up the very top of your lungs and this causes the shoulders to rise slightly. If done correctly, the shoulders will rise all by themselves because of the continued expansion of the lungs. Some people help a little by raising the shoulders, then lowering them to add compression when they play, especially for loud or high playing.

All Together Now, 1-2-3

It takes a whole lot more time to explain this type of breath than it does to perform it. At times this breath has to be very fast, and even when you have the time it should take less than two seconds to fully tank up on air.

In order to do this breath quickly, your throat must be open. Check your posture, maybe push your jaw forward a little, and go through the three stages slowly at first, then more quickly until it's automatic and fast. There is a tool called a *breathing tube* which will help get your throat open and help to speed up the process. Learn about it below.

Be sure to spend time at the beginning of each practice session to focus on breathing correctly. This means doing the exercises above, using the breathing tube which is explained next, and doing the breathing exercises listed below.

The Breathing Tube

This isn't a snorkel. It's a piece of 1-inch PVC tubing (or any type of tube, like the cardboard in a roll of toilet paper or a rolled up file card) which will help teach you how to take a good breath. I have my students wear one around their neck and use it for a few years or until the breath is good and big and automatic. I still use mine during warm-ups to remind myself.

Place the tube in your mouth over your tongue and put it at least an inch or more into your mouth. This may be uncomfortable at first, but as long as you don't gag, you'll be okay. If you *do* gag, I apologize. Don't put the tube in quite so far.

Okay, your tube's in? Now take a *slow* 3-step breath. Exhale. Now do a *quick* 3-step breath

Did you feel how quickly you got a lungfull of air? The air should fall right into your lungs quietly, with very little effort and nearly instantly. This is what taking a good breath feels like. Practice slowly, going through all three stages. Speed up until you can do this quickly. As you practice, you might want to sit down because taking in this much air will probably make you feel light-headed. If this happens, wait until the feeling passes before you continue.

Some Breathing Exercises

1 Sit-ups. Yes, something as simple as sit-ups will help improve your breathing. Playing trumpet not only involves breathing, but also blowing and sometimes blowing very hard. Strong stomach muscles are essential to blowing on trumpet when playing loudly. Plus, doing sit-ups is good for your lower back. In fact, exercise in general is great for your trumpet playing and your life. Do some today!

2 Take a piece of typing paper and draw a bull's-eye in the center of it. Hold the paper out right in front of your face and blow towards the center of the bull's-eye as though you were blowing soap bubbles through a wand. When the paper moves outward, hold it steadily with your air so it doesn't flutter around. Do this several times and be sure to sit and/or take a break if you begin to get dizzy or light-headed. Gradually move the paper further out with each new breath until the paper is at arm length. It will be more difficult to keep the paper pushed back and steady the

further away it is, but keep the air flowing and you'll have good success. Tape the paper to a stand so you can back up further. Continue backing up to about 10-15 feet or until the paper doesn't move. The distance you'll be able to move the paper will increase the more you practice this exercise.

3   A more difficult variation of the above: Sit in front of a candle in a windless room. Take a correct deep breath and blow. Focus your air stream on the candle and try to bend the flame without blowing it out. As with the paper, keep the flame bent back to the same spot and don't let it waver. This will take some practice to perfect. Back up and do it again. See how far away you can be and still effect the flame (10-15 feet is good). Keep at it. The benefits are worth it even if you can't feel them yet.

4   Set up a metronome to beat at mm=60, or keep track of the seconds on a watch. Breathe in fully and deeply for two beats (two seconds), then focus your airstream like you did with the bulls-eye exercise and blow for six seconds. Get rid of *all* your air by the time the sixth beat ends, take another two-beat breath and do it again. After two repetitions, increase the "blow" count to seven and do that twice also. Increase the count to eight, then nine, then ten. Be sure to do each twice. Learn to conserve your air and use as much of it as you can in the time given. If you start to feel light-headed, stop until the feeling passes.

5   Stop and rest if this one makes you light-headed or dizzy. Breathe in for two counts, focus your airstream, and get rid of all your air in five counts as before. Two beats of deep inhale and exhale all of your air in four beats, then inhale two and blow three, then inhale two and blow two, and finally inhale one and blow for one. Repeat each twice. Be sure to keep your airstream focused, like you were blowing soap bubbles. It will be much more difficult to get rid of all that air in one beat. Your stomach muscles should get a nice little workout with this exercise.

6   Hold a small piece of paper against the wall, stand back about 6 inches, take a good 3-Step breath and blow. Hold the paper against the wall with your air stream. Take a breath and move back an inch or two (be sure to hold the paper with your hand as you breathe in :-). Keep backing up with each breath. How far back can you stand and still hold the paper against the wall?

7   So far you have had no resistance to your exhale. Playing trumpet involves resistance to the exhale. Take a deep breath and exhale (3 times). Then after the inhale, blow through the trumpet without the mouthpiece (3 times). Then blow 3 times through the mouthpiece alone (no embouchure). Then put the mouthpiece in the horn and blow 3 more times (still no embouchure). Finally form an embouchure (but don't make a buzz!) and blow three more times after a good 3-Step breath. You should feel the resistance increase with each step in this exercise.

When to Breathe

When to take a breath is an important skill to learn because it can't happen just anywhere. Because a breath takes some time even at its fastest, and because your horn won't make any sound as you inhale, it's important to put the breath where it won't interfere with the melodic (or harmonic) phrase. If you took a breath in the middle of a phrase, that would be like   saying   a sentence with a bunch   of pauses in it and that would be   distracting to listen to or to   read.

Some music, especially for beginners, is marked with what are called *breath marks* which look a lot like commas (') and are written near the top of the staff. Often when you write them in your music, it's to remind yourself to take a Large Breath so you can make it through a phrase. The larger the breath you need, the larger the breath mark is drawn. And if you don't pay attention to it, you can make it bigger, circle it, highlight it, or whatever else it takes.

On the other hand, there are also times when you need to break the habit of breathing in the wrong place and chopping up the phrase. In this case, write a large **NB** where you usually take the forbidden breath. This stands for, you guessed it, **No Breath**.

When You Have Too Much Air

Oboe players have a very difficult job. They have to take big breaths but because they're pushing their air through a tiny little reed, they almost always have extra air in their lungs. They not only have to breathe in, but they also have to breathe *out* to get rid of the old stale air. You'll also have to do this occasionally, but lucky for you not as often as oboe players.

It's important to have a good volume of air in your lungs to get the compression you need to play. But once that air is used up by your body, you have to get rid of it and replenish it with fresh air. The longer you play, the more you'll learn to use you air, and identify such places. Use your judgement.

Using Gadgetry to Help You Breathe

It's fun to mess around with odd-looking contraptions, especially if they help you breathe better. The breathing tube was a very simple gadget compared to what comes next. These gadgets will help you become more aware of your breath. They're great tools to get you thinking about your lung capacity, your state of relaxation, lengths of inhales and exhales and other important aspects of a good breath.

Apply what you learn with these tools to playing on the horn. A good teacher can and should help you with this, and a good teacher will probably have some of these devices. Even with the greatest teacher in the Universe, it's still ultimately up to you. A good breath is a habit you must work to develop and continue to monitor.

Watch the bouncing ball. Most of these devices use a ping-pong-like ball which rides on the column of air you provide, whether you're inhaling or exhaling. For your own version of this, try putting a ping-pong ball on your mouthpiece cup. Carefully blow through the shank of the mouthpiece and you'll notice the ball will "stick" there in any position, as long as you're exhaling. You can find links to all these gadgets, as well as links to my videos on how to use them at www.sol-ut.com. On to the gadgetry!

The Voldyne

I chose this one first because it has a cool name, like something out of an old Flash Gordon movie. The Voldyne allows you to check the strength and volume of your inhalations. It has two chambers which measure air volume and pressure. There is a gauge which tells you how many milliliters of air you can take in and a marker which marks the high point of your lung capacity.

Before you inhale be sure to empty your lungs completely so you'll get a more accurate measure of your lung capacity. When you inhale, do it as quickly as you can. This will measure the strength (pressure) of your inhale.

A Voldyne will set you back about $17.

The Breath Builder

The breath builder was invented by bassoonist Harold Hansen and is a tube with a ping pong ball in it and a straw-like tube coming from the top. The tube has three holes in the top so you can vary the resistance.

You inhale or exhale into the tube and the ball goes up to the top of the tube and stays there as long as you're inhaling or exhaling at the minimum amount of pressure (14 ounces). The device helps to maximize inhalation and exhalation and is also a great way to practice keeping your airflow steady and smooth. They cost around $18.

Inspiron

Another Flash Gordon name. This device is also known as the incentive spirometer. A friend of mine had a collapsed lung and when I went to visit him in the hospital, he had one of these devices next to his bed to help him recuperate. The Inspiron allows you to visualize how much air you can inhale and, when you turn it over, how much air you can exhale. There is also a gauge to help measure resistance.

The Inspiron also has a ping pong ball which measures your lung performance. Set the resistance to maximum, inhale and move the ball to the top of the column. Just before the exhale, turn the device over. A mouthpiece can also be attached to the tube for further study. Cost is about $16.

The Air Bag

This is a simple device which allows you to see how much air you're able to hold in your lungs. The bags come in 5 and 6 liter varieties and will give you a rough idea of your vital capacity. A benefit to using the air bag for several breaths in row is that you'll avoid hyperventilation by re-breathing air that has less oxygen in it. An air bag costs about $25.

Variable Resistance Compound Gauge

This is a device invented by Arnold Jacobs and is used to measure the inhalation/exhalation cycle. Its use will also train you to increase both the inhalation and exhalation. The device will help you increase your actual vital capacity. After practicing with the VRCG, go back to the Voldyne and you should notice improved capacity.

Of all these devices, this one is the most expensive, around $100.

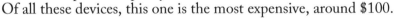

An Encouraging Word

Stick with this breathing thing. Get feedback from your teachers, either your teacher at school or your private teacher. Get feedback from other players, too. Often other people who are wrestling with the same things you are will give you insight into what you're trying to accomplish. Talk with other interested musicians about these things. Your education is out there and you don't necessarily have to have a teacher to get it, just pay attention and ask questions and experiment with yourself. Thich Nhat Han said, "This life is the instrument with which we experiment with Truth."

Get out there and experiment!

Resources for Further Study

Book Title	Author (Publisher)
Arnold Jacobs: Song and Wind	Brian Fredrickson (Windsong Press)
Brass Playing is No Harder Than Deep Breathing	Claude Gordon (www.claudegordonmusic.com)
Brass Wind Artistry	Paul Severson and Mark McDunn (Accura Music)
The Art of Breathing	Nancy Zi (Bantam)
The Science of Breath	Yogi Ramacharaka (Yogi Publication Society)

Up Next

Next is an interlude that has nothing to do with trumpet playing directly, but without it, you'll never improve. It's that dreaded word called *practice*. And it shouldn't be dreaded, but embraced. There are tried and true methods for reaching your goals with the trumpet. Find out some of them in the following Interlude, called *The Practice of Practice*.

INTERLUDE:
THE PRACTICE OF PRACTICE

I never practice; I always play.

~ Wanda Landowska, 1952

In This Chapter

- Where to Practice
- When to Practice
- How to Practice
- What to Practice
- Why Practice?
- Warm-up Exercises

Terms to Know

etude: (AY-tude): A piece of music studied to improve technique.
metronome: A mechanical device used to keep perfect time.
tuner: A mechanical device used to monitor correct pitch.
pedal tone: A note below the normal range of the trumpet. Excellent for warming up the chops.

Don't Say the *P* Word

Johann Sebastian Bach once said, "There's nothing remarkable about it. All one has to do is hit the right keys at the right time and the instrument plays itself."

It sounds sarcastic, but he was right. Music is easy! Keep telling yourself that, because it's true. With enough repetition anything becomes familiar and easy and trumpet is no different. With the right approach, playing trumpet will eventually take little or no effort, as difficult as that may be to believe right now. But believe it and believe that you'll get there, because that's when music gets really fun!

But you do have to put in the time. If playing an instrument well or singing well could happen only by wanting it badly enough, there would be many more great musicians in the world than there are, but that's not how it works. To learn an instrument you've got to practice. Oops, I said a bad word.

I don't like the p-word. When I think of the word "practice," what usually comes to mind is a boring task, one which I'm forced to do repeatedly. I prefer a friendlier p-word. Play. Which would you prefer saying, "I've got to go practice." or "I've got to go play." I don't know about you, but I like the second much better.

What does *play* mean? You play music. It's *supposed* to be fun. If it's not, something might be wrong. I say *might be wrong* because no matter what you do in this life, no matter how much you like it, if you do it often enough there will be times when it doesn't seem so pleasant. This is especially true when you push yourself toward improvement. It's bound to get frustrating once in a while. Not to worry, the feeling will pass.

> Why did Mozart have to get rid of his chickens?
>
> They ran around the yard saying, "Bach, Bach, Bach."

In order to do something well, you have to spend a lot of time doing it. This may seem obvious but you'd be surprised by how many students—especially the younger ones—don't quite understand this. Whether it's sports or art or business or any old thing you care to name, to become something more than a beginner takes focused effort and some time. According to Dizzy Gillespie, it takes ten years of practicing your butt off to achieve Mastery. His statement has been backed up by scientific research which shows that to reach a very high state of mastery, a task should be repeated about a *million* times, which takes about ten years. Better get busy!

Keep in mind there are some people out there who are so naturally gifted that they need little time to master a skill. They're the type of people who can pick something up—art, sports, music, dance, mathematics, Spanish—and start doing it well almost immediately. They're the kind of people we admire and envy. They're the kind of people we secretly want to strangle.

What this section is geared towards is you and me. People with average abilities, average intelligence and average coordination. And even so, if you *are* one of those rare and gifted individuals, this section will help you too, so don't skip it. No matter how smart or good your are, you can always learn more.

A Note on Private Teachers

No book can teach you everything or teach it as well as a good private teacher can. The fastest way to learn anything is one-on-one, just you and the teacher in a room. Half an hour each week is pretty standard for beginners, but an hour is better. A good trumpet teacher can save you years of time and show you tricks that make playing much easier and more fun. A good teacher knows what songs you can handle, knows which ones are fun, and will show you things you aren't doing quite right as well as how to do them better. A good teacher also provides positive feedback and encouragement to you, the student. This is perhaps the most valuable asset of a teacher.

A good teacher is invaluable. Find one. Study with him or her until you've soaked up all you can (usually 2-4 years), then find another and do it all over again. You'll learn the most this way, the fastest this way, and you'll never regret the money you spend. It's well worth it.

Good teachers aren't cheap though, and if you can't afford one you have several options. One good alternative, especially if you're a beginner, is to find someone who plays your instrument and is further along than you are (high school and college students work well). Another way is to find musicians that will let you hang out with them while they play. You can pick up a lot of free tips this way, often just by listening and watching.

How Much is Enough?

Keep in mind that the more time you spend on trumpet, the quicker you'll get better. Play that thing as much as you can. You should be aware of a few things: your desire to play, your ability on the instrument, and how much time you can *make* to play (I purposefully didn't say, "how much time you can *spare*," because nobody can spare time—everyone is always busy).

The very best answer is: play as much as you feel like. That may seem like a cop-out answer, but let me explain. Playing is supposed to be enjoyable, first and foremost, never forget that. When you learn something new, there is a very high possibility of frustration. Avoid this like the plague. If you begin to feel frustrated, keep at it another couple minutes to see if the frustration goes away, and if it doesn't, stop. It's that easy. Pick the horn up again later in the day or tomorrow.

Come on Baby, Light my Desire

The single most valuable thing you have is your desire to play music. Foster it. Imagine yourself playing somewhere. Anywhere. You could be on stage in front of 10,000 screaming fans, you could be at Carnegie Hall, you could be at the local coffee shop, you could be playing a song for a loved one or even in a room alone playing for yourself. There are many excellent players in the world who play only for personal enjoyment. Use your imagination to see yourself performing, keep with it and you'll get to experience it!

Desire will keep you motivated through exercises and repetitions and slumps in mood. The only problem with desire is that it's not like a metronome. You can't bop down to the local music store and pick some up, so you've got to foster it, be aware of it, help it grow. You can't buy it, but there are ways to increase it.

Live Music is Best

The single most beneficial thing to your development as a musician is to go see and hear music performed live. It will increase your desire to play more than any other thing you can do. There are many places to hear live music: coffee shops, concerts, even just sitting around in a friend's living room and listening to her play. Somehow, seeing music being done right in front of you makes it more real, more within reach. Recordings are great, but live is better. Ask your teacher where to find live music around your town.

> Take a music bath once or twice a week for a few seasons, and you will find that it is to the soul what the water bath is to the body.
>
> **Oliver Wendell Holmes, Jr.**

Your Stereo is Next Best

Listening to good music is important and can be very inspiring, especially if you realize the musicians you listen to were once as clueless as you may be right now. So listen as much as you can.

If you like grunge rock, get the best there is and listen to it. If you like speed metal, find the best and listen to it. If you like classical music, find the best symphony orchestras under the best conductors and listen to them. I could go on, but I'm sure you get the idea. Find the best.

The best is simply what you *like* best. Don't give up. There is so much music out there that much of it will do nothing for you. But on the other hand, there is so much music out there, you're bound to find something you love to hear. And you'll love to play it, too. Keep your ears out and wide open.

If you're not sure what kind of trumpet music you like, or you'd like to explore further, don't forget Chapter Two in the front of the book (see "Why Listen?" on page 17). In there you'll find all kinds of music that has trumpet. Take a look and a listen and you might find music that will become a good friend for life. It doesn't have to have trumpet in it either. Just find what you like and those sounds will influence your trumpet playing.

How to Get Better

Beginnings are Delicate Times

If you're a beginner, it's essential to take things slowly. As a beginner you're trying to get the hang of a very complex task that involves many different and challenging skills, and it takes time. Stick with it. You'll get it. I have *never* run into someone who has said, "Gee, I'm sure glad I quit playing my trumpet." It's always the opposite.

Tack up encouraging notes to yourself. On my music stand I have a fortune cookie message which says, "Be persistent and you will win."

As a beginner, your playing sessions might be ten to fifteen minutes, three or four times a week. The less you play, the longer it will take to get better. Remember this. It seems to be common sense, but I see it all the time with new students—playing is difficult and unfamiliar at first so they don't play much or not at all and it *remains* difficult and unfamiliar and frustrating. Pick that thing up and put some sound into it!

The less you play, the longer it will take to get better. There is no getting around this. Once a week will simply not cut it. Of course it's better than nothing, but it's too easy to forget all that information over a week's time and when you get back to your instrument, very little will have changed. This will be very frustrating. Avoid frustration by playing more often. Am I repeating myself? Yes, I am.

Play as long as you can, but don't push it too hard. Remember that the best indication of when it's time to stop is your frustration/boredom level, or the soreness of your chops. You have your whole life to work on this. Don't be lazy, but don't overdo it either.

If you're taking private lessons, the very best time to practice is right after a lesson while that information is still fresh in your head. Record your lesson or take notes if you can't play immediately afterwards.

As you continue to play, you'll become better and better and the amount of time you spend on your instrument will naturally increase. This will happen for several reasons: you'll be able to play more songs, your understanding of what you need to do will increase, your skill exercises will take longer to go through, and the very best part is that it will become more and more fun!

Don't Beat Yourself Up

Remember that it usually takes a long time to sound *really* good, and the progress is incredibly gradual. Anyone who plays an instrument has been a beginner at one point, and let's be honest—beginners make some really funny noises: squeaks, blats, bellows and bleats. We've all done it. It's part of the process of becoming better. Have the patience to wait out your frustrations and the funny sounds you might make. Things will get better, I promise they will, but only if you stick with it.

Start a New Habit

We are creatures of habit. Starting new ones is easy enough, and breaking old ones is sometimes painful. If you can make playing music an old habit, you'll never have to worry; it's a habit you'll never want to break.

One way to grow this habit is to choose a specific time every day to play. Have a routine. This will take some time to figure out and will change as you discover what works for you. Try different times of the day. Some people like early mornings and sit in a quiet house with a latté and strum their guitar, some play right after dinner or after school, some like to play just before going to bed (this option doesn't work well for trumpet players, unless you live alone and far from others or have a great practice mute).

Take at least one day off a week, two at most, to give yourself a rest—take a hike, read a book, take a swim, a nap, anything. Of course, if you don't *want* to take a break, that's also a good option. There are no rules.

Television

My first piece of advice is to throw the time-bandit out. No? You're unwilling to do that? Okay then, use it to your advantage. During one hour of prime time television there are over twenty minutes of advertisements. That's twenty minutes you could use to play. And besides, you don't need to buy all that stuff people are trying to sell you. Save your money and buy a nicer trumpet instead. Press the mute button and play! (This technique also works best for single people, or those with a good practice mute…)

When in Doubt, Leave it Out

I leave most of my instruments out and ready to play. I have to be careful when I pick one up because once I do, often it's tough to put it down again. By leaving your instrument out you can pick it up at a random moment and toss off an exercise or a song. If you do this with trumpet, be sure that you have already performed a warm-up at some earlier time. Five minutes later you're back to what you were doing before. You can find a trumpet stand at your local music store.

Where to Do It

When I was a kid and had to practice trumpet (I use the *p* word on purpose—back then I didn't know the difference), my parents finally ended up sending me to the garage. It sounds cruel, but it was an excellent thing. They didn't have to hear my squawks and blats, and I didn't have to feel self-conscious about making so much noise.

When you start to play an instrument as a beginner, your self-image as a musician is very fragile. You'll feel self-conscious, maybe a little silly, and you'll be very aware of how bad you sound.

Yes, it's true. You *will* sound bad at first. That's part of it. For some it can feel embarrassing, and for others simply uncomfortable. Only a rare few don't care. If you're one of these, consider yourself lucky. If you do feel uncomfortable playing with others around, the solution is to play when you have lots of privacy, either when nobody else is home or in a separate building. Even a closed door is better than nothing.

Repetition: the Mother of Success, the Father of Irritation

Charles Reynolds, a master teacher and man of great enthusiasm coined the first part of the above phrase, and I added the second. When you're learning to play a song, you must play it over, and over, and over, and over, often hundreds if not thousands of times. And not the whole song at once, but measure by measure until you've got the whole thing. Then you get to play the whole thing over and over and over.

It's a lot like jet skis—plenty of fun for the one doing it but not fun at all for anyone who has to listen to it. Even if you're Brian Lynch or Charlie Schlueter, the same phrase or scale or exercise played over and over and over again will drive even the most patient person bug-nuts.

Get a private place to play if you can. Those you live with will love you for it and will enjoy your music more when you're ready to perform it for them.

How to Do It

There are as many ways to play as there are people who play, but all of them share some similar characteristics. There are certain tools which can make your progress on trumpet much faster.

Some of these tools are crucial, some are less so, but all of them will put you further down the road toward trumpet and musical mastery if you use them correctly.

Equipment

Here's another musical myth that may or may not be true: Arturo Sandoval, a world-renown trumpet player, man of screaming range and prodigious chops, grew up very poor in Cuba. He wanted to play very badly. He would walk miles to the next village where someone had a copy of *Arban's Complete Conservatory Method for Trumpet*, a book that is hundreds of pages long, crammed full of thousands of exercises and songs; the trumpet player's bible. Because he couldn't afford the book, Sandoval kept returning to the distant village until he had the whole book memorized.

All you really need is your instrument and desire. The rest will come. However, here are some things which will make your experience much more pleasant and more successful in a shorter time. In order of importance they are:

- **instrument**: Get the best instrument you can afford and treat it well. Learn how to care for your trumpet in see Interlude Two, *Clean Up Your Axe on* page 151.

- **metronome**: Apart from your instrument, this is the most useful tool you can own as a musician. Get one early on and use it often. I'll discuss its use later in this chapter.

- **music**: This is both method books and sheet music. Not every playing session will require music. There are many things that can be done without it.

- **music stand**: There are many different types, from inexpensive fifteen dollar wire stands which fit in an instrument case to beautiful and expensive hardwood stands which aren't so portable.

- **pencil**: This will be used to mark up your music with notes to yourself and also to record your sessions if you choose to do so. Keep several in your case so you'll have one when needed.

- **practice journal**: A spiral notebook in which to keep a record of what you play, how long you play, and how you feel about your playing. This is a valuable tool to look back on. Not a requirement, but a good idea. Find blank, photocopyable sheets for a journal in this book's appendix. Also in the appendix are forms to track progress on specific exercises. Use 'em!

- **tape/CD player**: A very useful tool. Not only to provide good music to listen to, but also something you can play along with. Trying to figure out a favorite song is good training for your hand-ear coordination. There are many recordings which leave out the trumpet part so you can play it.

- **tuner**: A tuner can tell you exactly what pitch you play, and whether it's in tune or not. You're now in the world of sound and a small change of pitch is audible to most listeners. Certain notes on the trumpet are notoriously out of tune. With a tuner you'll know how much to correct them. For more information, see "Basic Trumpet Tuning" on page 117.

- **tape recorder**: Not essential, but very helpful. Hearing yourself recorded is much different than hearing yourself while playing, and you'll be surprised how many mistakes you hear that you weren't aware of while you recorded. The tape recorder tells no lies.

- **instrument stand**: Not essential, but useful. If you leave your trumpet out you'll pick it up and play more often. My trumpet, guitars and flutes are always out on their stands.

The Ideal Practice Session

Basic Information

A great practice session is divided into three sections:

1 The warm-up: warming up the horn and yourself physically and mentally.

2 Technical exercises: scale studies, lip slurs, tonguing, and a million other things to work on.

3 Musical material: etudes, orchestral excerpts, songs, or whatever it is you'll be performing. This is where you get to really play and this should be the most enjoyable part of your session.

Rest as Much as You Play

Trumpet is a physically demanding instrument. The muscles used for trumpet are small muscles that tire easily. Piano players can play for many hours in a day because they're using large muscles which don't tire like your face does. Resting while practicing trumpet is crucial!

As a general rule, you should rest as much as you play. Resting means not having the horn on your face. This doesn't mean that you should just stare at the wall while you rest. Use the down time to practice fingerings, tap out a difficult rhythm, sing some of your parts, oil your valves, or whatever is most helpful. During your play time, try to be actively learning *something* when the horn isn't on your face.

The Best Time

Directly after a lesson is the very best time to practice. When all that new information is fresh in your head, take the time to go over it again on your own. If there is something you don't understand, write down any questions or problems you may have so your teacher can explain them in your next lesson.

Pre Warm-up

Anne Morrow Lindbergh said, "A note of music gains significance from the silence on either side." and in that spirit, take a few seconds or a minute to sit quietly and think about your progress on trumpet, your goals, and how you will chip away at them during this practice session. This is an important and helpful way to start your session because it gets you mentally prepared and focused.

Then make sure your instrument works properly and you have all you need for the coming session (metronome, valve oil, metronome, music, metronome, mutes, pencil, etc.—don't forget your metronome).

A good way to get blood flowing to your lips and to get your air moving is to do the loose lip flap. This sounds a little funny, kind of like a horse whinny or an outboard boat motor, but is great for loosening up your mouth and lips. Keep your lips loosely closed and blow lots of air through them. This is not like the buzz because the lips are MUCH looser. Do this for fifteen to twenty seconds.

Take a proper 3-step breath and blow warm air through your horn to warm it up. See "Some Breathing Exercises" on page 56. This will help you think of the proper way to breathe while you warm up the horn. The pitch of a cold horn is lower than the pitch from a warm horn, so if being in tune is important to you (it should be), the horn must be warm before it can be in tune.

Warm-up

A warm-up is essential for trumpet players. Not only does a good warm-up get the blood flowing to your chops, a warm-up also gets your mind focused and helps with your concentration as you go through your session. This is general information. Specific music for warm-ups can be found at the end of this chapter, See "The Practice Session Details" on page 71.

Start Your Session with a Buzz!

Start buzzing with your lips alone. If you're a beginner, just buzz a steady, comfortable note. As your muscles get stronger, you can vary the pitch. Go from a steady note to a low note. Go from high to low and low back to high. Experiment.

Buzzing on the mouthpiece is also a great way to warm up. Just like buzzing without the mouthpiece, experiment to find your own variations. Keep the range low and the volume medium to loud with little to no pressure on the lips from the mouthpiece. Buzz for a couple minutes until you have no gaps or stops in the sound. See "Buzz with the Mouthpiece" on page 34.

Exercises

If a playing session is a meal, this section is the broccoli. You may not like the taste (unless you use lots of cheese), but it's good for you. Do the exercises religiously—it will pay off with increased ability, strength, dexterity and musicality.

This is when you do your scales, lip slurs, long tones, interval studies, chord progressions…whatever your teacher assigns you. The list is nearly endless, but your time is limited. Keep time spent on exercises down to about 1/3 of the total playing session. Don't skimp on this part of your playing session. Dessert is coming up.

For more information about where to find exercises, see "Essential Method Books" on page 198.

The Heart of the Session

Here is where you will do most of your work. This is the longest part of your playing session. This is where you work on the song you're learning to perform. Use the *tuner*, the *metronome* and the *tape recorder*.

The Metronome (or: The Torture Device)

There is a legend about Chinese Water Torture. I have no idea if it's true, but it makes for a good story. You're strapped down to a table and above you is a barrel full of water. The barrel has a small hole in it through which a tiny drop of water falls every minute or so down onto your forehead. This goes on for a long time, finally driving you mad. The metronome is kind of like that, only it's actually *good* for you.

A metronome is a mechanical foot-tap which keeps perfect time. Each metronome has a series of gradations on it, usually from around 40-200 *beats per minute (bpm).* The higher the number, the faster the clicks. You set the metronome on the tempo you need and away you go.

Close your eyes and repeat three times, "The metronome is my friend."

Metronomes come in many different shapes and sizes. Because trumpet can be such a loud instrument, there is a type of metronome you *don't* want, which is the wind-up pendulum variety like the one in the margin of this page. What you want is the electronic variety with an earplug that will send the clicks right to your ear. This is also a good option if you live with others: the repetitive clicks of a metronome can send others to the loony bin.

Nobody likes being wrong. That's one of the reasons metronomes are so neglected. They keep perfect time and we humans do not. But if you think about it, we learn the most when we're wrong, as long as we're paying attention. So really, being wrong can turn into a good thing.

Of course *staying* wrong is *not* a good thing. You use a metronome to fix mistakes in rhythm.

How to Use the Metronome

When you're learning a song, use the metronome on only a short section at one time—several measures at the most, two notes at the least. It's important to *start slowly*. Whatever you learn is what you will play, so *if you set the metronome at a speed which is too difficult, you will learn mistakes*.

1. Set the metronome to a tempo that is slow enough so your playing feels comfortable and easy. Play the short section through a few times at this tempo. If you're making mistakes, the tempo is too fast. Slow it down some more until you find an easy tempo. Play 5-10 times correctly before going on.

2. Click up to the next fastest tempo. One click only. The clicks may not *sound* any faster, but when you play the passage you'll notice the difference. Play at this tempo until it's easy. Play 5-10 times perfectly.

3. Click up to the next fastest tempo. One click only. Play the section several times at the new tempo. It may take more repetitions to get the passage perfect. Keep at it. If it's too hard at the new tempo, go back one click until it's perfect again. Play 5-10 times perfectly.

---

4 Continue with this process until the correct tempo of the song is reached. This may take several days, weeks or months.

Remember, you're in this for the long haul. Don't bash your head against something for too long. If you become very frustrated or discouraged, go back to a slower tempo and play it a few times correctly before you quit.

William Powell, by Leo Kottke was the first song I learned on guitar. It was much too difficult for my abilities and I probably shouldn't have chosen it, but I did. At first, the song was so incredibly slow it was unrecognizable. It took about three or four days (of two hours a day) to get each 4-measure passage up to a decent speed. Using the metronome as mentioned above, I learned the song, but it took me six months.

You may not be so foolish as to choose such a hard piece at first, but if you do, using the metronome works very, very well. Try it. Play with it. Come up with your own variations. There are no rules.

The Tape Recorder Tells No Lies

I got my first stereo when I was eleven. It had a tape deck with a microphone attachment. During my enforced *practice* sessions, I came up with a plan to get away with not practicing. I'd record something on the tape deck, then turn up the volume and play it back, sometimes twice. That way everyone in the house would think I was still playing. *Ha! That'll show them*, I must have thought. *I'm not actually practicing.*

But I was. Listening to yourself play an instrument on a recording is a lot like listening to your *voice* on a recording. It doesn't sound anything like what you thought it sounded like. Every little wobble and flub and mistake is painfully obvious. Again, we learn the most from making mistakes.

But as with the metronome, don't let those mistakes stand. Fix 'em.

Try recording yourself. You'll be surprised, and you might like doing it. You will definitely improve!

You Can Tune a Trumpet but You Can't Tuna Fish

A *tuner* is a valuable tool. You will use a tuner to make sure your trumpet is generally in tune, and also to check all the notes on your trumpet to see whether *they* are in tune. For all the grimy details about notes that are out of tune on trumpets, See "Basic Trumpet Tuning" on page 117.

The best type of tuner for this sort of thing is an analog tuner, one which has a little arm that swings back and forth to show how sharp or flat you are. If the little arm is straight up at "0," you're in tune. For a picture, go to "Tuning The Whole Trumpet" on page 118.

There are many types of tuners. Visit your local music store for a demonstration and decide which will work best for you. Most stores will let you try out the tuners in a back room, so take your instrument.

Other Ways to Play

You aren't limited to playing only during your daily session. There are opportunities throughout the day to hone your skills, and you don't even need your instrument.

There's always buzzing. Do it both with and without your mouthpiece. Buzz along with songs on the radio in the car, or at home on your stereo. Buzz from high to low and back as many times as you can in one breath. Hold a high buzz for as long as you can. Hold a low buzz for as long as you can.

you can in one breath. Hold a high buzz for as long as you can. Hold a low buzz for as long as you can.

Trumpet playing is a very muscular activity, and just like any activity in which muscle strength is important, you have to exercise the muscles to get them stronger. Your lip workout regimen will revolve around the buzz. Don't neglect it.

Using only your lips (no teeth), hold an unsharpened pencil out parallel to the ground for as long as you can. If a new pencil is too heavy, try a shorter one at first. This will also strengthen your pucker muscles.

When I learn scales (there are hundreds of them and always more to work on), I practice the fingerings when away from the horn. To practice fingerings, you can get a set of valves from an instrument at the pawn shop and carry that around instead of the whole instrument; or simply do fingerings on your thumb or palm.

These are just a few suggestions. Use your noggin to think up some other options. There is a lot of "down" time in a day that you can use to improve your playing.

Trumpet is Just the Beginning

Many famous musicians started on one instrument and continued to learn many others. Lenny Kravitz, Stevie Wonder, Prince, and Beck play *all* the instruments on their early albums. Beck still does it. Those three are only a few. There are many more. Nowhere is there a rule that says you can only play one instrument. Heck, learn 'em all if you want to. A new instrument can light the fire inside you again.

If you can read music, learning songs on a new instrument is much, much easier. Music theory is another almost limitless topic. The more you understand music, the better music you'll be able to make. For a good start on music theory, get a copy of *Basic Music Theory: How to Read, Write, and Understand Written Music*.

On the next couple pages you'll find warm-ups and sources for exercises. For even more information on music to play, See "Where to start?" on page 197. You'll find information about songs, etude books, and other performance pieces to practice during the final third of your playing session. Have fun!

The Practice Session Details

Warm-up: Mouthpiece Buzz

Of course, you've already checked to make sure your horn's working properly, you've got your valve oil, mutes, music, metronome, recording equipment and anything else you'll be using for this session. We'll start with buzzing. To improve your sound even more, buzz the following exercises with the same fat, full sound and check the pitches with the piano if you have access to one. Use the piano keyboard in the back of the book to tell which pitches you're playing.

Interlude Example 1:   Simple mouthpiece glissando buzz.

8vb

Buzz close to the pitch shown here (8vb means 1 octave lower, so that last note should be in the basement. Keep the sound/air full and constant as you slide up and down. Pay attention to dynamics.

Do this exercise with a full, fat sound until there aren't any gaps or stops in the sound throughout your range. Go lower on each repeat.

Warm-up With the Horn

Once you've got a solid mouthpiece buzz, slide the mouthpiece into your horn and play the following. If you're a beginner, some of these low notes may be a little difficult. Stay loose, use warm air, and keep the air-flow steady. If the notes don't sound right away, keep at it until they do. For information about tonguing (separating the notes), see "Use My Tongue for What?" on page 91.

Interlude Example 2:   Tongue warm-up exercises. Keep the tempo slow at first. Focus on your airflow and your tongue strike. Once the notes are memorized, try the exercise at different speeds from slow to fast

The Practice of Practice

Interlude Example 3:   More warm-up exercises. Keep the tempo slow at first. Once the notes are memorized, try the exercise at different speeds from slow to fast.

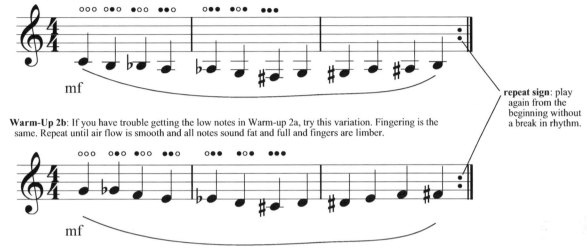

Warm-Up 2a: Repeat until air flow is smooth and all notes sound fat and full and fingers are limber. Vary the speed from slow to fast. Fingerings are provided, but try to read the note and not the fingering!

Warm-Up 2b: If you have trouble getting the low notes in Warm-up 2a, try this variation. Fingering is the same. Repeat until air flow is smooth and all notes sound fat and full and fingers are limber.

repeat sign: play again from the beginning without a break in rhythm.

Practice Part II: The Exercises

There are so many things to work on that it's more than a little intimidating to think about, let alone tackle on the horn, but if you chip away at problem areas every day, you'll be a master trumpet player in a relatively short time. Your teacher will help you wade through the material and help you focus on what you need to work on most. Be persistent! Practice with intelligence and a critical ear. Use the skills checklist in the Appendix to keep track of what you need to learn.

There are so many exercises that there isn't space to include them all here—you'll have to get them from other books! The more the merrier. A companion book to this called *Sound the Trumpet: Exercises to Blow Through Your Horn,* is due out in 2006. For lots of info about exercise books you can get right now, See "Essential Method Books" on page 198. You'll have these books for life, or longer. I've been playing for over 25 years and still use many books, and buy more all the time. Start digging in!

Practice Part III: The Fun Stuff!

This section of your session where you get to play actual songs. What a concept! Like the exercises, there are so many options here that it's hard to know where to start. Your teacher will be of great help to you in this. To get a start on sorting through your choices, see "Un-Boggling Your Mind" on page 197.

Forget the Written Music and Use Your Ears

Remember that music is *not* about notes on the page, but *is* about sounds and the emotions that those sounds can evoke. Take time during this part of your practice session to play along with a favorite song or piece of music so you can train your ear-finger-lip coordination.

But beware! This is easy to say, and not as easy to put into practice. You'll have to play the song you choose over and over and over again, and each time you go at it, you'll figure out a little bit more of the song. As your ear becomes sharper, this will take less time. If you want, write down what you discover so that you won't have to re-learn it next time. When you get bored or want to go on to a new song, do it! This will keep you fresh and interested and excited about learning. However, if you *always* move on before learning a tune completely, this can be a problem. Try to follow a song through to completion.

Mistakes and How to Deal With Them

When you practice, because you're pushing yourself, you are going to make mistakes. What's important is not that you made a mistake, but how you deal with the information. A mistake indicates a place where your abilities are not what they could be. What will you do with this information? Many of us simply ignore our mistakes because it shows us where we are lacking, and few of us are strong enough to really, truly face our shortcomings. That's too bad, because as far as trumpet playing goes, mistakes are pretty easy to fix. You've just got to do it, is all.

Repetition is the Mother of Success

When I'm learning a phrase or passage, I play it 10 times perfectly *in a row* before going on to the next phrase or passage. If I'm working on getting a passage up to a certain speed, I'll play it ten times perfectly at one metronome setting before increasing the speed by a click or two. This means that if I mess up on the 9th try, I have to go back to number one again. As the passage becomes more familiar, I may decrease the repetitions to five.

When I make a mistake, I take this same approach. It's not good enough to practice just the note that you missed, but the entire phrase surrounding that note. Back up to the beginning of the phrase which contains your mistake and play the whole phrase ten times perfectly.

This kind of repetition is important. If you make a mistake and go back through the phrase just once, odds are that you haven't truly fixed the mistake and it's very likely you'll make it again. You must fix the mistake many times before the fix sticks.

How good do you want to be? This is an important question. Answer it as honestly as you can and be prepared to take the steps necessary to follow through with your answer. If you want to be great, you must fix your mistakes. This will take time, effort and more time. But what are your options? Quitting? No way!

Take the time and care that is necessary to play your notes perfectly. It will pay off, I promise!

Practice Awareness

Playing correctly is more about awareness than just about anything. Often a student will play a simple passage that is well within their ability, yet they mess it up. When this happens, I point out that the phrase just missed is not difficult and not beyond the student's skill. Then I have them play it again. Often, on the second repetition, the phrase is correct and much more beautiful. This is the point where I ask the question, "What was different about that time through the phrase?" Often the student doesn't know, so I ask "Are your skills suddenly better?" They shake their heads, no. "Have you acquired some special ability you didn't have the first time you played the phrase?" Again, they shake their heads, no.

Finally, the student realizes that what is different is their awareness, their concentration level and focus. This is often a "light bulb" experience for many students. Playing music beautifully at your current skill level is more about awareness and focus than anything else. How aware are you? How much can you focus?

Sources for Further Study

Learning how to practice is one of the most important things to perfect. Without a decent approach to practice, your road to improvement may become a dead end. Here are some books to help your journey. You can find reviews of most of these on my practice blog, http://intentionalpractice.wordpress.com. As with the other chapters, links to these resources is at the *Sound the Trumpet* web page at www.sol-ut.com.

Book/Article Title	Author (Publisher)
The Musician's Way: A Guide to Practice, Performance, and Wellness	Gerald Klickstein (Oxford University Press)
Effortless Mastery	Kenny Werner (Jamey Aybersold Jazz)
Systematic Approach to Daily Practice for Trumpet	Claude Gordon (Carl Fischer)
The Art of Practicing: A Guide to Making Music From the Heart	Madeline Bruser (Bell Tower)
The Mastery of Music: Ten Pathways to True Artistry	Barry Green (Broadway)
The Practice Revolution: Getting Great Results from the 6 Days Between Lessons	Philip Johnston (Practicespot Press)

More Better Practice Advice

The advice in this chapter is solid. Some of it is essential. But I wrote it nearly 10 years ago, and since then I have earned my candidacy for a PhD in music education, from Northwestern University, a fantastic university full of incredible minds. My dissertation is on practice, and so my knowledge about practice—as well as my experience of it as a practicing musician and teacher—has grown and changed dramatically. I've got a blog on practice and around late 2011, I'll have a new book out called *The Practice of Practice*. It'll be filled with research on practice and interviews with both well known and barely known professionals, as well as amateurs and beginners. Find out more at the Sol Ut Press web site and the blog site, www.IntentionalPractice.wordpress.com.

Up Next

Okay, that was a pretty long chapter, and a very important one. Be sure to come back and review it now and then to be sure you got it all.

Up next is Part II: Getting Into It. You'll find a whole bunch more tips about playing trumpet in this part, including things like written notes on trumpet, how to use your tongue, lip slurs, high and low range, endurance, and some simple tunes to play. Lots of good stuff!

PART II GETTING INTO IT

WHAT YOU'LL LEARN IN THIS PART

- Written Notes for Trumpet
- Use of the Tongue
- Lip Slurs
- Trumpet Intonation
- Pedal Tones

- How to Increase Your Range
- How to Increase Your Endurance
- Trumpet Sound Effects
- Interlude: Clean Your Horn

SolUt Press

Musician-friendly Resources.
www.Sol-Ut.com

CHAPTER 7

TAKING NOTES

The notes I handle no better than many. But the pauses between the notes—ah, that is where the art resides.

~ Arthur Schnabel (1882-1951)

In This Chapter

- Basic Note-Reading Skills
- Find your starting Note
- C and G
- The first 5 notes of the C scale
- C scale Variation
- The C blues scale

Terms to Know

Staff: The five lines and four spaces on which music is written.

ledger lines: Small lines used above and below the staff to extend its range.

A, B, C, D, E, F, G: The letters used to name musical pitches.

treble clef: a symbol at the beginning of the staff that sets the letter staff.

open: No valves pressed down.

fermata: A musical symbol indicating a hold or a pause.

stepwise: Moving from one note to the next available note up or down. Also known as diatonic.

Warning! Take Your Time

If reading music is new to you, it will take some time before it makes sense. You should refer back to this chapter as often as you need to, and don't feel bad about spending two to three weeks or more on this chapter alone.

Continue to just mess around with the trumpet. You'll be able to play things naturally that would seem very difficult if you had to read the musical notation. For example, play an open note (no valves down) and then fan your second valve (that means push it up and down as fast as you can). This is called a *trill*. It sounds cool and is easy to do. However, the notation for a trill isn't taught in any beginning trumpet book or band method that I know of. To find out about more of these devices, see "Ornaments Aren't Just for Christmas" on page 171.

So keep messing around and making up your own sounds on the horn while you chip away at the skill of reading music. Onward!

An Ultra-Brief Intoduction to Written Music

If you've never read music before, prepare to be a little bewildered by the information and terms I'm about to throw at you. Don't panic! You only have to remember one or two key concepts at this point and you can give yourself a review any time you need it. For more in depth instruction in how to read music, pick up a copy of *Basic Music Theory: How to Read, Write, and Understand Written Music* at your local independent book seller or music store. The following information was taken from *Basic Music Theory*.

So far in this book I've avoided written music because you've got enough to deal with already. Making music is *not* about written notes on a page, it's about sound. If you feel more comfortable just playing the trumpet and don't want to read music yet, by all means wait a few more weeks, but don't wait too long.

There are millions of excellent musicians in the world who don't read music. It's not a requirement, but written music is such a great tool that it would be silly to avoid it. If you're reading this book, you possess more than enough skills to read music. It might be confusing at first, but stick with it because it will open up a whole universe of music for you to play. Here we go!

The Staff

Music is written on a *staff* (plural *staves*) which is five horizontal parallel lines. The five lines create four spaces between them.

Example 7.1 Blank staff.

Lines and spaces are numbered from bottom to top.

Example 7.2 Staff with lines and spaces numbered.

Names of the Notes

You'll be happy to find you only need the first seven letters of the alphabet for written music.

The music alphabet uses **A, B, C, D, E, F,** and **G**. You'll never find an "H" in music, or a "Q", or anything other than **A through G**. This is one of those few rules that has *no exceptions*! Below you can see the names of the notes on the staff for trumpet. Notice how the note names repeat again after the 7th note.

Example 7.3 Trumpet note names on the staff. Notice that in sequence notes alternate between lines and spaces.

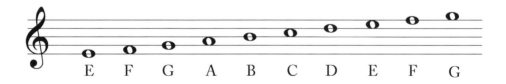

When notes go higher or lower than the staff, *ledger lines* (also spelled *leger*) are used to extend the staff. Ledger lines are short little lines on which you can write notes. Below are examples of trumpet ledger line notes below the staff. Ledger lines also occur above the staff, but you won't have to worry about them for some time.

Example 7.4 Trumpet leger line note names below the treble clef staff.

G   A   B   C

You Got Rhythm!

Rhythm is the essential glue that binds music together. Rhythm is so important that without it music wouldn't exist. The rhythm of a piece can be felt through the *beat*.

The beat of nearly any piece of music is easy to feel. It's what sets your toe tapping, it's what makes you dance. The beat is a regular pulse, like your heartbeat, which lasts throughout a piece of music. You'll use the beat to define the length of notes.

There are only three different note lengths you have to know at first. You'll notice that the half notes and quarter notes have two examples, one with the stem down (high notes on the staff) and one with the stem up (low notes). From longest to shortest the notes are:

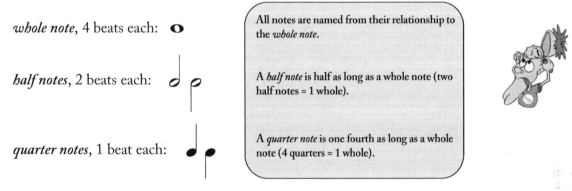

whole note, 4 beats each:

half notes, 2 beats each:

quarter notes, 1 beat each:

All notes are named from their relationship to the *whole note*.

A *half note* is half as long as a whole note (two half notes = 1 whole).

A *quarter note* is one fourth as long as a whole note (4 quarters = 1 whole).

The Rests of the Story

Silence in music is as important as sound, and of course we crafty humans have invented a way to show this silence in music. *Rests*. Rest lengths and rest names are the same as the note lengths you learned above. They are *whole rests*, *half rests*, and *quarter rests*.

Whole rests hang from the 4th line, are 4 beats long, and look like this:

Half rests sit on the third line, are 2 beats long, and look like this:

Quarter rests are one beat long and look like this: . On the staff, these rests look like this:

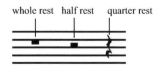

whole rest   half rest   quarter rest

Whole or Half, Hole or Hat

Whole rests and half rests look very much the same and they can be easily confused with each other. Here's a way to remember which is which. The whole rest, looks like a *hole* in the ground, like so:

The half rest, looks like a *hat* (I know, *half* and *hat* don't sound the same, but work with me here):

C and G: Your First Notes

Even though you only have to deal with seven letters in written music, I'll make it even more simple and limit your first notes to two: C and G. Both of these are fingered "open" (no valves down) and you will find one of these easier to play than the other.

If you've been practicing your buzz you'll have little trouble playing either of these notes. In fact, if you've been practicing your buzz, you'll probably be able to play even higher than these two notes, but we'll get to that later.

The "C" is the lowest open note on the trumpet and is usually the easiest note for beginners to play. For some however, the "G" comes out more easily. See if you can play both of them. To find out if you've got the right notes you have a couple options. You can go to the Sol-Ut web site for the sound clip 7.5 (www.sol-ut.com). If you have access to a piano you can find out the pitch of the G and C on the piano by referring to the following keyboard diagram. The final and best option is to have a trumpet player (your teacher) play these notes for you.

If you already know the notes on the piano keyboard you'll notice that the notes you see written on the keyboard are not the correct names for the notes on the piano. Don't worry. Trumpet is what's called a B-flat instrument, and this means its notes are different from those on piano, which is a C instrument. Don't sweat it right now if that seems confusing (and it is confusing). To learn more about this, see "Trumpet is a Bb Instrument" on page 187.

Example 7.5 These two notes will be your first written note on trumpet. Hear them at www.sol-ut.com, clip 7.5, or play them on the piano or keyboard if you have one. The piano keyboard shows the trumpet notes C and G. Use the keys in the middle of the keyboard.

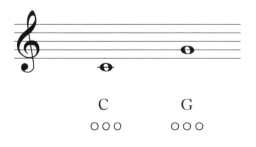

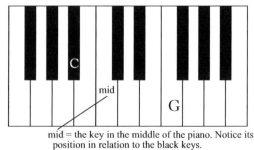

mid = the key in the middle of the piano. Notice its position in relation to the black keys.

You can see on the keyboard that there are six other notes between G and C. There are also six other valve combinations between the open notes. Can you discover what they are without looking at the fingering chart in the back of the book? Try. Use your ears and your brain to discover what they are. It's more fun to pit your wits against such a challenge and learning in this way is often more rewarding than simply finding the information. In addition, you'll remember better if you work it out for yourself. (Hint: 2nd valve changes pitch a half step, 1st valve changes pitch a whole step, and 3rd valve changes pitch a step and a half.)

We won't deal with all six combinations just yet. Practice the C and the G until you can get them both easily and can tell the difference between the two. You should be able to tell the difference both by how the notes sound and how it feels to play them.

More Notes: D, E and F

Remember above I said there were 6 combinations between G and C? Well, you'll only need three of them for a while. The three combinations you'll learn are the notes D, E, and F.

Example 7.6 D, E and F by themselves with fingerings and side by side. Check your pitches with a piano or keyboard.

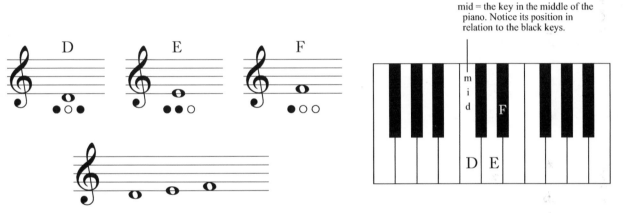

Including the C and the G, these notes are the first five notes of the C major scale. The major scales are very important in music because all other scales and most concepts of harmony use the major scale as a reference. For now, memorize these first five notes until they're entirely automatic.

I'll say this many times in the hopes that it will stick: "Music is *not* about notes on the page, but it *is* about sound." Don't worry about getting the right number of beats per note in the examples below. Simply hold out each note with the most beautiful tone you can muster for one full breath, then go on to the next.

Memorize these notes as quickly as possible, both in the way they sound and how they feel to play. Practice them forwards and backward and in as many combinations as possible. You'll begin to discover songs that use these notes. Start on E and play "Mary Had a Little Lamb." Don't worry about how songs will look written down. Just find the notes. You know the rhythms and pitches you need to hear. Trust yourself!

When practicing these notes, only glance at the fingering to get it right. When playing, focus on the note. If your goal is to read music, this is essential. If you stare at the fingering underneath the note, *that* is what you'll learn. When it comes time to read the notes without fingering you'll be lost because you memorized the fingering and not the note. Check the pitch of these notes with a keyboard.

Be prepared to spend some time on this part. It will take at least a week, and probably more if you really want to get it down. One time through is great, but you'll have to do it many more times for this information to become memorized. Don't let this frustrate you! It's normal, so get used to it. Whenever you learn something new on trumpet, you have to spend quite a lot of time practicing before it begins to feel natural. Keep at it and you will succeed.

Example 7.7 The first five notes of the trumpet's C major scale (sol-ut.com sound clip 7.7). Play low to high, high to low and any other combination you can come up with. Below are a few examples. Hold each note for one full breath.

Fermata: a symbol used to tell the performer to hold out the note as long as necessary. In this case, one full breath.

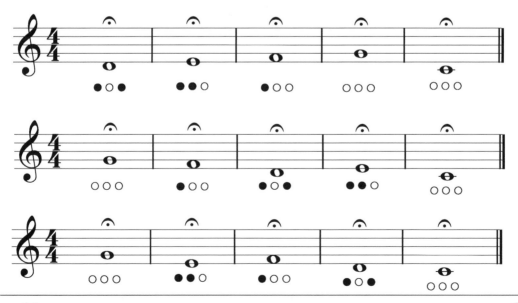

Example 7.8 The first five notes of the trumpet's C major scale in random order (sol-ut.com sound clip 7.8). Hold each note for one full breath. Can you name the notes?

Taking Notes

Once you have these five notes memorized, begin to vary the speed and the order in which you play them. Tap your foot to keep it rhythmic and use a metronome to keep yourself steady. To find out how to use the metronome, see "The Metronome (or: The Torture Device)" on page 69.

There is an endless variety of songs you can create using just these 5 notes. Change the rhythm, change the order, repeat some notes, play others only once, skip notes and come back to them later, play some softly and some loudly, etc., etc. Be creative. Make up songs. Don't be afraid to experiment. That's where the joy is! Let go!

Reading the Music

In all of the examples above there is no rhythm. You were simply holding each note out for one full breath. Pretty easy. Now you'll add rhythm to the notes you've learned. Tap your foot so you can get the count right on all the notes and rests. The rests between the notes are provided to give you a chance to prepare for the next note. Look ahead, push the right valves and get your chops ready so you can play exactly on the first beat of the next measure. We'll start simple and go from there. All the examples to now had pretty big notes so it could be easily read. For the rest of the book, the written music will be a more standard size, which is a bit smaller.

Example 7.9 Read the notes and not the fingering of the note. Tap your foot. Whole notes/rests get 4 beats. To hear it, get sound clip 7.9 at www.sol-ut.com

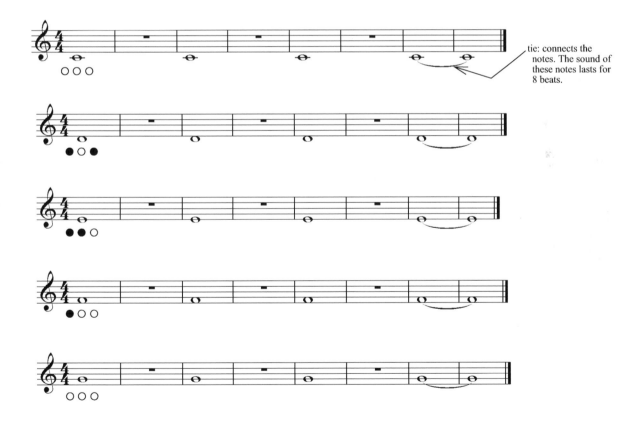

tie: connects the notes. The sound of these notes lasts for 8 beats.

Changing Notes

The above exercises were about as simple as written music can get. The exercises below are a little more difficult, but are still pretty darn simple. Look ahead and change fingerings during the rests. I've included the fingerings for these first exercises, but by now you should have the fingering memorized for each note. If they're not memorized yet, you've got your first project to work on.

Example 7.10 Whole notes and whole rests. Tap your foot to be sure each gets 4 beats. Look ahead so you can change fingerings during the rest. Sound clip 7.10a at www.sol-ut.com.

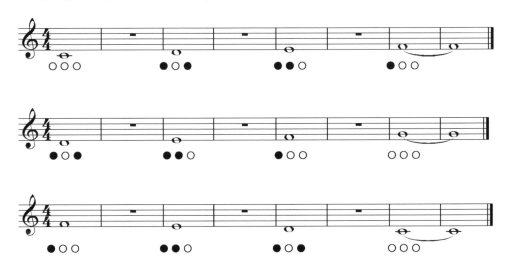

All the examples before this have been *stepwise*, or *diatonic*, which means they move from one note to the next line or space note higher or lower. In the examples below, there are skips between notes, so be careful when reading ahead during the rest so you know what's coming up. Try to hear the note before you play it. Use your tonguing skills to articulate the beginning of the note.

Set the tongue and use the air to blast it open when you say "too." When the air and tongue are coordinated, notes come out cleanly and clearly. Sound clip 7.10b at www.sol-ut.com.

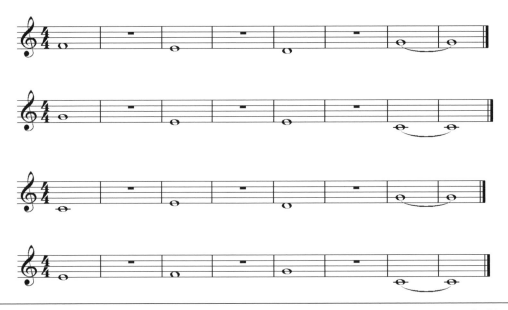

Taking Notes

Simple Duets

Playing an instrument by yourself is pretty fun. When you start to play with others, it's even more fun. However, when you play with others it's easier to get distracted by what the other person is playing. Not only that, but your rhythm needs to be exact when you play with others so that you're playing together. If you leave out or add beats, the parts won't line up and the music won't sound as good as it should. These are two great reasons to play music with other people.

Below are some duets to help you start playing with others. If you have access to the Internet, you can get these sound files for free and play along with them. Go to www.sol-ut.com. You can also buy a CD with all the examples from the book at the web site.

Learn both parts and play with a friend. If your friend plays an instrument other than trumpet, clarinet, baritone horn, or tenor sax (all B♭ instruments like trumpet), they will have to *transpose* their part to get the right sound. If you're not concerned about that, just play. It will sound interesting, and you might even like the results. To learn more about transposing, see "Trumpet is a Bb Instrument" on page 187.

When more than one person is playing, starting together is important. One of you will have to count off or give some signal to start you together. A good way to start is to count at the speed you want to go. For example, "One, two, three, four." If you want to go fast, count fast. To go slowly, count slowly. Another option could be, "One, two, ready, go," or "one, two, you know what to do." Whatever works.

Example 7.11 Duets #1-4. Sound clip 7.11-1 is duet number one, part A, then part B. Sound clip 7.11-2 is duet 2, both parts. Etcetera, etcetera.

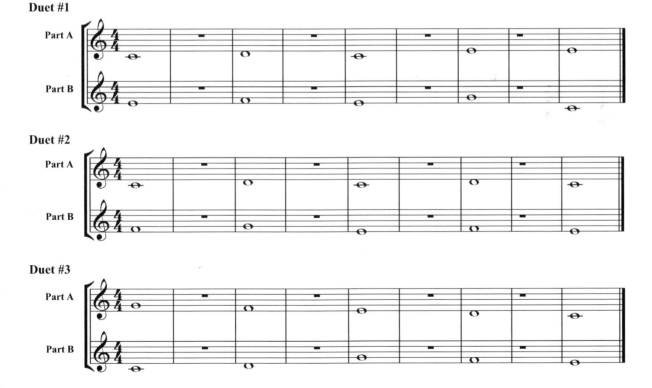

Duct #4

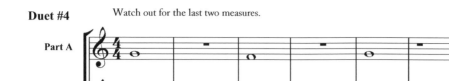

More Notes!

The first five notes you've been practicing are important, but there are many more notes, too. If you've got those first five notes memorized, move on to the notes below. Just as with the first notes you learned, play these for one full breath and focus in on the quality of your tone. Play them many times until you have the feel and sound and fingering of the note memorized. Search out songs which use these notes to get in some practical use. Better yet, make up your own songs using these notes.

Example 7.12 Use the C you already know to get your ears working, then try for the lower notes. Use warm, slow air, like you're making steam come from your mouth on a cold day. Sound clip 7.12, www.sol-ut.com

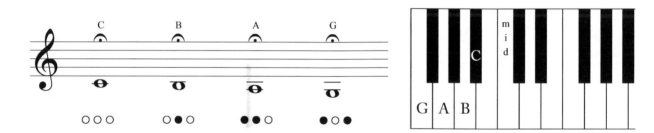

Playing Higher: Notes Above G

Playing higher takes good air, correct embouchure formation and some muscle strength. If you've been doing your buzzing both with lips alone and with the mouthpiece, you'll probably have no trouble with the following notes. If you haven't been doing buzzing exercises, ask yourself the question, "How good do I want to be?"

Even if you have been doing the buzz, the following notes will take some effort, and to get them to sound beautiful will take a lot of critical listening and long tones, just like with all the other notes you've learned.

Take large breaths because higher notes need faster air. The only way to get your air faster is to take more of it into your lungs and compress it before blowing. This means you have to work to push that air out faster and when you're doing this correctly, you'll feel it in your stomach muscles and your face might turn a little red.

Don't use pressure on your lips to get these notes! If you've been doing your buzz exercises, you should need very little pressure to get these notes. For more information on increasing your high range, see "What is the High Range?" on page 129.

If you get these notes easily and want to learn more, check out the fingering chart in the back of the book and get yourself a song book that uses notes higher in the range. And good job, keep it up!

Example 7.13 The A, B and C above 2nd line G.

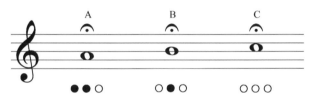
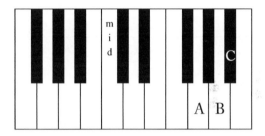

You have probably noticed that we've begun to repeat some note names, like C, A, and B. Remember there are only 7 letter names for notes in music. As you go higher, note names repeat at the *octave*, or every 8 notes. There is a reason for this repeat of note names. All A's, B's, etc., will blend together so well that you'll have a hard time separating one from the other unless one is very high and one is very low. The reason the notes have the same name is because they blend so well.

Coming soon is a chapter which has a bunch of simple tunes so you can get some practical use out of these notes you've learned.

Up Next

I hope you're able to get all of these notes to come out the end of your horn. Keep at it until you can. Most of the examples you've had so far involve notes spaced apart from one another to keep things simple. When one note immediately follows another, the notes need to be separated and to do this you use your tongue.

The next chapter teaches all you need to know about using the tongue to separate notes. Most of it is very simple, common sense stuff, but there are also a couple advanced techniques that will take serious study before they're mastered. What better time to start than right now?

Chapter 8
Tongue Tips for Trumpet

While thou livest, keep a good tongue in thy head.

~ William Shakespeare (1564-1616)

In This Chapter

- Why Tongue?
- Basic Tonguing
- Double Tonguing
- Triple Tonguing

Terms to Know

articulation: The use of the tongue in a wind instrument to separate notes in various ways.

legato: Smooth and connected. Shown by a line (_) above or below notes.

slur: No tonguing. Notes are connected with the air stream only.

staccato: Short and detached. Shown by a dot (.) above or below the note.

double tonguing: Using the "t" and "k" to articulate music that is too fast for single-tonguing (using just the "t").

dorsal tonguing: A style of tonguing in which the middle of the tongue strikes the roof of the mouth (say "goo-goo-ga-ga" and you've done it).

Use My Tongue for What?

The tongue plays an essential role in trumpet music; it allows you to separate notes cleanly and clearly. It will also allow you to play very fast, will help you play higher, and with it you can do some cool sound effects on trumpet. You'll learn about all the details of tonguing in this chapter. Be aware that some of these techniques, like double and triple tonguing, will take a lot of practice to master.

The tongue is one of the strangest muscles in the body. It allows us to speak, to taste things, and to show dislike when we stick it out. And it's only attached at one end, unlike most other muscles. But, like any muscle, the tongue can be trained to be quicker and stronger and more limber. Kind of a weird concept, isn't it? A workout program for your tongue.

When musicians talk about note lengths and styles, the word *articulation* usually comes up. Articulation is a word for different types of tonguing. In a slow, sweet song, the articulation would be smooth and light with notes connected, also known as *legato*. In a march, the articulation would be shorter, more forceful, and with the notes separated, or *staccato*. In a jazz band or a rock 'n roll horn section, you'd use another kind of articulation. The cool thing is that no matter what style of music you end up playing, use of the tongue is crucial to get the kind of sound you need.

Basic Tonguing

The only hard and fast rule about tonguing is that when you do it, whichever style you're using, don't let your jaw move *at all*. If you jaw moves, this can throw off your embouchure and your air stream and will cause more difficulties that you want. Keep your jaw still. In the beginning it's a good idea to practice the following in front of a mirror to make sure your jaw isn't moving.

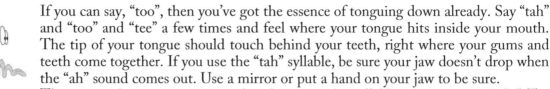

If you can say, "too", then you've got the essence of tonguing down already. Say "tah" and "too" and "tee" a few times and feel where your tongue hits inside your mouth. The tip of your tongue should touch behind your teeth, right where your gums and teeth come together. If you use the "tah" syllable, be sure your jaw doesn't drop when the "ah" sound comes out. Use a mirror or put a hand on your jaw to be sure.

There are other ways to tongue besides using the syllables that start with "t." Try using a "du" or "doo" sound. Compare where you tongue hits when you use this syllable. It should strike your soft palate; that flat part just back from your teeth. Also try "thoo" or "the", with the tongue touching the bottom edge of the top teeth. Other options are "ka" and "la." Try these and other syllables and see what sounds you come up with.

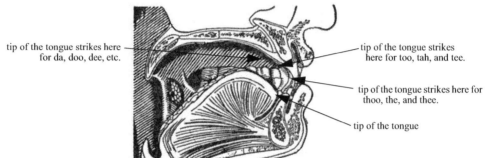

tip of the tongue strikes here for da, doo, dee, etc.

tip of the tongue strikes here for too, tah, and tee.

tip of the tongue strikes here for thoo, the, and thee.

tip of the tongue

In classical music you want the cleanest, clearest articulations you can get, so the "t" or "th" syllables are best for this. In jazz, often the softer articulations are preferred, like a "dah" or "doo" tonguing. Some use one and say the other is incorrect. Try them all and use the one *you* like best. It's a good idea to be able to do *any* kind of tonguing, so learn 'em all and you'll have that many more tools to rely on.

You can practice tonguing wherever you have your mouth. Use your the buzz either with or without the mouthpiece and add the tonguing. If you don't have easy access to a mirror, put a couple fingers on your chin and say, "Ta, ta, ta, ta," or "tha, tha, tha, tha." You shouldn't feel your lower jaw move at all.

The Air Stream and the Tongue

Imagine you're holding a garden hose turned on full blast. The water streams out of the end of the hose in a solid arc across the grass. Quickly chop your hand back and forth through the stream of water, then look at the stream of water as it arcs out over the grass. The stream of water is chopped into small chunks even though the flow of water is constant.

Do you get the analogy? Your air stream is the water and your tongue is the hand breaking the stream into small chunks. It's *VERY IMPORTANT* to keep that air stream going, just like the flow of water in the hose. The air stream is what gives your sound power, strength, and allows you to change cleanly from one note to the next. Without a strong steady air stream, your sound will not be full and present and it will be much more difficult to play consistently.

It's a common mistake to spit the notes out when learning to tongue, using the "tut, tut" syllable. Keep that air flowing and let the air pressure blast the tongue out of the way after tonguing. For learning about how to maintain a proper air stream, see, "Avoiding Bad Breath" on page 53.

The tongue is a muscle and muscles need to be warmed up before they're worked. Do this with some slow tonguing on the mouthpiece, and then slow low notes on the horn. Below are some exercises to do with the buzz alone and/or with the mouthpiece. *Keep the air moving* through the tongue strike. With the third and fourth exercises, gradually speed up until your tongue gives out. As you practice, your tongue speed will gradually increase. Below the buzz tonguing warm up exercises are some tonguing warm-up suggestions on the horn.

Example 8.2 Some exercises for buzz tonguing warm-ups. Sound clip 8.14 at www.sol-ut.com.

Whole Notes = four beats each.
Tongue the first part of the note, then hold the sound out for 4 beats.
Don't stop the air between notes!
Repeat several times.

Half Notes = two beats each.
Tongue the first part of the note, then hold the sound out for 2 beats.
Don't stop the air between notes!
Repeat several times.

Quarter Notes = one beat each.
Tongue the first part of the note, then hold the sound out for 1 beat.
Don't stop the air between notes!
Repeat several times.

Eighth Notes = two per beat.
Tongue evenly, with one note right on the downbeat, the other on the upbeat. Fit the notes evenly within one beat.
Don't stop the air between notes!
Repeat several times.

Example 8.3 Tonguing warm-ups on the horn. Sound clip 8.15 at www.sol-ut.com.

The Tongue's Role in Playing High and Low

Be aware of your tongue for a few moments. Say "ahh" and feel where your tongue is in your mouth. Now say "eee" and feel what happens with your tongue to produce this sound. The back of your tongue is down during the "ahh" sound and it raises toward the roof of your mouth for the "eee" sound.

When you use these syllables while playing, it's very easy and natural for your jaw to drop down for the "ahh" sound and raise up for the "eee" sound. This is great if you're simply talking, but very bad if you're playing. Moving the jaw will disrupt your embouchure and air flow and will generally make things difficult for you. Keep your jaw still when doing the following. You'll notice I repeat these instructions frequently because it's very important. Don't move your jaw. If you don't have a mirror, put a hand on your jaw to monitor it.

Now keep your mouth closed with your teeth slightly apart as though you were going to play trumpet. Keep your jaw relaxed but don't move it as you do the following. Silently say "ahh" then "eee" again and feel how your tongue moves. Go back and forth between the two very slowly at first (it would sound like aahhhhhhheeeeeeeeee). Do this several times until you've got a good feel for it. Now do it quickly so your tongue snaps back and forth between the lower and upper position. Do this in a mirror or with a hand on your jaw to make sure your jaw doesn't move.

Okay, now you'll add the buzz to the mix. Buzz a low note and use the "ahh" shape with your tongue. Make the pitch go higher gradually and as you do so, change from the "ahh" shape to the "eee" shape. Do this several times. Then make an abrupt switch from low (ahh) to high (eee) and be sure your jaw doesn't move.

It may be difficult to coordinate at first but keep trying. You'll need this skill, so practice it until you've got it. Practice with a mirror or with a hand on your jaw to be sure your jaw doesn't move.

Add the mouthpiece and do the same thing as above. Do I need to say it? It's said that it takes seven repetitions before something sticks in our heads. Be sure your jaw doesn't move! ;-)

Example 8.4 Graphic of the tongue techniques mentioned above. Remember it's more difficult to go from low to high than it is from high to low. Don't move your jaw! Sound clip 8.16 at www.sol-ut.com.

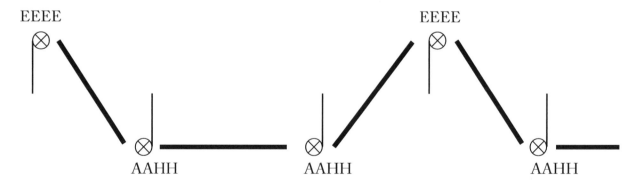

Tongue Placement: Low, Middle, High

Studies have shown that the tongue placement changes depending on where in the trumpet's range you're playing. When playing low, the tongue strikes between the teeth, and in some cases, even all the way up to the lips. As you go higher, the tongue moves further back behind the teeth. For very high playing the tongue moves back even further, often striking the soft palate behind the upper teeth. For altissimo playing (very high), some players use *dorsal tonguing*, where the middle of the tongue strikes the roof of the mouth. Experiment with your own tongue to see which placement works best for you.

Tongue Use in Lip Slurs

A slur is moving from one note to another without tonguing, as smoothly as possible. All wind instruments use slurs, which are shown by a curved line connecting the notes. Trumpet players have an added challenge when the slur is between two notes with the same fingering, like between G and C. A slur between two notes which share the same fingering is called a *lip slur*.

Because they're a little tricky and because they're important, lip slurs get their own chapter. You won't have long to wait because lip slurs are covered in the next chapter.

The Oral Cavity's Role in Your Tone Quality

If all the above wasn't enough, the tongue affects the size of the oral cavity, and this affects your tone quality. If you tongue is up high in your mouth (small oral cavity) your tone will be less rich and warm than it could be. With your tongue down low (ahhh) and an open your throat (large oral cavity), the richer and more resonant your tone will be. Think of the difference between a little acoustic guitar with a small resonating chamber and a big dreadnought-size acoustic guitar. The bigger guitar will have a larger, more resonant and more pleasing tone.

Remember the breathing tube from the chapter on breathing? If not, see "The Breathing Tube" on page 56. When you use the breathing tube, it forces your tongue down and makes your throat open up, giving your the largest oral cavity you can have. If you play with the inside of your mouth very open like this, your tone will be more resonant and pleasing.

The trouble with using a very open oral cavity is that it becomes more difficult to play in the upper range. You have to compromise. Keep your oral cavity as large as you can without sacrificing range.

Double and Triple Tonguing

At times you may have to play a passage that is very fast—too fast to tongue in the usual manner (also called "single-tonguing"). In such cases, you'll want to use double, or even triple tonguing. This is an advanced skill that is not difficult at all to understand, but takes a while before it becomes natural and easy. Stick with it, do a little every day, and it'll come.

Your tongue is a muscle, albeit a strange one, and it will tire easily at first. It will also seem slow and stubborn at first, but the more you train your tongue, the quicker and stronger it will become. Many of these exercises you can do anywhere and you don't need a trumpet to practice them. You can even do them silently so people don't give you strange looks.

With these techniques, you're using both the front part of your tongue (the *tah*, *too*, *tee*, *the*, or *thoo* sound) and the back part of your tongue (the *kah* or *koo* or *kee* sound). Take a moment and say, "ka, ka, ka, ka," and feel where your tongue strikes.

Again with the jaw movement problem. As before, you don't want your jaw to move for all of the same reasons. Keeping your jaw still is more difficult with the "tah kah" than the others, so be aware of what your jaw does when using those syllables. Practice with a mirror or a hand on your jaw.

Double Tonguing

Do the following very slowly! Combine the two syllables you learned above and say, "tee-kee-tee-kee-tee-kee," and "too-koo-too-koo-too-koo," and "tah-kah-tah-kah-tah-kah." Go slowly and keep a hand on your jaw if you don't have access to a mirror. Don't let your jaw move. Keep the length of each syllable even. Below are some exercises to help with this.

Use a metronome with the exercises below and find a tempo at which you can say the syllables easily. On the third exercise, gradually speed up a few metronome clicks at a time. See how fast you can go before your tongue gives out. Record how fast you were able to go with the *Exercise Tracking Form* in the Appendix of the book. Practice double tonguing all week whenever you think of it and during your actual practice session with the instrument, then check in with the metronome when the week's up to see how much you've improved. Record your speed on the exercise tracking chart in the appendix and compare your speed to previous weeks. Continue to monitor yourself like this so you can see how much better you're getting.

Example 8.5 Buzz double-tonguing exercises. START SLOWLY! With the 3rd example, gradually speed up with your metronome until your tongue gives out. Rest a few minutes, then do it again. Do this daily and you'll have a fast tongue in a short time! Sound clip 8.17 at www.sol-ut.com.

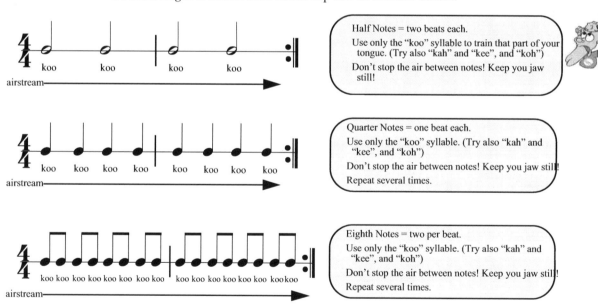

Now you'll do the actual double-tonguing with the buzz and the mouthpiece. Below are the same exercises as above, but with the syllables alternating. Strive to make the "too" and "koo" sound *exactly* the same. This is one of the challenging parts of double tonguing.

Tongue Tips for Trumpet

Example 8.6 Buzz double tonguing exercises alternating the *too* and *koo*. Also use the *tah-kah* and *tee-kee* syllables. Keep the air moving! Keep your jaw still! Do these both without and with the mouthpiece. Sound clip 8.17 at www.sol-ut.com.

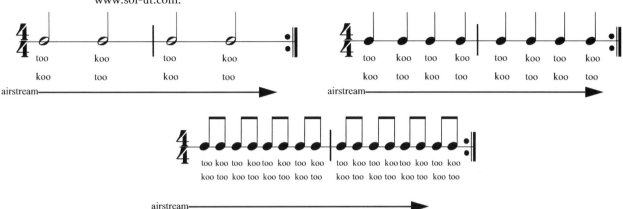

When you add the horn to your double tonguing, you'll be able to hear very clearly the difference between using the tip of the tongue ("too") and the back of the tongue ("koo"). Strive to make the two sound exactly the same by making that "koo" syllable as hard and explosive as is necessary. As before, keep the air flowing and keep your jaw still.

Triple Tonguing

There isn't much difference between double- and triple tonguing technique. You'll still use the "ta" and "ka" syllables. The rhythm of the notes will be different (usually triplets) and depending on which type of triple-tonguing you choose, the order may also be slightly different. What the heck does that mean? First an explanation and then some exercises.

Because you're dealing with three notes, you have two options for triple tonguing. The first is to use the double-tonguing pattern you already learned, but to group it in threes. That would sound like "ta-ka-ta, ka-ta-ka, ta-ka-ta, ka-ta-ka," etc. Notice that each group of three alternates between "ka-ta-ka" and "ta-ka-ta." It is this alternation which makes this type of triple-tonguing a challenge. Many players use it, so give it a try and see how you like it.

Another, and perhaps easier, way of triple tonguing is to use the pattern "ta-ka-ta, ta-ka-ta, ta-ka-ta," etc. This is also widely used and many find it simpler and cleaner that the above. Try this method of triple-tonguing and see how it feels compared to the first technique, then focus on one until it's learned. It's not a bad idea to learn both. Why not? Here are some exercises.

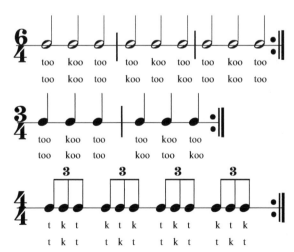

Practice variations of these exercises on every note in your range.

Multiple Tonguing While Changing Notes

Once you've practiced multiple tonguing on one note, it's time to practice multiple tonguing while changing notes. This is a little more challenging, but if you've got the basics down, it's not that hard to make the leap to double- or triple-tonguing a moving melody.

The technique is identical, but the challenge lies in coordinating the tongue and the fingers. As with any coordination challenge, you have to start very slowly to train the muscles to perform the movement correctly. Trying to double- or triple-tongue too fast is the mistake most often made. You must start slowly! Get it perfect at a slow tempo (use your metronome) and then gradually speed it up. It's that simple, you just have to do it!

As with any skill you're trying to learn on the horn, if you can double up the things you're practicing, you get double the work in half the time. What does this mean? Well, in the case of double- and triple- tonguing, you can use scales while practicing the tonguing. That way you get in scale practice *and* tonguing practice. Makes sense, right?

Below are just a few examples to give you an idea of what I'm talking about. Use your imagination and creativity (and method books) to double-up your practice.

Example 8.7 A few relatively easy double- and triple-tonguing exercises. Invent and find more. Sound clip 8.19 at www.sol-ut.com.

Sources for Further Study

If you don't have an Arban's Complete Method for Trumpet, go get one now. It has exercises for most techniques on trumpet, including many double and triple-tonguing exercises.

Title	Author	Publisher/Distributor
240 Double & Triple Tonguing Exercises	Salvo	Belwin
Articulation Studies	Chris Gekker	Colin Publications
Arban's Complete Conservatory Method	Arban	most music stores have it

Listening Examples of Multiple Tonguing

Some great recordings of double- and triple-tonguing can be found on Wynton Marsalis's album *Carnival*, especially the piece called *Flight of the Bumblebee*. Also find examples in the piece *Scheherezade*, by Rimsky-Korsakov, in Tchaikovsky's *Symphony IV*, the third movement of Hummel's *Concerto in Eb*, and many, many others. Find video clips for all these pieces on the "extras" page for this book at the Sol Ut web site (www.sol-ut.com).

Up Next

Since this chapter covered the tongue, the next chapter will cover special instances when the tongue is *not* used. When you don't use the tongue between notes, this is called a slur. When you slur between two notes that have the same fingering, this is a special type of slur called a lip slur. Learn all the details about this important skill in the next chapter.

CHAPTER 9

LIP SLURS & THE ORAL CAVITY

Smile. It's the second–best thing you can do with your lips.

~ Anonymous

In This Chapter

- Regular Slur
- What is a Lip Slur?
- Lip Slur Techniques
- Lip Slur Exercises
- Lip Slur Method Books

Terms to Know

lip slur: The technique of moving from one note to another using the same fingering without the use of the tongue.

oral cavity: The space inside your mouth and throat. Used to affect the sound you get on the horn.

What is a Lip Slur?

On a wind instrument, a regular slur is two different notes smoothly connected using the air alone, no tonguing. This is usually a pretty easy skill, but with brass instruments like trumpet, trombone, French horn and others, many notes share the same fingering. When one note of a slur shares the fingering with the next note of the slur, the change has to be made with the chops and the airstream alone. This is called a *lip slur*.

Lip slurs are an essential tool to have in your belt so be sure to practice them. There are a few tricks and tips which will help you master the technique of lip slurs and we'll cover them in this chapter. Be patient with yourself and your lips. It takes some time to get this skill automatic and smooth, but with persistence and the use of the following hints, you'll do well.

Example 9.1 **Top:** regular slurs. **Bottom:** lip slurs. A slur marking (also called legato mark or phrase mark) can be either above or below the notes it affects. In the lip slur example can you spot the one regular slur? Sound clip 9.1 at www.sol-ut.com.

regular slurs: fingerings from one note to the next are different.

slur marks

lip slurs: fingerings from one note to the next are the same. Which of these is a regular slur?

Before we get into any details about lip slurs, experiment with some to get a feel for what you can or can't do. Choose a valve combination (don't forget open) and see how many notes you can get on that combination without using your tongue to change notes. Keep the air steady. If you try to figure out for yourself how to do lip slurs you'll have a better understanding of what you need to learn.

Lip slurs are essential to playing trumpet. As you practice them you'll be increasing your flexibility and dexterity on trumpet. You'll strengthen your lip muscles and train them to respond more quickly and precisely. Lip slurs keep lips limber. Practice them regularly.

Lip Slurs and Physics: Downhill is Easier

Is it easier to go uphill or downhill? Does it take more work to climb a cliff or fall off one? These are no-brainer questions and they relate to lip slurs because lip slurs are also easier going down. Going from a high energy state (higher note) to a lower energy state (low note) requires no extra energy.

All these words may mean little to you. Try the following experiment. Take two notes which share the same fingering. For our example we'll use G and C, your first two notes from Chapter 7. Play the G and be aware of how it feels: how hard you have to blow, how flexed your muscles are, the sound of the note, how it smells, and anything else you can sense. Then play the C and do the same thing. You should notice the different sensations produced by each note. You'll do this for each of the examples below, too. It will help a lot when you do the actual slur.

Keep that air flowing at all times! Your sound should be continuous. At first you'll be going only from a higher note to a lower note. Try each valve combination several times. You may find some combinations easier than others. Tongue the first note of each slur. Check your pitch with a piano. Go slowly!

Example 9.2 Downward lip slurs. Repeat each valve combination several times. Check your pitch with a piano or online at www.sol-ut.com, sound clip 9.2.

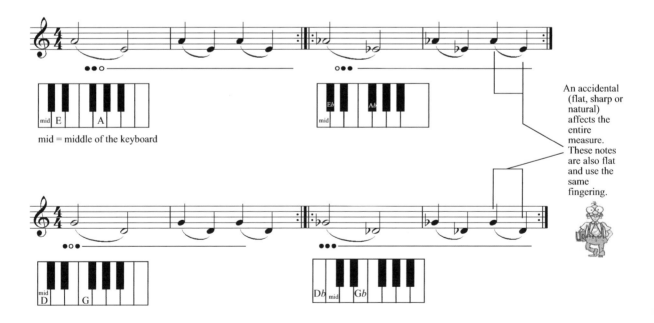

mid = middle of the keyboard

An accidental (flat, sharp or natural) affects the entire measure. These notes are also flat and use the same fingering.

If the higher note just won't budge, try mouthing the word "ahhh" as you change notes, but don't let your jaw move. To do this you must change the shape formed by the inside of your mouth, also known as the oral cavity. More on this next.

Example 9.3 More lip slurs. The interval between these notes is larger than in the last example. If you're using the "ahh" technique, be sure your jaw is not moving.Use a mirror. Check your pitch with a piano or online at www.sol-ut.com, sound clip 9.3. Go slowly! The lower notes may be quite difficult to get at first.

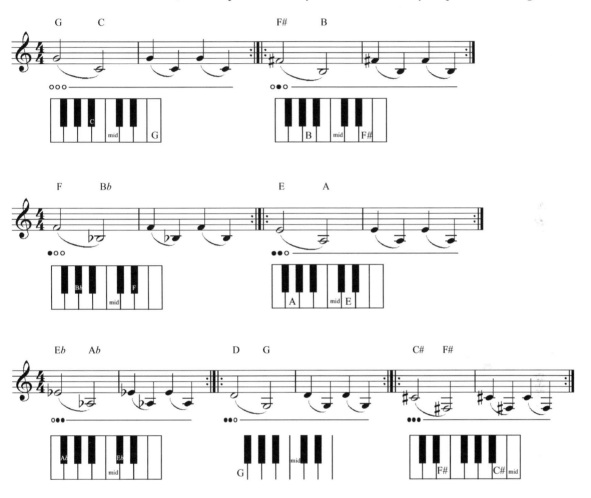

Lip Slurs: Going Up!

An ascending, or rising lip slur is more difficult, as you've probably already experienced. C'mon, admit it. You know you tried it. Did it work? Was it easy? If not, there are some things you can do to help. The first has to do with air stream, the second has to do with the shape of the inside of your mouth, also known as the *oral cavity*.

A lip slur from low to high requires extra energy. Playing from a low note to a higher one is usually aided by the tongue strike but since we're talking about lip slurs, you don't have that option. The first thing you must rely on is your airstream. As you do a lip slur from a lower note, give the airstream a push when you want to change to the upper note. Think of blowing a fly away with an extra puff of air, or blowing dust off something. Give a quick pulse of air. You'll have to experiment with just how much air it will take to get the results you want. In addition to the air stream, you can change the shape of the inside of your mouth (oral cavity) to get the higher note of the lip slur.

The oral cavity is not something you'll need filled by a dentist. It's the shape of the inside of your mouth and throat. The size of the oral cavity is changed by your tongue. Do this: without opening your lips or moving your jaw, mouth the word "ahhh" and be aware of where you tongue is. And again without opening your lips or moving your jaw, mouth the word "eeee" and feel where you tongue is. Finally, still with closed lips and stationary jaw, mouth "ahhh" and then "eeee" and feel the position of your tongue change. You've just changed the size and shape of your oral cavity with your tongue position. Not too difficult, is it? If you know how to whistle, you can already do this.

Raising the tongue causes the oral cavity to become smaller and this speeds up the airstream. It is the air speed that allows you to play higher. Faster air and higher notes go together like olive oil and Italian food.

Example 9.4 Cross section of the oral cavity. **Left:** ahhh. **Right:** eee. When you go from "ahh" to "eee" be sure your embouchure, jaw and lips don't move, unlike the drawings below.

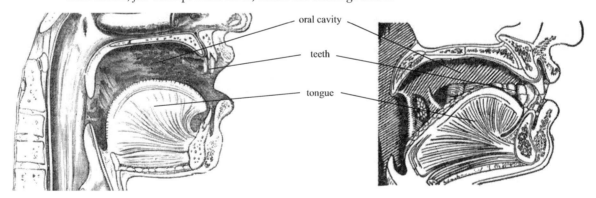

It will be tempting to use mouthpiece pressure to get to that upper note. Don't do it! Use the airstream and tongue position only. It will take some time and effort to master this skill and it's best to start with the smallest jumps between notes, like the following examples.

Do these exercises just like the previous ones. Tongue the half notes the first time and be aware of how each note feels. When you slur from the lower note to the higher, use the "ahhh" "eee" technique if you can't get the note to change with the airstream alone. Go slowly. Check your pitch with a piano or online at www.sol-ut.com.

Example 9.5 Ascending lip slurs, small interval. Use your airstream first! If that doesn't work, use the airstream *and* the "eee". ***Don't use mouthpiece pressure to change notes. Keep your jaw still.*** Go slowly! Sound clip 9.5 at www.sol-ut.com.

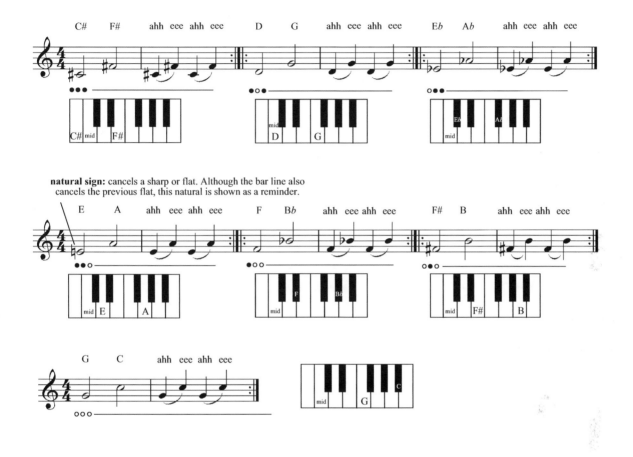

natural sign: cancels a sharp or flat. Although the bar line also cancels the previous flat, this natural is shown as a reminder.

Large Interval Lip Slurs

Some times it's necessary to do a lip slur between notes that are far apart. Because there are other notes with the same fingering between the two notes of the big slur, the challenge is to get the slur smooth without any of the notes in the middle. Confused? Here's an example:

Try the octave slur from high to low first.

Between the two Cs there is another note which also has no valves down. Do you know which one? It's the G on the second line. The challenge is to get from one C to another without hitting the G between them. Sound clip 9.4.

There are several things to keep in mind with a large slur that will make it much easier. The first is to hear the note you are going towards. If you can hold the sound in your mind before you jump to it, you body will often do exactly what is needed to make a smooth transition. To get the sound in your head, play each note separately. Focus on the sound and try to hear the next note in your head before you jump to it. Sing the interval several times and then try the lip slur. If you get hung up on the middle note or notes, there are a couple other things to try.

How each note feels is something to keep in mind. When you play that upper note, be aware of exactly how much air and lip strength it takes to play it. Do the same with the lower note and compare the two. After doing this a few times, try the slur and focus on making the air and the lips switch from the feel of the lower note to the feel of the upper note as quickly as possible. Did it work?

Airstream is your best friend with smaller lip slurs and it's no different with the bigger lip slurs. In fact, the airstream is even more important for these big leaps. Keep your air flow steady and blow through the notes so the horn does the work. When you go from low to high, bear down on that bottom note with your air just before you make the leap. This will help shoot you up past the G.

When you practice these large interval lip slurs, that middle note will probably be pretty obvious at first. As you practice more, the middle note will disappear to just a little blip of sound between the notes, and finally it will disappear completely. Keep practicing. Talk to your trumpet teacher about it.

Further Study

Many method books cover lip slurs, but the best is Earl D. Irons' *27 Groups of Exercises for Cornet or Trumpet*, published by Southern Music Company. Another great book is *Advanced Lip Flexibility Studies* by Charles Colin. Get a copy of each at www.sol-ut.com

Up Next

All of this talk about technique can get tedious. It's tough to escape at the beginning because you have so much to learn. In the next chapter we'll escape the tedium by playing songs. The next chapter contains simple songs to help you hone your skills of reading music. Finally!

Lip Slurs & the Oral Cavity

CHAPTER 10
SIMPLE TUNES

Do not follow in the footsteps of the wise. Seek what they sought.

~ Zen saying

In This Chapter

- Repeat Signs
- Breath Marks
- Pick-up Notes
- 8th Notes
- Flats
- E♭ and A♭

Terms to Know

repeat sign: Two dots at the end of a section telling you to repeat the section.

breath mark: A comma-shaped symbol telling you to take a breath.

upbeat: The second half of a beat, (the second of two eighth notes).

round: A song in which the same melody is played by all players starting in different places.

flat (♭): A symbol used to lower the pitch of a note by a half step.

sharp (♯): A symbol used to raise the pitch of a note by a half step.

natural (♮): A symbol used to cancel a flat or sharp.

Some Simple Songs

Below are songs that most musicians have played in the process of learning to read music. The songs are easy to play and you'll already know most of the melodies. Be sure to follow the notes, especially if you know the song well. I didn't write the fingering under the notes so you'd be forced to remember the fingerings. Of course you can write the fingerings in, but try to remember them instead. If you do write in fingerings, be sure you use a pencil so you can erase them later to test yourself.

Here's a reminder and something new to beef up your music vocabulary. You already got the lowdown on the *breath mark*. See "When to Breathe" on page 57. Placing the breath is important. If you put the breath in the wrong place, the pause needed to breathe will break up the musical phrase (this is a bad thing). Generally, you should take a breath every fourth measure if you can last that long. Take a big breath before you start to be sure you make it through four

measures. In some of the examples below, the breath mark is used every two measures. Not all music will show you when to breathe. Use your judgement. If you see **NB**, this means "no breath," so *don't* take a breath.

A *repeat sign* is two dots at the end of a section of music and these dots tell you to go back and repeat the previous section. Some times the repeat will be back to the beginning, some times a section in the middle of a song will be repeated.

Buzz These Tunes!

Perhaps you picked up this book for its discography, the information on pedal tones or several other reasons. If you've been playing for a while you may think these simple songs offer nothing for you, but that might not be true. Can you sing them perfectly in tune? Can you buzz them perfectly?

To challenge and strengthen your ability on trumpet, buzz all these songs with your mouthpiece. Start in a comfortable middle range and give it a try. If you need a little help, use a piano or your trumpet to get the right pitch in your ear, then go for it. Once you're able to buzz all of these on your mouthpiece, buzz the tunes with just your lips. This is an excellent thing for you to do! It might not be easy at first, but keep at it until you can buzz the songs easily. Almost everything worthwhile takes some effort. Buzz these tunes and you'll be rewarded with better tone, better range, better control of your sound and better listening skills. Why wouldn't you want all that good stuff?

The "NB" indication is seen only in music for beginners. Use your ears to tell when the musical phrase should continue without the break caused by breathing.

Mary Had a Little Lamb: This song is two lines long and repeats one time.

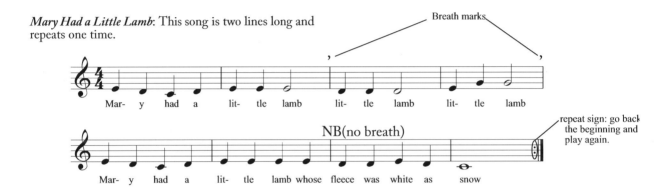

Go Tell Aunt Rhodie

Lightly Row: can you finish these 4-measure phrases in one breath?

Au Claire de la Lune: this tune goes up a little higher to the A.
Do you remember the fingering? (first and second valve.)

Simple Tunes

Twinkle, Twinkle, Little Star: the legend is that Mozart wrote this tune when he was five. Actually, he used the already-existing melody for a composition. Still pretty amazing.

Jingle Bells: You probably know this one.

Chiapanecas: Notice there are three beats in each measure (3/4 time). The quarter note still gets one beat. Keep your foot t at a steady tempo. Remember the fingering for low B? (it's 2nd valve)

Eighth Notes

Except for two spots in *Jingle Bells*, all of the songs so far have used quarter notes, half notes and whole notes. Now we'll get a little more interesting with eighth notes. There are two eighth notes in every beat, so in a whole measure of $\frac{4}{4}$ time (the most common), there will be 8 eighth notes.

When you tap your foot (you *are* tapping your foot, right?) the first eighth notes is played when your foot hits the floor and the second one is played when your foot is in the "up" position. The second of two eighth notes is called the ***upbeat*** for this reason.

In $\frac{4}{4}$ time, eighth notes are counted, "one-and-two-and-three-and-four-and." It's often helpful to count a difficult rhythm out loud to help you process the information before you actually play an example. If you run into a difficult example or a difficult song below, count it out loud first, then try to play it again. Continue the process (you can finger the notes as you say the rhythm) until you've got it.

Before we get to songs with eighth notes, let's give you a little practice on some simple examples. This will give you a chance to coordinate your tongue and your foot; then on to the real tunes.

Example 10.1 Simple eighth note exercises. Keep your foot tap steady and even. Sound clip 10.6 at www.sol-ut.com

foot tap: down up down up down up down   down up down up down up down   down up down up down up down

down up down up   down up down up down up down up   down up down up   down up down up down up down up

Notice the foot tap arrows on this example. I've only shown the downbeat for quarter notes. The upbeat is assumed.

Tunes With Eighth Notes

Hot Cross Buns: Notice there are only two beats in each measure ($\frac{2}{4}$ time). The quarter note still gets one beat. Tap your foot at a steady tempo.

Skip to My Lou

Neener Neener (swing it*)

*with a lilting, bouncy rhythm

Duets

When playing a duet and both parts have the same rhythm, it's pretty easy to stay together. When each part has a *different* rhythm you'll need more concentration to get your part correct, especially if your part is the one that holds while the other part moves. In the duets below you'll get to practice this. The "A" part will be the part that moves and the "B" part will be the one that holds while the other moves.

After the two simple duets is a **round**, another type of duet. In a round each person plays the exact same part but at different times. The round below is *Frere Jacques* and each person starts at a number. You can either all start at the same time, one person at each number, or you can have one person start and the next person comes in at the beginning when the first player reaches a number. Have fun. Go to www.sol-ut.com for sound clip 10.1 so you can play along!

Simple Duet 10.1

Simple Duet 10.2

Frere Jacques: This tune can be done as a round. Numbers mark where each player starts. Another variation is to have one person start and additional players come in at the beginning as the first player reaches the numbers. Repeat as many times as you want.

Just a Taste

These tunes are just a small selection to get you reading music easily if you don't do it already. You should find other sources for songs. There are hundreds of books out there with songs from easy to difficult in many, many different styles. More and more song books have recorded accompaniment with them to make playing the songs even more fun. Visit your local music store and see what they have to offer. If they don't have what you're looking for they can order it for you. You can also look online. Thrift stores are great sources for deals on music and if you go to a library, you can check out music for free!

Finding music you like is a lifelong task. I'm always looking for new songs and I buy new books of songs regularly. It's always fun to explore a new book. Start your collection of songs now! To find lists, see "Where to start?" on page 197.

Talk over your options with your teacher and get some suggestions of what might be good for you. If you haven't studied with a teacher yet, you really should. You'll learn a lot very quickly!

If you've got those first six notes down pretty well and want to learn some more, keep going. The notes covered next use flats, a musical symbol you'll learn about below.

More Notes! Eb and Ab

So far you've got 8 notes to choose from and after practicing the songs earlier in this chapter, you'll know these notes really well. In fact, you may become bored with them.

Below are some variations of the first five notes. We'll cover the C minor scale which is closely related to the C Major scale you learned in the last few pages. I can't stress enough that you look at the note and not the fingering. Look at the note and not the fingering. Look at the note and not the fingering!

As in the first examples, play each note with one full breath and strive for a beautiful tone (hint: keep your air moving and stay relaxed). Memorize these sequences of notes as soon as you can.

Change their speed, their rhythm and their order. Experiment! Look at the note and not the fingering.

For the complete scales, as well as patterns to use when practicing them, see "General Info About These Scales" on page 275 in the Codicil of the book.

But First, This Message

Before we get to the new notes, you'll need to know about *flats*. Flats are doohickeys that go before a note. Flats tell you the note following is to be lowered slightly. Remember this about flats: when you say the name of a note, you say, "E–flat," with the word *flat* coming after the letter. When you draw a flat for a written note on the staff, the flat must be placed *before* the note on the same line/space as the note to be altered. This is so you see the flat before getting to the note so you know it is to be lowered.

The note you'll be looking at is an E♭. The E♭ is slightly lower than the E which you've already learned. Play one then the other in the example below to allow your ear to hear the difference. Tap your foot.

Example 10.2 The E and E♭. The A and A♭. Listen carefully to the difference in pitch. Sound clip 10.7 at www.sol-ut.com

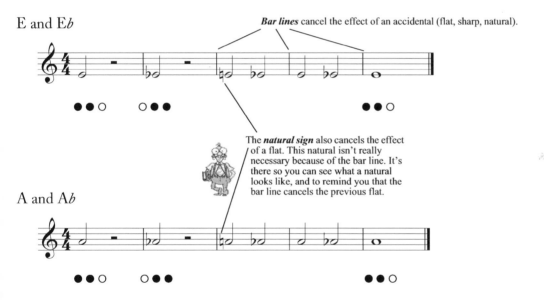

Example 10.3 A duet so you can hear the harmonic difference between a major third and a minor third. Go to www.sol-ut.com for sound clip 10.8.

Example 10.4 The first six notes of the C minor scale. For complete scales, see the appendix.
Sound clip 10.9 at www.sol-ut.com

C minor scale (1st 6 notes)

Some Minor Ditties

In music you'll often hear the terms *major* and *minor* thrown around a lot. Basically, major means a brighter, happier sound, and minor means a darker, sadder sound. To get this big emotional difference you only need to change two notes. In these first little tunes, you'll notice the E♭ is used instead of the E. This is the note that changes the feel of these songs from bright to dark. After playing the song with the E♭, try going back through the songs again and use E natural. Can you hear the difference?

The other note that is changed to make this more melancholy sound is the A. It is also lowered a half step to A♭. You'll see the A♭ in the third and fourth examples. Sound clip 10.10 at www.sol-ut.com.

A Challenge

Below is a great song called *Dark Eyes*. It has a Russian mother and a Gypsy father. It was originally a Russian folk song and was borrowed by Gypsies and spread throughout Europe. The Gypsy guitar virtuoso Django Reinhardt recorded this tune. It's fun and pretty easy at a slow tempo. Try to figure out the song from the written notes. If you get stuck, go online to www.sol-ut.com to hear Jazzology play this tune; sound clip 10.11. If you look for Django's version, it's in French, and the title is *Les Yeux Noirs*. I've added the chords in case you know a guitar or piano player who will play with you. Chords are in the trumpet's key, Bb, so you'll have to transpose them down a whole step to get concert pitch for guitar and/or piano. If this is confusing, see Chapter 18 about transposing. Also, the music below is in what's called "lead sheet style." The font is often used on jazz tunes. It has sort of a hand-written feel to it. If you're curious about jazz or how to read the chords below, check out my book *Basic Jazz Theory* for more information. You can find it at www.sol-ut.com.

LES YEUX NOIRS (DARK EYES)

TRADITIONAL

Up Next

Matching your pitch *exactly* with another instrument is a very important skill to learn. The trumpet's pitch can be changed slightly with the use of the slides. Some notes of the trumpet are chronically out of tune and you can use your slides to get the pitch of those notes correct. In the next chapter you'll get all the details of this important process.

CHAPTER 11

TRUMPET TUNING TIPS

Human beings, vegetables, or cosmic dust, we all dance to a mysterious tune, intoned in the distance by an invisible player.

~ Albert Einstein (1879-1955)

In This Chapter

- What is Intonation?
- Basic Concepts
- Tuning the Whole Trumpet
- Problem Notes on Trumpet
- Using Triggers for Tuning

Terms to Know

tuning slide: the largest slide on the trumpet. Used to tune the entire instrument.

flat: slightly below correct pitch.

sharp: slightly above correct pitch.

intonation: the accuracy of pitch.

leger lines: Small lines used below or above the staff for notes beyond the range of the staff.

concert pitch: International tuning pitch of A440. Some instruments in concert pitch are piano, flute, trombone, tuba, oboe, etc.

What's Tuning All About?

Sound is made up of invisible waves of vibration. When two or more instruments create sound, the sound waves mix together. If these waves aren't synchronized so the sound vibrates at the same wavelength, we experience this as being out of tune. The more sensitive you are to *intonation* the more uncomfortable and even unpleasant a listening experience can be if the music is out of tune. On the other hand, if things *are* in tune, a performance can be an incredible, even magical experience.

From the perspective of the performer, it is *much* easier to play and to really get into the music if everyone is in tune. When a group is perfectly in tune, the sound takes on a presence and a power that simply isn't there when the intonation is poor. The best musicians take intonation very seriously and so should you. It makes music much more beautiful and fun.

Basic Trumpet Tuning

tuning slide

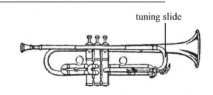

The pitch of any wind instrument is a factor of length. The longer a wind instrument is, the lower it's sound will be. Compare the lengths of a trumpet and a tuba to see what I mean. When you tune an instrument, you're changing its pitch very slightly. This is done by either shortening or lengthening the instrument a small amount. For brass instruments like trumpet, this is done with the *tuning slide*.

Pull the tuning slide out and the pitch gets lower as the instrument gets longer. Push it in and the pitch goes higher as the instrument gets shorter. Experiment with your tuning slide: pull it almost all the way off, play a note and as you're playing, push the slide in. Listen to the sound. Do you hear it getting higher? How small of a difference are you able to hear?

If you're unable to move the slide, see "Trouble-Shooting" on page 154 for advice on how to get your slide unstuck. If your slide is stuck, be sure you take care of it right now because tuning is very important.

Tuning The Whole Trumpet

When you move the tuning slide, you're changing the pitch of the entire horn. Trace the path of the air through the horn and you'll see that it always goes past the tuning slide before it gets redirected by the valves. Most trumpets are naturally a little bit *sharp* (high in pitch), so ***the tuning slide should be pulled out slightly whenever you play***, even when you practice by yourself. This will train your ear to the specific pitch of your horn. All horns are different, so you'll have to find out exactly how sharp your trumpet is.

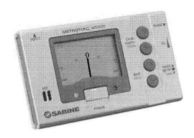

Don't guess about tuning. Be specific. In order to do this, you'll need a tuner. There are many different tuners out there. Be careful not to buy a guitar tuner as they only tune six specific notes. You want a chromatic tuner that will read any pitch. Also look for an analog indication of pitch. This is a little arm that changes as your pitch changes. If the arm is left of 0, your pitch is low, or *flat* (push your tuning slide in); if the arm is right of 0, your pitch is high, or *sharp* (pull your tuning slide out. If you can, get a tuner that is also a metronome. Sabine makes a good one, the MT-9000 seen here.

Before you tune, make sure you and the horn are warmed up. When you tune your horn, pick an open note (no valves down) for tuning. G is a good choice because it's low in the range and easy to play. When you tune you want to be warmed up, relaxed and blowing freely without any strain.

This will give you a correct reading on the pitch. Play the G into the tuner. If your tuner shows the letter name of the note you play, you'll notice that when you play a G, the tuner will tell you it's an F. Not to worry. Trumpet notes are one letter away from *concert pitch*, which is what the tuner shows. You'll learn more about this under "Trumpet is a Bb Instrument" on page 187. For now don't worry about the different note name, just watch where your pitch falls in relation to the "0" mark.

Sometimes you will adjust the pitch with your chops automatically and this will give you an incorrect reading. To avoid this, close your eyes and play the note. When you're relaxed, the air is flowing freely and the note is steady, open your eyes and check the tuner. This will give you a much more accurate reading than watching the tuner as you play the note.

If the arm is left of 0, your pitch is too low (or your instrument is too long), so you need to shorten the trumpet. Push the tuning slide in. If the arm is to the right of the 0, your pitch is too high (or your instrument is too short), so you need to lengthen it. Pull your tuning slide out. Close your eyes and play again. Check the pitch and continue to adjust until you're right on the 0. If you've got it, you're in tune. Well, *usually* in tune. Read on....

How the Pitch Can Change

In the above tuning exercise you tuned the trumpet to the note G on the second line of the staff. Technically this means that only the G is in tune at that moment. All other notes on the trumpet may be out of tune for several reasons. The most common reason a trumpet will go out of tune is that the horn isn't fully warmed up. Because sound travels faster at warmer temperatures, as the horn warms up there is a rise in frequency which is the same as a rise in pitch, also known as *going sharp*. Other reasons the pitch may change are improper breath support, very loud dynamics, very soft dynamics, high in the range, low in the range, and how tired your lips are.

Try this with your tuner. Play the same G and watch the tuner. Your note should be in tune at first. Close your eyes and play as loudly as you can. Don't worry if the sound isn't all that pleasant. Before you run out of air, open your eyes and check the tuner. Which way did the pitch go? Do the same exercise again, but this time keep your eyes open as you get louder and keep the little arm centered on 0. Could you do it? Keep trying until you can.

Do the same exercise, but this time playing very softly. How did the pitch change?

High Pitches Tend to Be Sharp

Try playing high in your range. How does the pitch change up there? Most players are sharp in their upper register. This can be caused by a few things, the most common being mouthpiece pressure, especially pressure on your top lip. Some players tuck their chin down and in when playing high and point the bell of the trumpet up. Sometimes we stretch the lips and use more of a "smile" embouchure when playing higher. These habits also cause the pitch to rise.

To fix these problems, keep your head level and lower you bell slightly. You may not like how this feels at first because you're not used to it. You may even lose a couple notes from your upper range. That's okay. You'll have a much better, fuller sound on the notes you *can* play and they'll be much more in tune. Hold the corners of your lips down and in. This will also fatten up your tone. Practice upper notes with the tuner. Get help from your trumpet teacher.

Low Pitches Tend to Be Flat

How about low in your range? Most players are flat down there, usually because not enough lip is vibrating inside the mouthpiece. The very best thing you can do is sing the notes before you play them (use a piano or your tuner to get the correct pitch of the notes—many tuners including the Sabine shown earlier will generate a pitch for you to hear). If you can sing the note in tune, often your body will automatically fix the pitch of the note. Amazing but true!

There are a few other things that will help raise those low pitches. Use soft, slow, warm air down low in your range. Pretend you're making steam come out of your mouth on a cold day. Say, "Haaaaah." Keep the volume soft at first to help stabilize the pitch. To raise the pitch slightly, shape your oral cavity with the "eee" vowel (raise the back of your tongue like you're saying "eee"). Practice low notes with your tuner. Get help from your trumpet teacher.

The Left Hand's Role in Tuning

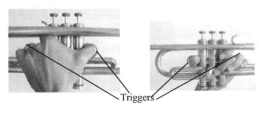
Triggers

Another way to change the intonation of a trumpet is with the slides connected to valves one and three. Most trumpets have *triggers* on these slides which are used to move them in and out. If your hand is loose and relaxed you'll be able to move these slides quickly. Well, as long as your slides are *clean* you can move them quickly.

To get your slides zipping in and out with ease, be sure they're clean and greased with slide grease. You may have to add a drop of valve oil to each "prong" of the slide while moving the slide in and out. Work the valve oil in and add another drop if the movement is still sluggish. Keep doing this a drop at a time (no more than 2-3 drops). If you gave the slide more than two or three drops of oil and it still isn't quick, you may have a problem.

As a *very* last resort you can use a steel wool pad to buff the slide. If you decide to do this keep in mind that too much scrubbing could ruin your horn, so scrub carefully with that steel wool. Give each prong of the slide 4-6 passes with the steel wool. Each time you do this use the same number of strokes for each prong of the slide. When you're done scrubbing the slide, lube it up and pop it back in to check the action. If it's still stiff, repeat until it's not. To avoid the hassle and risk, take it to an instrument repair person.

Out of Tune Notes on Trumpet

Even if your horn is perfectly warmed up and perfectly in tune, you still have to tune some individual notes. This is because there are certain notes on trumpet that are chronically out of tune. A trumpet is built so that as many notes as possible are in tune. This leaves a few notes permanently out of whack. Not only that, but certain overtones are naturally out of tune. The good news is that they're all pretty easy to fix.

The Sharp Notes

The first and worst out of tune note on trumpet is the low D♭, also known as C#. How can two notes have the same pitch and the same fingering? They're called *enharmonic notes*. To learn more about them and music theory in general, check out *Basic Music Theory: How to Read Write and Understand Written Music* from your local library. For now, just know that both notes have the same fingering and the same pitch.

Because it's more common, I'll call this pitch C# from here on. If your horn is generally in tune, check the low C# with your tuner. Is it sharp or flat? I'll wait while you check it.... You'll notice this note is very sharp, or high in pitch. Before I show you the easy way to fix the pitch of this note, try to get the little arm to "0" with your chops alone. Takes some work, doesn't it? Tips on how to do this better are coming soon on page 122.

The slide coming off the third valve is called the third valve slide. No big surprise there. You'll use this slide to get that pesky C# in tune. Because that note is sharp, you'll need to make the trumpet longer to lower the pitch. Play the C# and extend the third valve slide out until your tuner says it's in tune. The exact amount the slide should be extended depends on your horn. Use the middle or ring finger to extend the slide, whichever you normally have in the finger ring.

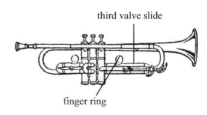

third valve slide

finger ring

Check the tuner as you push the slide out and be aware of how far out the slide is when the C# is in tune. That's how far you need to extend the slide *every time you play C#!* Don't neglect this. Get in the habit of doing it every time and you'll never have to stop to think about it.

You don't however, need to extend the slide for *any* 123 valve combination, for example the low, low F#. Use your ears to listen for your intonation.

Some horns have a slide stop on them. This can be handy because when you find exactly where your C# is in tune using the third valve slide, you can set the screws at that spot and when you kick the slide out it'll stop exactly where it should be.

D

The next worst out of tune note is the low D. It's also very out of tune, but not quite so much as the C#. Check it with the tuner. Which way is it out of tune? It should also be sharp.

You'll fix the D with the same technique used to fix the C#. Kick the third valve slide out until the D is in tune. Make a note of where that is and *every time* you play a low D, kick the slide out that much.

There you go. You can now play the worst notes on trumpet in tune every time. Make that slide kick a habit for these notes!

E   A

The next notes we'll deal with are the first line E and the second space A. Just as before, check these two notes with your tuner and try to lip them into tune. You'll see that these notes are also sharp, but only a little bit, so they won't need as much change as the previous notes did. However, these notes occur a little more often, so be vigilant, especially if they're held out for a long time.

You'll also use a trigger to fix the pitch for these notes, but this time use the first slide ring to extend the first valve slide. With your tuner, play the E and gradually extend the first valve slide until the note is in tune. Be aware of just how far you have to move (usually less than 1/4 inch). Do the same thing with the A. The distance will be about the same.

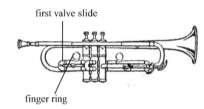
first valve slide

finger ring

If you don't have a first valve slide ring (or a U-shaped saddle), use the third valve alone to lower the pitch(∘∘•). The sound quality isn't as good with the third valve alone, so using your chops to lip the note down is a better option if you can do it. Lipping the pitch of a note is covered in this chapter under "Changing the Pitch Without a Slide" on page 122.

The Flat Notes

The flat notes on trumpet are flat because of the way the Universe works, believe it or not. The harmonic series is a series of pitches (called *partials*) with special relationships between them. We won't get into details here, but for a good book on the subject, check out *On the Sensations of Tone* by Herman Helmholtz. Anyway, a partial is one of the notes of the harmonic series. For example, the low C and the second line G are the second and third partials for the open valve combination on trumpet (the first partial is a pedal tone C). The fifth partial of the harmonic series occurs naturally a little lower than we like to hear it. So the notes we'll be fixing are the fifth partial of the harmonic series on trumpet.

E   Eb   E

That paragraph above may have been overkill for you. If so, my apologies. All you really need to know is that the D, Eb, and E at the top of the staff are slightly flat. By now you should know the drill. Be sure your horn is warmed up and generally in tune first, then check these notes with the tuner to see how flat they are.

To fix these notes we can't use the slides because the slides only allow us to lower pitches. We need to raise the pitch of these notes. There are a few things you can do. The first and best thing to do is to sing the note perfectly in tune. Find a piano or use your tuner to generate the correct pitch. Sing the note and internalize that sound. Can you hear the pitch in your head? Play and match the pitch.

Here are some techniques to use for raising the pitch slightly. First, use the shape of your oral cavity to raise the pitch. Use the "eee" shape inside your mouth. The raised tongue will help raise the pitch. Check with your tuner to see if that's enough. If not, try playing a bit softer. This helps focus the notes better. Raise your eyebrows. Strange as it may seem, this actually helps. Check with the tuner.

As a last resort you can use these alternate fingerings. Use these alternate fingerings as a last resort because the sound quality isn't nearly as good as the regular fingering. A benefit of using alternate fingerings is that you can use the triggers to change the pitch downwards if necessary. I know I sound like a skipping CD, but I'll say it again anyway. Use the tuner to check.

Changing the Pitch Without a Slide

You can change the pitch of a note on trumpet with your lips alone. You can probably do this without any instruction. Play a steady G into the tuner and then make the pitch go lower (also called *pitch bending*). Did it work? What did you do to make it work? How low can you make a note go before it drops down to the next note below? How slowly can you bend the note? Try a different note and make it go lower also. How low can you make that one go before it breaks to the note below? How slowly can you do it?

If you can't get the note to change at all, try lowering your jaw, loosening the muscles at the corners of your mouth, use a very deep "aaahh" to make the oral cavity as big as you can, and focus your air downward. Did that help?

Just like with lip slurs, changing the pitch upward is more challenging than lowering the pitch. Take the same G and try to make the needle of the tuner move to the right, or sharp. Could you do it? What did you do? You'll notice how much more difficult it is, I'm sure. To help get that pitch to rise, speed up the air, shape your oral cavity using the "eeee" syllable, tighten the muscles at the corner of your mouth and focus your air upward. It's like an upward lip slur, just before the lower note skips to the next higher note.

Bending the pitch up or down is a valuable skill to have because it allows you to fine-tune the trumpet. You can use this skill when you're playing with others and need to quickly get a note in tune. You can use it to bend the pitch of a note while playing an improvised solo. Someone adepts at pitch-bending can make the trumpet sound very beautiful, like a voice. Pitch bending is also helpful when you're tuning the trumpet without a tuner, and we'll cover this next. Practice pitch bending so you can bend the pitch of any note up or down.

Tuning Without a Tuner

When an orchestra tunes up, the oboe player usually plays an A and the orchestra tunes to that note. In a concert or symphonic band it is often the tuba player who sets the tuning note, usually a concert B♭, and the rest of the group tunes to that note. Tuning to another instrument is much different than tuning to a tuner; it takes more awareness of pitch. For these reasons it is both better and worse to tune in this way. It's better because tuning to another instrument will force you to listen very carefully. It's worse because it's a lot harder and the person you're tuning to may not be perfectly in tune.

Sound is vibration. To show this vibration visually, we use a wave shape. When you are out of tune, the sound waves interfere with each other. This produces a periodic repeating fluctuation in the intensity of the sound. That's a mouthful, so we'll just say "beats" in the sound from here on out. On the other hand, if you *are* in tune, the waves match perfectly and the sounds blend together. If the

Trumpet Tuning Tips

sound is made by two like instruments (say, two trumpets), the tones will blend so much that they'll sound like one instrument.

A representation of sound from two different instruments. When combined, the slightly out-of-tune notes produce the interference we hear as beats, shown with the thicker line.

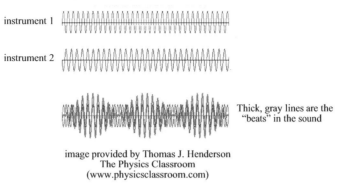

instrument 1

instrument 2

Thick, gray lines are the "beats" in the sound

image provided by Thomas J. Henderson
The Physics Classroom
(www.physicsclassroom.com)

A Sound Experiment

If you're not used to listening for it, the beats in out-of-tune sounds can be difficult to hear. In order for you to hear these beats, you'll need a partner, preferably one who plays the same instrument as you. If that's not possible, try for a partner whose instrument is in the same range as trumpet. Clarinet, Oboe, viola, or alto saxophone would be good choices. (If you're playing with a clarinet player, they'll also play a G. If playing with an oboe, viola, or bass clef instrument, they'll be playing an F to your G. Saxophones will be playing a D.) If partners aren't available at all, use a piano and play an F, the white key just to the left of the three black keys in the middle of the keyboard.

Use a tuner separately and make sure you're both exactly in tune. Once you're both in tune, play the same note together and you'll notice how well the sounds blend, especially if you're playing with another trumpet player.

trumpet's G

Now one of you (preferably you) will go out of tune. Push your tuning slide all the way in. Play the same note together again and this time you should be able to hear the beats in the sound. The beats are there, so listen hard for them. If you still can't hear them after a few tries, pull your slide out further than "in tune" and try again. If you still can't hear the beats, pull the slide out a little further. If you still can't hear the beats, keep trying. The beats *are* there and it takes careful listening to hear them. Keep trying and you'll hear them. It could be that your partner is unconsciously matching your pitch. If possible, have the partner look at a tuner and keep their pitch perfectly in tune while you play.

Fixing Poor Intonation By Ear

You're still with a partner and each of you will play the same note. Push your slide all the way in and listen for the beats. As you're playing, bend the pitch downward slowly. You'll hear the beats slow down and eventually disappear. This is because as you bend the pitch downward you gradually make the sound waves match frequencies and the beats disappear, also known as being "in tune." You may bend the pitch too far downward and in this case the beats will slow down and disappear, then start up again as you go beyond where the notes are in tune. Listen for this and try to do it. Take turns.

Go the other way this time. Pull your slide out past the spot where the horn is in tune. Both of you play again. This time you'll have to bend the pitch upward to get the pitch in tune. This is more difficult. Listen for the beats and make them disappear. Take turns.

In both of the above experiments you know exactly which way to bend the pitch to get the horn in tune. In real life you may not know. This is where pitch bending comes in handy. If you can't hear which way to go to get in tune, guess. Try bending the pitch down and listen for the beats. If the beats get slower and disappear, then lower is the way to go and you need to pull your tuning slide out. If the beats speed up as you lower the pitch, then that's *not* the way to go and you should push your slide in. Continue this process until an easily blown, relaxed note is in tune.

It's easiest to hear whether you're in tune when it's just you and another instrument. If you're in a band or orchestra with many people getting in tune at once, it's much more difficult to hear yourself. In this case you must focus intensely on the instrument playing the in-tune pitch. You must also focus intensely on your own sound and ignore all the others playing around you. This isn't a great way to tune. If you have the time, especially before a performance, warm up your horn and tune yourself individually with a tuner.

Difference Tones

This is a great experiment to do with another trumpet player. One of you plays a C in the third space, the other plays an F on the top line. Play the notes with a full tone at a loud volume. If you're in tune you'll hear another note ring in your ear. If you're *not* in tune, all you'll hear will be a buzzing noise. One of the players must lip his or her note up or down to find where the intonation is good. When you're in tune, you'll know it because you'll hear that extra note, called a ***difference tone***. To learn more about difference tones, go to http://hyperphysics.phy-astr.gsu.edu/hbase/sound/subton.html.

Up Next

Practice these intonation skills every chance you get because it takes time to master them, but playing in tune is a valuable things to learn as a musician. Once you learn this and can automatically play in tune, everyone who plays with you will appreciate your intonation.

Up next you'll learn a special technique on trumpet to play very low notes. In fact, these notes are so low that they aren't part of the trumpet range used in most music. These low notes are called pedal tones. Why learn such low notes if they aren't used? Good question. Pedal tones will help you in several ways. To find out, read on.

Trumpet Tuning Tips

CHAPTER 12

HOW LOW CAN YOU GO? PEDAL TONES

I don't care too much about music. What I like is sounds.

~ Dizzy Gillespie

In This Chapter

- What are Pedal Tones?
- Benefits of Pedal Tones
- Pedal Tone Exercises
- Double-Pedal Tones

Terms to Know

pedal tone: A pitch below the normal range of a brass instrument. Named after the foot pedals (very low notes) on the pipe organ.

leger lines: Small lines used below or above the staff for notes beyond the range of the staff.

Put the Pedal to the Metal

If you've ever seen an organist in action, you've seen their feet dance around underneath the keyboard. The organist's feet are working the bass pedals of the instrument. The organ pedals are arranged like the piano keyboard and are for the very low notes that rattle your teeth.

Pedal tones on trumpet are notes that go below the normal range of the trumpet, which is low F#, seen here. If you've messed around with your horn a lot you probably got some notes that were a lot lower than low F# and they probably sounded like maybe you shouldn't have had that second helping of baked beans. You played a pedal tone. If you haven't experimented with very low notes, grab your horn and give it a try right now.

low F#

Don't worry too much about pitch at the moment, just see how low you can get your horn to go. Use very loose lips and warm, slow air. Lower your jaw. Try different fingerings. If you have trouble, try using only your upper lip in the mouthpiece. Using just one lip is a fun, but to get the most benefit from pedal tones you've got to use both lips. Have your teacher or another trumpet player let you listen to some pedal tones if you're still having trouble.

What are Pedal Tones Good For?

Pedal tones are beneficial for several reasons. They allow your embouchure to relax and they help get blood flowing to the muscles used for playing. Pedal tones take a whole lot of air to produce and this will get you into the habit of taking good breaths and using your air and airflow with *all* your notes. Pedal tones are also good for ear-training because the pitch of pedal tones doesn't "lock in" like normal notes on trumpet; you have to use your ears to get the pitch just right.

Tone and range are also improved through the use of pedal tones, and they're an ideal warm-up technique. Pedal tones are part of my warm up every day for all of the above reasons. My chops don't feel right until I've played pedal tones for a good five minutes or more. Start practicing them now and you'll benefit from them right away. Coming up are some exercises and tips to help you out.

Pedal Tone Exercises

Because pedal tones are tricky to produce at first, we'll pair each pedal tone with its chord tones. Don't worry if you don't know what this means. Basically, chord tones will help you to hear the low pedal tone you're shooting for.

Some pedal tones are easier to produce with a different fingering than you may expect. The easiest fingerings are shown first. In the exercise below you'll work down to the first pedal tone by playing the notes leading down to that low F. This will get your chops used to playing low, will help your ears hear the pitch, and will give your eyes practice reading all those leger lines.

Do this exercise slowly. Take a HUGE breath and play (see "The Correct Breath" on page 54); keep your air flowing as you descend and hold the final low note until you run out of air. Then take a HUGE breath and to it again. If at first you have trouble finding the pedal tones, get as close as you can. Use a piano or keyboard to check the pitch if you have one. After a few weeks working at pedal tones, you should be able to get them fairly easily. Be persistent.

Example 12.1 Pedal tone exercise one. Easiest fingering is shown first with alternate fingerings below. Sound clip 12.1 at www.sol-ut.com.

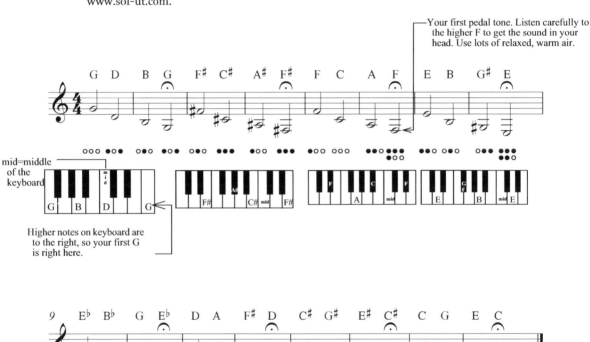

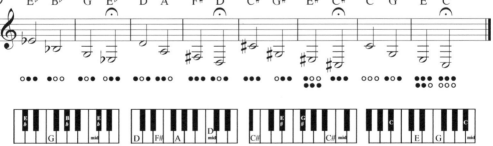

Pedal Tone Exercise #2

This second pedal tone exercise uses the major scale to help you get the pitch correct down low. You'll be performing double duty by practicing your scales while working on pedal tones. When you get into the pedal tone range you must listen carefully and make the trumpet produce the right pitch. If you've been practicing your buzz, especially buzzing tunes and pitch matching, this exercise shouldn't be too much trouble. Listen! Use the piano to check your pitch. Keep at it.

Example 12.2 Pedal tone exercise #2. Keep your air flowing all the way through these notes. Listen to the pitch. Pedal tone fingerings are marked. Sound clip 12.2 at www.sol-ut.com.

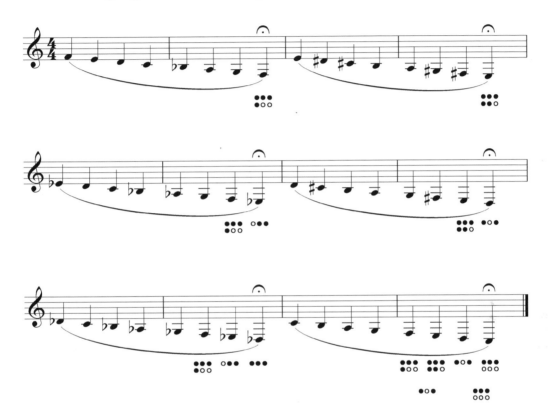

Lower Your Standard: Double Pedal Tones

I first discovered pedal tones in high school. In rural Alaska trumpet teachers are hard to find so I had to figure pedal tones out for myself. I didn't get them quite right until I got to college and was corrected. The pedal tones I had been playing were actually an octave *lower* than they should've been.

Pedal tones go lower than that pedal C you played above. In fact, these ultra-low pedal tones are often easier to play. It helps to play the note an octave or two higher to get the pitch in your ear before you do the pedal-pedal tone (also known as double-pedal tones). Use your ears and a piano keyboard.

It may be that the double-pedal tones are easier for you and if they are, go ahead and do them but keep working at playing the pedal tones you learned above. After a month or two of practicing on pedal tones a few minutes a day, you'll have no trouble with them.

Sources for Further Study

As with any technique, you should read up and explore as many different ways to perform the technique as possible. Here are a few method books that have many more exercises/etudes on pedal tones and low notes in general. Find them all on this book's "extras" page at www.sol-ut.com. Enjoy!

Title	Author
Low Etudes for Trumpet	Snedecor
Warm Ups Plus Studies	James Stamp
The Original Louis Maggio System for Brass	Carlton McBeth
Trumpet Pedal Register Unveiled	Dale Olson

Up Next

Now that you know how to extend your range downwards on trumpet, it's time to learn how to extend your range upwards. Up next you'll learn tips, tricks and several exercises to help strengthen and increase your high range, something most players are eager to do.

Chapter 13

Home on the High Range

The rung of a ladder was never meant to rest upon, but only to hold your foot long enough to enable you to put the other somewhat higher.

~ Thomas Henry Huxley

In This Chapter

- What is High Range?
- How to Increase Range
- Basic Range Exercises
- Range Method Books

Terms to Know

high C: A term used by trumpet players. C two leger lines above the treble clef staff.

double high C: Also used by trumpet players. The C that is 5 leger lines above the treble clef staff.

set: Specific position and flexion of an embouchure to produce a certain note. Playing high uses a different *set* than playing low.

What is the High Range?

For the purposes of this book, high range is whatever seems high to you. For a beginner this will usually be the notes above the second line G. For an average middle school player, high notes may be those above the fourth line D. For high school players, the high notes might be above the A, first leger line above the staff. For many more accomplished trumpet players, the high range could *start* at high C. For others, the high range is up an octave beyond that, or double-high C, believe it or not. Here are those notes as written.

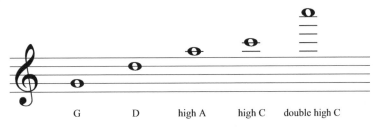

G   D   high A   high C   double high C

Don't worry about where your abilities fall in that range of ranges. Many trumpet players will never play a double high C and the majority of us won't *need* to play up that high. Probably more than 90% of trumpet music is below high C. The important thing is that no matter how high your range is, it can always be extended further. There is no ultimate high note on trumpet.

For great players with astounding high range, listen to Maynard Ferguson, Cat Anderson in Duke Ellington's band, Phil Driscoll, the Haydn trumpet concerto, the Brandenburg Concerto by Bach, Brian Lynch, and Doc Severinsen. These are just a few options.

The other important thing is not to compare your range to someone else's range. That can be someone with either more or less range than you. Concentrate on your *own* growth as a player and find a way to let someone else's ability inspire you. Let someone else's *lack* of ability inspire you to teach them.

Don't Get Hung Up on High Range

It's important to stress that although high range is a desirable thing for all trumpet players, it's not as important as good tone, musicality, flexibility, dexterity and a few other techniques. Often trumpet players have a mentality that higher, faster, and louder is better. This is not necessarily true. Better is simply better. What this means is that *all* aspects of trumpet playing should be paid attention to, and not just range. You can have a screaming range and still be a player not many folks will want to hear. Strive always for beauty.

Okay, I had to say that. Sometimes beauty involves the power and impact of playing high, but just sometimes. Don't get hung up on acquiring a screaming high range. Range is something that takes a lot of time to acquire, often years. It's kind of like doing an Iron Man Triathlon. It's not something you walk out your front door one day and decide to try immediately. You'll fail miserably, get all embarrassed, and probably cause yourself a lot of physical pain and possible injury, too.

One of the biggest obstacles to increasing your range is a lack of patience. It takes time to train the muscles and hone the reflexes needed to play up high. For example, from second line G to a high C takes most players four to nine years! Building range can be done but it will take time. Expect that and embrace it and all will be well.

If you add a whole step or two to your range each six months to a year, you're doing pretty well. As you first start to practice the following exercises and make them part of your routine, you may add several notes to your upper range immediately. As you settle into the routine the progress will be less dramatic, so don't be discouraged. Just keep practicing.

Beware of Lip Injury!

When playing in London, Louis Armstrong, at the end of his shows, would play 77 high C's in a row. One night he pushed himself a little too far and severely split his lip, drenching the front of his white shirt with blood. After that he had to take a long break to let the lip heal and it gave him some trouble for the rest of his life. Bobby Shew tells the story of seeing blood squirt out from his mouthpiece when he played high with a lot of pressure.

It's pretty easy to mess up your delicate lip tissue and give yourself an injury that will take time to heal even if it's not permanent. When practicing your high range, use as little pressure as you can get away with. It's better to sacrifice a note or two of range than to cram the mouthpiece into your face to get those last two notes. This is easier to say than it is to do. Use your judgement. Work with your teacher on your range.

High range is affected more by your air support than lip strength. More air support will help you avoid mouthpiece pressure. Start doing sit-ups or abdominal crunches two or three times a week. In fact, regular cardiovascular exercise of some sort will help your overall playing, including your high range. Better muscle tone will improve your endurance and stronger lungs will improve your tone, your coordination, your high range, and more. And if that weren't enough, a little regular exercise will give you a longer life which means more time to play great music.

Another excellent way to avoid injury is to rest as often as you play during each practice session. Resting gives your lip time to recover. In the short term, rest allows oxygenated blood to replenish the muscles in your chops. In the long term, rest allows your muscles to repair and rebuild themselves more strongly.

A Brief Word on Special Range Techniques

There are several horn manipulation methods out there for getting higher notes, like the pivot system and the mouthpiece twist. There is a lot of discussion as to whether some of these methods are beneficial or not. Some people swear by them, some swear at them. I won't cover these methods in this chapter but will list a few books at the end of the chapter which cover these and other related topics so you can do your own research and experimentation.

The best method for acquiring a higher range is to focus on breath, air pressure and volume (quantity, not loudness), airstream speed, and chop strength. This chapter contains a few basic exercises that train you in these skills, have worked for many people, and don't require special techniques or manipulations of lip or horn to get results. Let's get to them.

The Loose-Lip Flap

It's appropriate that we start not with an endurance exercise but with a resting technique. You'll use this trick when you've been playing hard and your lips begin to feel like mincemeat.

The loose-lip flap is a skill you may already be doing because it's natural, especially when your chops get that burning, tight feeling. This technique sounds kind of like a horse and looks pretty funny. For those reasons, if you do this when in front of an audience you may want to put your hand over your face and do it quietly. Or not. Your audience will get a laugh out of it.

To do the loose-lip flap, push your lips out slightly, keep them loose, and push air through them on your exhale. They should flap together and make a sound like an old biplane or Model T Ford, or a horse. Experiment with how far you need to push out your lips to get the flap started. Less is better, but at first you may need to push them way out to get the flap going. Experiment.

You want *all* the lip and surrounding muscle to flap in your breeze, including your cheeks. The flapping is what massages the muscle and gets much-needed blood to your tired face. The loose-lip flap will get the blood flowing to your chops which will clean out the lactic acid causing that burn you feel. When the burn goes away, continue with the exercise you're working through.

Can You Say "Oo-Ee?"

Make your chops do funny things and get odd looks from strangers. Go back and forth between the "ooo" and "eee" shape of your lips. To increase the chance that this technique will help your range, use a technique weight-lifters use. Keep the muscles very firm throughout the movement using *isometrics*. This pits each muscle against another and will increase the "burn."

The Lip Buzz

Here's your old friend again. The lip buzz is great because without the mouthpiece, you *must* use the muscles necessary to produce a sound. When you buzz, strive to make the corners of your aperture move in closer. The corners of

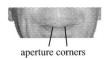

aperture corners

the aperture are not the corners of your lips but the edge of the buzz itself, where the lips stop vibrating.

Buzz whole notes at mm = 60. Rest four beats between each note. Go up by half steps until you can go no further, then turn around and come down by half steps. If you're using a piano to check your pitch (you should), don't forget to use the black keys and don't skip any notes.

Example 13.1 Strive for fat, warm, steady tone. Go back down after going as high as you can. Buzz this exercise both with and without the mouthpiece. When using the mouthpiece, avoid excess pressure.

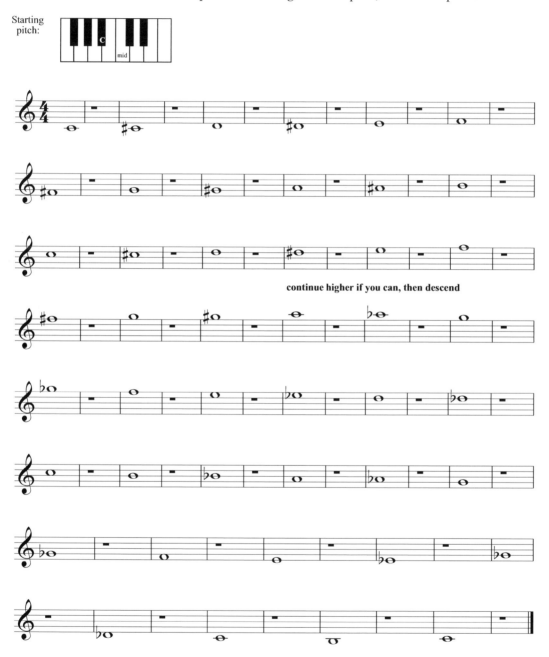

continue higher if you can, then descend

Home on the High Range

The Pencil Exercise

General Info

This exercise may seem silly, but give it a try for a few months and see if it helps you. You'll need a few pencils of different lengths at first so you can find one that is the right length for your current chop strength. This exercise works the muscles of your embouchure that are responsible for producing the buzz. Let's review them. Pay special attention to the M. buccinators at the corners of the embouchure. These are the ones you'll be working most with the pencil exercise.

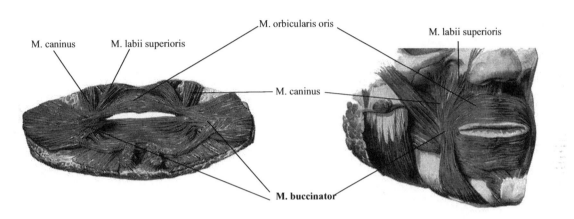

Just as with any weight lifting program, it's easy to over-do this exercise and cause damage. Take it easy at first and even when your muscles are built up, don't spend a whole lot of time with this exercise. Do it three times a week *at the most*. Use your judgement and monitor how this exercise affects your sound. You may find that for the first several weeks your chops may be stiff and unresponsive and you'll have a fuzzy sound. If you find this is the case for you, spend more time practicing on the horn instead of doing this exercise.

The Exercise

Before you give your chops a good workout you'll need to get a feel for what it is you'll be doing. Take your shortest pencil and put the eraser end between your lips, in front of your teeth. Be sure the pencil is centered. Clamp your lips on the eraser and lift the tip of the pencil until it is parallel to the floor, or pointed slightly upward. Do this by pushing your lower lip toward your upper lip. Be careful not to thrust your jaw forward, especially as you start to get tired. Use lip strength only. Keep your teeth slightly open and unclenched. Feel the muscles flex at the corner of your mouth.

Okay, did you get a feel for it? Now take a pencil of longer length and give that a try. Move towards an unsharpened pencil once your chops are strong enough to handle it. Don't expect to hold that pencil up for very long. Players who can play the scream book all night are said to hold the unsharpened pencil up for only 4 minutes! Hold the pencil until your muscles fail. Flap your lips and stretch them out to relieve the stiffness you feel, then do it again. Here's a step-by-step breakdown.

1 Do the loose-lip flap and stretch before starting
(to stretch, open your mouth as wide as you can).

2 Start with medium or short length pencil. Pens also will work and are often lighter than pencils.

3 Center the pencil between the lips, in front of the teeth.

4 Hold the pencil parallel to the ground or at a slight upward angle.

5 As you begin to tire, don't thrust your jaw forward.

6 Hold the pencil in position until your lip muscles fail and the pencil drops.

7 Do the loose-lip flap and stretch your lip muscles until any stiffness or soreness fades.

8 Repeat only once or twice.

9 Go practice on the horn.

Variation

You can make the above exercise a little more intense by raising and lowering the pencil until your lip muscles fail. Don't let the pencil either drop or raise beyond a 45 degree angle and make the movement slow and steady without thrusting your jaw forward. The slower the better (and harder) the exercise will be.

Further Study

If you're interested, there is a device that takes this pencil exercise a step or three further. It's called Chop-Sticks and is like a weight-lifting set for your lips. The Chop-Sticks come with a booklet containing suggestions and tips for use and a workout plan. For more information or to get yourself a set, go to this book's extras page at www.sol-ut.com

Lip Failure Study

The Concept

In the following exercise you'll continue to play a little beyond where your lip fails. Towards the end of this exercise your sound will be pretty horrible, but don't let that stop you. This isn't about getting a great tone (for that you should do long tones), but *is* about breaking down the muscles of your chops so they'll build up stronger.

This study is based on the work of the brass teacher Carmine Caruso. I've adapted it to be more accessible to beginning students. For more extensive range-building exercises, get the great book which covers these concepts and more: *Musical Calisthenics for Brass* by Carmine Caruso. Order it from your local music store.

The Foot Tap

You *must* tap your foot for this exercise. If your foot tap isn't automatic already, this exercise will be a good way to get it so. Remember, you're training your reflexes and that's all about timing. If you're a beginner, use your metronome to help you keep steady. If you're not a beginner it's still a good idea to use the metronome so your timing is perfect. Just because the metronome is going doesn't mean you're excused from the foot tap. Using the metronome is the best way to train your foot to tap in perfect time. How good do you want to be?

When you switch notes, strive for perfection. Slam down those valves precisely on the first foot tap of each note.

The Embouchure

During this exercise the embouchure will stay *set* the entire time. That is, your lips will be in contact with the mouthpiece the entire time and the chops will be flexed to play the entire time. *This includes rests!* There are several reasons for this, the most obvious being that keeping the muscles in tension continuously will tire them more quickly. In addition to this, if you keep your embouchure set you won't have to re-form it for each new note. For beginners this makes it easier to get a note started because there is no re-positioning involved.

To aid your chops as you get higher in the range, set the embouchure at the beginning of the exercise as though you were going to play the high note. With that embouchure set, relax into the first note. You may find it a little more difficult to get the lower notes out and the sound quality on the lower notes may suffer a little, but stay relaxed and don't be too concerned about sound quality. Setting your embouchure in this way will allow you to play higher more easily later in the exercise.

The Breath

Because your embouchure set is continuous throughout this exercise, you'll need to take a full, deep breath through your nose only during the rests. It's a good idea to give your nose a good blow before you start this exercise so you can benefit from the full breath.

Lower in the range you may find you need less air. If this is the case, use the rest to exhale any excess air. Learn to gauge how much air you use so your lungs are emptied in the 8 beats of playing. That way you can pull in a full, fresh breath during all 4 beats of rest.

The Airstream

The importance of the airstream can't be stressed enough. Without a full breath through the nose as described above, the airstream won't produce the results you need. Be sure to take a deep breath. That deep breath will help provide support. This support is not so you can blow more air through your horn, but to give you the pressure you need to make the airstream very fast. Playing high actually involves *less* air moving through the horn than lower notes, but the speed of the air is much greater.

Keep the air flow fast and steady. This is important. Keep the air flow fast and steady! Think of blowing *through* the note instead of blowing the note itself. A steady, fast airstream will be heard as an unwavering, vibrant sound. This will be more difficult as your lip tires, but keep the airflow continuous throughout the exercise.

Things to Remember

1 Slur between all notes. No tonguing.

2 Avoid excessive mouthpiece pressure!

3 Keep the embouchure firmly set during the rests. Keep the mouthpiece on the chops.

4 Don't worry about sound quality as you begin to get tired.

5 Don't force the notes. When you can't get any sound out, rest.

The Lip Failure Exercise

1 Play as high as you can until no sound comes out. Do the loose-lip flap for 20 seconds, pick up where you left off and continue until no sound comes out.

2 Do the loose-lip flap. Rest for 15 minutes. You can continue with other studies during the rest period.

3 Repeat.

Take a nose breath here during the rests. Keep the embouchure firmly set. Tap your foot!

continue as high as you can

Variations

When you get bored with the key of C, try this exercise with the other 11 major keys, too. Then the minor keys. Try a Byzantine scale when those get boring, or the Lydian augmented scale.

Also, instead of playing a Major 2nd between notes, try 3rds, 4ths, 5ths, etc. (if you don't know what this means, brush up on your music theory).

Pianissimo Playing for Range

Believe it or not, when you play very, very quietly (pianissimo), you're using the same techniques for notes high in the range. Playing quietly with a good sound requires a fast, narrow airstream. This means your air should to be under compression. Focusing a very tiny thread of that high pressure air requires strong chop muscles. These are the same skills used playing high, so a great way to improve your high range is to practice at a low or medium range as quietly as you can.

If you're not used to using these techniques for playing quietly, it takes some getting used to. If you usually drive a 1969 Volkswagon Bug and then get behind the wheel of a turbo-charged 5-liter

Mustang, you'll notice there is a lot of power to control. If you're not used to it, the power is difficult to direct at first. You'll tend to play too high, so you must work at focusing that power to keep the pitch where you want it. Keep at it.

You Are An Air Compressor

Learning how to compress your airstream is one of the most valuable things you can learn as a trumpet player. The funny thing is, most of us already know how to do it. Remember when you'd make your face turn beet red, amusing your friends and alarming your parents? If you don't know what I mean, just ask any middle-school-aged boy and he can probably show you what I'm talking about. To do it take a huge breath, close your mouth tightly and try to push all the air out of your lungs, but don't let any air out. The pressure will build instantly, veins will begin to stand out on your neck and forehead and you'll start to turn a lovely shade of red. Don't do it too long or you'll pass out.

To play very quietly, use this same type of pressure but only let a thin, ultra-fast stream of air pass between your chops. This will lessen the reddening and vein-popping effect a bit. Air under this high pressure is very fast and that fast airstream is crucial to playing either high or softly. In fact, without that type of fast air, a soft dynamic will be out of tune and sound weak. Experiment with how much air pressure you need.

Chop Strength for Pianissimo Dynamics

When your air is under compression, it wants to blast apart anything in its way, including your chops. Your chop muscles must be nice and strong to control the high-pressure air stream needed for quiet playing. These are the same muscles used for high range playing.

Just about any trumpet player can play loudly. It takes more skill and control to play quietly and playing quietly is a skill that can make your music much more dramatic, whether you're playing a soft passage in a classical solo, playing softly in a wind ensemble or jazz band, or using a soft dynamic for effect during an improvised solo. People often don't expect a trumpet to be quiet and when it is, folks are pleasantly surprised. It's simply an added bonus that while practicing ultra-quiet dynamics you're also working on your high range.

Cat Anderson was the high note specialist for Duke Ellington's band. To hear him in action, listen to Duke's band wail at the Newport Jazz Festival on the tune *Diminuendo and Crescendo in Blue*. Some screamin' trumpet at the end of that tune. Cat Anderson said the only thing he practiced to help his range was a 20-minute G. He'd play second line G for 20 minutes at a very soft dynamic. I'm sure he stopped for air, but 20 minutes is a long time to hang on one note. I've been trying it and have noticed an improvement in range. Give it a try yourself. If nothing else, the exercise will teach you patience.

Three Pianissimo Exercises

Below are three examples of pianissimo exercises to do. These exercises are in the key of C, but you should do them in all keys with all scales and using as many different patterns as your wonderful mind can create. If you're stuck and need pattern ideas, try Herbert Clarke's *Technical Studies*.

Pianissimo Exercise Reminders

1 Take a large breath.

2 Firm embouchure. Control the aperture. Make it small!

3 Use your chops to focus a thin stream of *fast* air.

Exercise 1: *do in all keys*

Exercise 2: do in all keys

Exercise 3: do in all major and minor keys, use augmented scales, blues scales, Byzantine scales, whole tone scales, etc.

Variations

Try combinations of slurring and tonguing to make these exercises more interesting and more challenging. Be creative with them! Strive always for beautiful, musical sounds!

The 2 Octave Scale Exercise

Imagine you're taking a long bike ride on a cool summer day. You're about to go downhill before climbing a bigger hill. What do you do? You pedal like mad to gain speed and make the ascent of the bigger hill easier, right? This exercise is a lot like that.

It's often easier to reach the higher notes in your range if you work up to them instead of trying to nail them with no preparation. The 2 Octave Scale Exercise will help you with this. Just as with the other exercises, this one does double duty by helping you practice your scales. Below you'll see the G Major scale used as an example. Use all scales to practice this technique (Major, minor, diminished, Dorian, Mixolydian, Byzantine, and any others).

DO THIS WHILE LOOKING IN A MIRROR! A full length mirror is best. This is a *very* important aspect of the exercise. If you monitor yourself in the mirror, you'll catch things you're doing which you may not be aware of otherwise, like problems with your embouchure, a pivot of the horn as you go higher, poor posture, or tension in your body. Tension is a vampire which sucks out your tone quality, endurance, intonation and range. Stay relaxed.

Each time you do this exercise, and you'll repeat it many times, go through the following checklist and be sure you're practicing with a mirror! Even a slight movement or pivot of the trumpet will negate the effect this exercise, and you don't want to waste your time. Have I mentioned you must use a mirror?

1 Stand or sit up straight and relax your entire body. Shrug your shoulders to help stay loose.

2 Form a good, balanced embouchure (say "mmmm") with firm corners and set for a medium-high note. As you play the exercise, check your lips outside the mouthpiece to be sure they are not bulging out even slightly. Embouchure should be firm all the way to the corners. Flat chin.

3 Play #1 below. Take a large breath. As you descend to the low G, don't pivot the trumpet or let your embouchure relax. The tone may be poor, but keep the embouchure firm. Use warm, slow air to improve tone, as though you're making steam come out of your mouth on a cold day, "hahhhhh."

4 Repeat several times and in the mirror, monitor your embouchure, horn and posture. Be critical. Don't continue until you can do #1 in a relaxed manner and with all the correct embouchure and posture traits. Don't rush things. Take your time until you've got it.

5 Shrug your shoulders again to relax and monitor your body and face for any tension. Relax further if you find any tension.

6 Take a *large* breath, set your embouchure for the G on top of the staff, then play #2. Monitor yourself in the mirror. As before, don't pivot the horn, keep the embouchure firm.

7 As you move higher, speed up the air (use *cooler* air than with low notes), focus the muscles of your embouchure towards the center as you go higher. Blow! (If you can't make it up to the G, turn around at your highest note.)

8 Repeat as many times as necessary until you can play #2 in a relaxed manner, with correct posture, embouchure and relaxation.

9 As you gain mastery over this scale and the range, go one half step higher (A♭) and repeat the process. For more work on G, try the other scales starting on G: minor, blues, dorian, mixolydian, byzantine, bebop scales, etc. For a special challenge, use the chromatic scale.

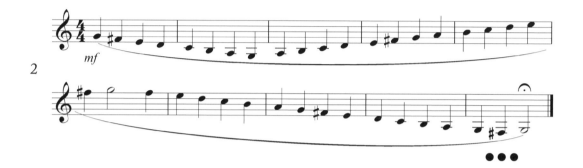

Trumpet is one of the most physically demanding instruments you can play. Take the time to be positive you're doing everything correctly. When all is correct, you'll have a powerful sensation of your sound beamed like a high-pressure stream of water shooting out from you and through the horn into the corners of the room. It's a powerful sensation. Strive always for beauty of tone and expression, not just the high aspect of pitch. Stick with it!

Scheduling Your Range Workout

Although I mentioned it a few times before, it's important enough to be repeated again; you don't want to do these exercises every day. Your muscles need time to recover and rebuild themselves. If you have no performances in the near future, take a one-day-on, two-day-off approach. This will give you three lip workouts each week and still allow enough time to let your muscles heal and rebuild.

If you have a performance coming up, lay off any range exercise at least a week before the gig. This will ensure that your chops are at their strongest when the time comes to show your stuff.

A Final Word on High Range

Placido Domingo, the famous vocal tenor said, "The high note is not he only thing." Don't be too caught up in acquiring a high range. Work at it steadily and you *will* progress. Investigate all information, both from the books above, other sources, and from real life players. Good luck!

The exercises in this chapter are very basic and limited and are meant to give a beginner or intermediate player some simple information to get started. If you're looking for something more advanced, check out *Sound the Trumpet's* companion book: *Sound The Trumpet: Exercises to Blow Through Your Horn*, available Spring 2006, or any number of books listed below which deal with range.

Resources for Further Study

Below are a few books to experiment with. Some may work for you, some may not. Be sure to discuss them with your trumpet teacher and be cautious with your chops; you don't want to damage them. Find all of these at www.sol-ut.com on this book's "extras" page.

Title	Author (Publisher)
A New Approach to Altissimo Trumpet Playing	John Lynch (C. L. Barnhouse)
Chops Builder (other books, too)	Clint McLaughlin (www.bbtrumpet.com)
Embouchure Enhancement (book 1&2)	Roddy
Exploring the Trumpet's Upper Register	Kendor (www.kendormusic.com)
Learn How to Play Double High C in Ten Minutes	Walt Johnson (www.great-music.net/waltdhc.html)
Pedal Tone Approach to High Notes	Louis Maggio
Sail the 7 C's: An Easier Way to Play Trumpet	Clyde Hunt (B Music Production)
Take the Lead	Dominic Spera (Houston Pub.)
The Alexander Method (150 min. video)	Jane Kosminsky (Wellspring Media)
The Balanced Embouchure	Jeff Smiley (www.trumpetteacher.net)
The Cat Anderson Trumpet Method	Alfred Publishing (www.alfred.com)
The Truth About How to Play Double High C On Trumpet	Knevitt (Ultra-Trumpet Ministries)

Up Next

All this talk of range. Range is great, but it's possible to be able to play a double high C and yet not be able to play a full gig without losing your face. That's where endurance comes in. Endurance is a crucial element in your trumpet playing if you want to perform. Learn about what you can do to increase your endurance in the next chapter.

CHAPTER 14
ENDURANCE

Beyond talent lie all the usual words: discipline, luck—but most of all, endurance.

~ James Baldwin

In This Chapter

- What is Endurance?
- Why Endurance is Important
- How to Gain Endurance
- Resting and Endurance
- Endurance Exercises

Terms to Know

perseverance: The ability to keep at something.
set: The specific set of the embouchure for a particular note.
degree: Tones in a scale. The first note of a scale is known as the first *degree* of the scale, the second as the second *degree*, etc.

How to Endure

Endurance is one of the keys to being a good trumpet player. Endurance means being able to play through an entire concert or gig and still have chops strong enough to play what needs playing on that last piece of music.

The two most important things you need in your quest for greater endurance are simply patience and perseverance. It takes time to build up the muscle strength you'll need to play a long gig, and the only way to get that endurance is by working on endurance one or two practice sessions per week.

There is nothing particularly special about endurance that you need to know, but it's *essential* that your fundamentals are securely in place. If you have problems with embouchure or breathing, your endurance will suffer. Even if you're struggling with a fingering or don't have a tune entirely down, your endurance will suffer because you won't be relaxed. An important part of endurance is efficiency and it's tough to be efficient when you're tense. If you're having trouble with endurance, check with a good teacher to be sure your fundamental skills are under control.

I'll assume your skills are all in place and working properly. Now all you need to know is how to build up endurance and how to conserve your chop strength so you have staying power. Like any other skill, both of these are done through specific exercises. We'll get to them soon.

Why Resting and Endurance Are Best Friends

With the following exercises, you're breaking down muscle so you can build up muscle. In order to build up strength, muscles need time to rest and recuperate. Resting is equally as important as playing. It's easy to over-do endurance, range exercises, or playing in general. If you've experienced overplaying, you know that for a few days afterwards your chops are stiff and unresponsive. To avoid this unpleasant experience, be sure to rest early and often.

A trumpet student asked Wynton Marsalis what he does when he gets tired. He said, "I stop playing." Hey, if it works for Wynton, you should do it too. Resting helps.

When doing the exercises below, you'll start to feel a "burn" at the corners of your mouth. This is lactic acid building up in your muscles and means you're pushing your endurance. Let the burn continue briefly, then rest and do the loose-lip flap.

Endurance Exercise Schedule

Resting is also important on a larger scale. ***Don't do these exercises every day!*** You'll need at least a couple days of rest to let your muscles rebuild. Doing an endurance practice sessions two or three times a week is plenty, and any more than that probably won't help you much and may hinder progress and possibly damage your chops.

Also, if you've got a gig or concert coming up, lay off the endurance practice at *least* a week before the show to ensure you'll be at your optimum chop-strength for the performance. Maurice André advocates short periods of practice throughout the day to build strength and avoid injury.

The concept of resting is something we all understand but often ignore, usually because we believe *more is better* and because we want to get better and stronger as quickly as possible. Remember earlier I spoke about patience? You need it, because building endurance takes time. So let's not waste any more of it and get right to the exercises.

Memorize

If you're tense or are concentrating on reading music, you won't be able to monitor your breathing very well. If your music is memorized, you will free up concentration that can be used to monitor relaxation and breathing. This doesn't mean you have to do without the music. By all means, have the music in front of you as you perform. But if that music is memorized, your confidence will be greatly increased. Increased confidence means more relaxation and more ability to focus on breathing.

Start the memorization process by memorizing the following exercises. They're simple and you should be able to memorize them in just a few sessions. If the exercise is memorized, as you get tired you can monitor breathing, body relaxation, and mouthpiece pressure.

Long Tones

Remember these? Are you noticing that a lot of exercises build more than one skill? Long tones are no exception. Long tones should be your best friend if you're a beginner, and an old friend if you've got some experience under you belt. You'll see a similarity between these long tones and those you did with your first notes.

When you practice the following long tones you'll breathe through your nose, just like with the range-building exercises in the last chapter. Keep your corners firm and embouchure set all the way through the breath. This will cause your muscles to get a continuous workout and tire more quickly. When you start to feel the burn, finish whatever note you're playing, take the horn off your face, do a loose-lip flap until the burn subsides, then continue. Limit your time on this exercise to 10-15 minutes or less, depending on your current level of endurance.

Because this book is geared toward the beginning and intermediate player, the examples below begin low in the range. You can (and should) start these long tones higher in the range, especially if you have little fatigue playing the lower version of the exercise. Enjoy!

Endurance Exercise 1

Example 14.1 Long tones. No tempo. Hold each note for one full breath and hold each rest until you're completely tanked up on air. Keep your corners set during the nose inhale. Rest with a loose-lip flap when the burn gets intense. Begin where you left off and go till you feel the burn again. For variety, do this with all scales in all patterns.

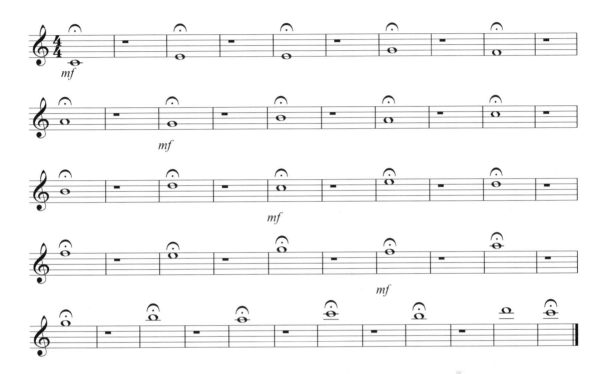

Double Duty

Did you notice the pattern in the last exercise? Because we all have limited time, it's a great idea to combine exercises to get the most benefit in the smallest amount of time. That's the reason these endurance exercises follow the patterns they do. Endurance Exercise 1 used an interval pattern of thirds (if you don't know why it's called a third, brush up on your music theory). The following endurance exercise uses the C major scale and the pattern is 1, 5, 2, 3 (these are the *degrees* of the scale and in the key of C would be C, G, D, E). Minor scales use the pattern 1, 5, 4, 3.

When practicing your endurance exercises, change the key in which you play to gain the benefit of working through a key signature while you strengthen your endurance. Always try to combine exercises in this way and your improvement will be that much quicker!

Endurance Exercise 2

The previous exercise had no strict tempo. This one does. Set your metronome to about 90 (slower if you want a better workout), and be very strict with yourself about obeying the tempo precisely. Be sure to slam down your valves at this slow tempo to insure clean note changes. Keep your corners firm throughout this exercise, *especially* in the rests when you'll breathe through your nose.

In this exercise, when you start to feel the burn, continue for another measure before stopping to do the loose lip flap. Once the burn goes away, continue and repeat this process.

Example 14.2 Endurance Exercise 2 (MM = 90 or slower). Keep corners firm. Breathe through your nose in the rests when needed. When you start to feel the burn, continue an extra measure before the loose-lip flap, then continue.

Endurance Exercise 3

This endurance exercise involves a crescendo and a decrescendo. Start as softly as you can and crescendo to the point just before your tone starts to spread and get ugly. Hold that volume for two beats then diminuendo back to your original soft volume. When you can't make a sound any more, rest by doing the loose-lip flap for 20 seconds, then continue until you can't get a sound again, do the loose-lip flap for 45 seconds to a minute, and stop. Also be sure to do the variations listed after the exercise. Memorize this as soon as possible. You'll pay better attention to everything (posture, breathing, count, etc.) if you're not reading music. Music is about sounds, not notes on a page.

Example 14.3 Endurance exercise #3. Set your metronome for 60 bpm or slower (slower is better). Be sure to hold your loudest volume for two beats before starting the decrescendo.

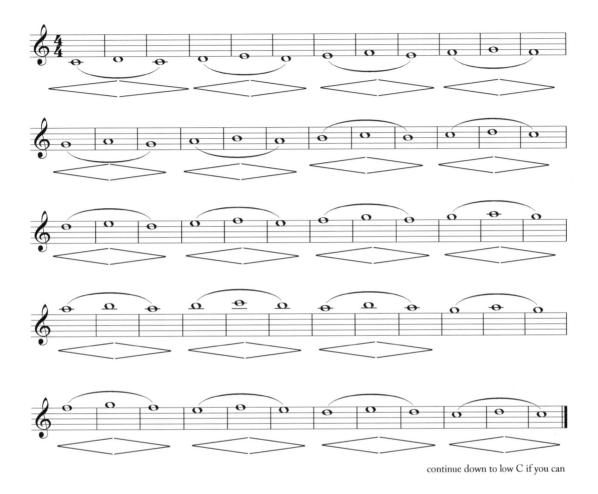

continue down to low C if you can

Exercise 3 Variations

Here are some variations to work through with the above endurance exercise. Practice to your weaknesses! The more double duty you can get in with your exercises the better!

* Use intervals other than the Major 2nd shown above (minor 2nd or half step, Major and minor 3rd, Perfect and augmented 4th, Perfect and diminished 5th, Major and minor 6th, Major and minor 7th). If you don't understand these intervals, study some music theory. Go to www.sol-ut.com for a free theory book.

* Use other scales (11 other Majors, harmonic minor, melodic minor, modes, exotic scales, etc.)

* Change the dynamic markings from ⬤ to ⬤

* Go as high as you can, then go back down until you get to low C.

* Make up your own variations.

Ways to Save Your Chops

Techniques used to save your chops from getting tired go hand in hand with the above exercises used to strengthen your chops. Endurance is not simply an issue of how strong your chops are, but also how you use that strength. Endurance is more an exercise in being efficient than it is a test of strength. There are a few tricks that will help save your chops so you can make it through a four hour gig or that concert of Sousa marches.

The Breath

Remember the student who asked Wynton Marsalis a question at the beginning of this chapter? Well, after Wynton said that he stopped playing when he got tired, the student asked what he did if stopping wasn't an option. Wynton said, "I concentrate on breathing more deeply."

Because it's covered in much more detail elsewhere in the book, I'll just mention the breath here. Without good breath support, you'll tire yourself out MUCH more quickly. You should always be aware of your breath and strive to use that air to make your music. This will help save your chops more than anything else you do. As you get more and more tired, focus on your breathing! For more info about breathing, See "The Correct Breath" on page 54.

Take It Off Your Face

A simple way to save your chops is to remove the mouthpiece from your chops whenever possible, even for as short a time as an eighth rest! This technique is advocated by David Baldwin, trumpet professor at University of Minnesota. He also has other tips to help you with endurance in his book *The Seven Secrets of Endurance*.

The Set of the Embouchure

The *set* of the embouchure means the way your chops are positioned for a particular note. For example, higher in the range the embouchure has a different set than for notes low in the range. Using the set for a low note while trying to play high will negatively effect your range and endurance. If you're prepared for this problem, you can extend your endurance significantly.

Imagine you're about to play a phrase that has a range wider than a fourth (if you don't know what this is, better bone up on your music theory). Before playing the phrase, you should note where the highest pitches are and set your embouchure for those high pitches. This may make the lower pitches sound a little less full, but the benefit is that you won't have to produce the high pitches with the embouchure set of the low notes, which is more tiring. Here's an exercise to help you with the idea.

This exercise uses both the Major and minor pentatonic scale. The Major pentatonic scale uses the Major scale degrees 1, 2, 3, 5, and 6. The minor pentatonic scale uses the natural minor scale degrees 1, 3, 4, 5, 7. Instead of memorizing both major and minor, just memorize the Major pentatonics. If you play the Major pentatonic starting on the 6th degree (6, 1, 2, 3, 5), you'll have played the minor pentatonic. For all of the pentatonic scales, see "Pentatonic Scales" in the Codicil at the back of the book.

Example 14.4 Embouchure Set Exercise. Always look ahead so you know how high you have to set your embouchure.

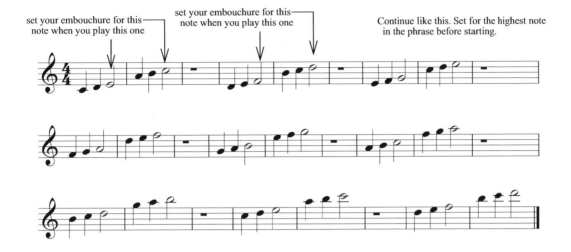

Embouchure Set Exercise Variations

As before, there are many variations to this exercise.

- The above is based on the C Major pentatonic scale. Use all other scales.
- Add dynamics (crescendo, decrescendo) in various combinations.
- Invent another pattern instead of 1, 2, 3, 5, 6 for Major and 1, 3, 4, 5, 7 for minor.

Sources for Further Study

These are just three simple endurance exercises. Of course, you can (and should!) use all 12 major scales, minor scales and other exotic scales with these exercises. There are many other endurance exercises out there, and you can easily make up your own to keep things interesting. Here are a couple books to help you in your quest. Find them on this book's "extras" page at www.sol-ut.com.

Book/Article Title	Author (Publisher)
Musical Calisthenics for Brass	Carmine Caruso (Hal Leonard)
The Seven Secrets of Endurance	David Baldwin (International Trumpet Guild Journal, December 1996)

A Final Word About Endurance

I can't stress enough how important it is that you rest when you practice. Your muscles need time to recover and rebuild themselves. It's also important that you rest for three or more days after doing an endurance session. This does *not* mean don't practice at all, just don't do another endurance session for three or more days. Your lips (and your audience) will thank you.

As with range, it takes time to develop your endurance. If you're conscientious about doing endurance exercises, you'll notice some improvement in just three or four weeks. Keep at it and in six months you'll have much more staying power and will be able to play at your peak for much longer. Keep it up!

Up Next

So, you've been doing all this playing on your horn, maybe for several months, and from day one strange and slimy things have been living and growing inside your horn. No, it's not science fiction, it's biology. Warm, wet areas are prime locations for growing cultures of.... well, slime. In fact, take a moment right now to pull out your tuning slide and mouthpiece and peer down the lead pipe. Yum! It's time to learn how to clean your trumpet. The next chapter will get you through the process and help avoid damage to your horn.

INTERLUDE:
CLEAN UP YOUR AXE

Cleaning anything involves making something else dirty,
but anything can get dirty without something else getting clean.

~ Laurence J. Peter (1919-1988)

In This Chapter

- Why Clean?
- Routine Cleaning
- How to Take Apart the Trumpet
- How to Fully Clean the Trumpet
- How to Put Your Horn Back Together

Terms to Know

axe: Slang for your instrument. Originally meant a guitar but now means any instrument.
mouthpiece brush: A brush used to clean inside the mouthpiece.
slide grease: Lubricant for the slides on the trumpet.
snake: A device used to swab out the inside of the trumpet.
valve casing brush: A brush used to clean inside the valve casings.
valve oil: Oil used on the valves to keep them moving smoothly.
lacquer: A clear sealant that keeps your horn shiny by preventing oxidation of the brass.

Why Clean My Trumpet?

My high school biology teacher gave us an assignment: we had to run a Q-Tip over some surface, then rub that Q-Tip over mucilage in a Petri dish. If any bacterium is present, it will grow quickly on the mucilage. I swabbed inside the lead pipe of my trumpet. My classmates swabbed bathroom floors, gym lockers and other nasty places.

At the time, I cleaned my trumpet maybe once every three or four months and a good buildup of greenish slime was inside my horn. My Petri dish had more prolific bacterial growth than any of the others. A *lot* more. After that, I began washing my horn more regularly.

But cleanliness isn't the only (or the best) reason to keep your horn clean. Your trumpet sound is produced by air flow and the more buildup of slime you have in your horn the less well that air is able to flow. Also, that gunk will get into your valve casing and cause your valves to stick. Cleaning your horn will make it easier to play, and you'll probably sound better.

Another reason to clean is that the slime in your horn actually eats away at the metal and in time will eat a hole right through it. Keeping your horn clean will make it last much longer before repairs are necessary.

There are two types of cleaning you'll do to your horn, the routine cleaning and a monthly overhaul which cleans the entire horn. Don't be like Bix Biederbecke, one of the early jazz cornet players. He *never* cleaned his horn because he thought a clean horn sounded "hard." I can only imagine what was growing in his horn. If slime had ears, that slime in Bix's horn would've heard some great music!

Routine Cleaning

If you clean certain parts of your horn every few days, you'll have less of a job when the monthly cleaning session rolls around. Here's what to do: before putting your horn away, empty the spit valves. If you have Amato water keys (the push-button type), take the tuning slide all the way off and shake it out until it's dry. What you're emptying isn't really spit, but condensation from your breath. The more damp a place is, the more likely something will grow there.

Polishing

The oil on some people's hands is corrosive enough to eat through the lacquer and even the metal of the trumpet. Others' hands have oil which is less caustic, but it still can wear through brass over time. It's a good idea to wipe your trumpet down after you play it. Music stores sell polishing cloths made specifically for instruments, but don't get an abrasive polishing cloth or use a brass polish! It will peel off your *lacquer*. Lacquer is the clear sealant that keeps your horn shiny by preventing oxidation of the brass.

I've always kept a soft cloth in my horn case to wipe away finger prints and oils from my horn. Any cloth will do, but a soft cloth is best so that you won't scratch your horn's lacquer.

The Mouthpiece

The mouthpiece is an easy part of the trumpet to clean and is also one of the parts that needs cleaning the most. It's easy. Simply swab it out with your mouthpiece brush while holding it under running water. Presto, you're done. If you're in a hurry or don't have water handy, you can use just the brush.

mouthpiece
brush

Oiling The Valves

A Word Of Warning: valves are the most delicate part of a trumpet and are machined to be extremely precise. Even *very* slight scratches, bends or dents may ruin your valves. When handling them be very careful.

During an honor festival concert in high school my valves began to stick badly. Like the amateur I was, I had no valve oil with me. I used spit instead. It worked, but not very well. Valves need occasional oiling to keep them from sticking. Be sure to always have your valve oil handy, *especially* during a performance. Valves usually need oil only once every few days, depending on how much you practice.

There are several ways to oil the valves, and the very *worst* way is to squirt oil through the holes in the caps at the bottom of the valve casings. The holes in the valve caps are there not so you can put oil in them, but so dirt will fall *out* of them. Dirt collects in the caps and if you oil your valves through the holes you may be putting that dirt back into the valve casing. This is bad and will cause your valves to stick even more. Also, the oil has little chance to lubricate the valves and drips back out the hole, marking your pants with "trumpet tracks."

The best and quickest way to oil your valves is to take off the correct slide and drop one or two drops in each hole. Push the valve up and down a few times to distribute the oil and you're done. One of the reasons this is the best and quickest is that the valve is protected and you don't have to worry about reseating the valve properly after taking it out.

Interlude Example 1: The best way to oil your valves is through the slides.

If your valves are really dry, they may be very securely stuck. If you run into this problem you should play more! To fix valves with this problem, pull the slide that goes with each valve and put several drops in each hole. Try the valve again. If that doesn't work, you may want to pull the valve and oil it. See "Trouble-Shooting" on page 154.

When you put the valve back in, line up the number on the valve so it faces the mouthpiece (see picture on page -156). Before screwing the cap back on, twist the valve slightly until it clicks into place and won't move. This is important because if you *don't* do this, when you go to blow you'll probably give yourself a hernia. If the valve isn't aligned correctly no air will go through the horn. If this happens, twist the valve until it seats properly and try again. If you give yourself another hernia you might have the wrong valve in the wrong slot. To find out how to fix this see "Replacing The Valves" on page 156.

The Slides

Slides will rarely give you troubles between your monthly cleaning. The only time these slides will need attention is if they're sticking or are difficult to move or take off.

If one of your slides is a problem, place a little grease all the way around the farthest end of the inner part of the slide, the unlacquered part. Work just one side of the slide in and out of the horn until it's well-greased. Wipe up any extra grease and then do the same with the other side of the slide. Wipe up again and put the whole slide back on the horn. You might need to wipe up extra grease one last time. Shown below are only two of your slides. If the other two are stuck, grease them the same way.

Interlude Example 2: Place a small amount of slide grease at the base of the slide to avoid a gooey mess.

 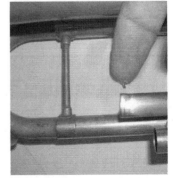

The third valve slide performs a vital function and needs to move quickly and smoothly. It's a good idea to add a drop of valve oil to each arm of the slide so the slide glides easily. Pull the slide almost all the way out, apply the drop, and work the slide in and out until the action is quick and smooth. If necessary, use another drop of valve oil. If you've forgotten why the third valve slide needs to move so quickly, See "Tuning The Whole Trumpet" on page 118.

Trouble-Shooting

Sometimes, especially if the horn hasn't been taken care of, slides, valve caps and even valves will become stuck. The thing to always keep in mind when working on your trumpet is that brass is a soft metal and will bend or dent easily, so be *very* careful. Don't use force. Your wisest option is to visit your local instrument repair person.

Slides

To loosen stubborn slides take a towel or piece of cloth and wrap it through the slide. Give a gentle pull and gradually increase the pressure until the slide comes out. If necessary, give some sharp tugs to loosen the slide. Hold the trumpet firmly *only* around the valve casing as you do this. If you hold the horn anywhere else, you'll probably bend it.

Valve Caps

If your valve caps are stuck, try running warm water over them. If you use pliers of some sort (this is generally a *VERY BAD* idea), wrap the horn with cloth so you don't damage it. Also, **do not** squeeze very tightly or you'll warp the valve casings and ruin your horn. If you're nervous about doing any of these things (and you *should* be), take your horn to a professional repairman.

Valves

If your valves are stuck, don't yank, bang, thump, thwack or otherwise abuse your valves. You will very likely ruin your trumpet. The best way to loosen stuck valves is to squirt some valve oil into them through the slides. Don't unscrew the top of the valve and put valve oil there. You'll cause a mess and the oil won't get where it needs to go. If this doesn't work, let the valves soak in the tub while they're in the horn (see below for instructions), then take them out and clean them after soaking.

The Monthly Overhaul

This is a process that will take about an hour, but by the time you've done it once or twice you'll be able to do it more quickly. On the following page are the things you'll need:

- a sink
- a bathtub, or something that will hold enough water to allow you to submerge your trumpet.
- dish soap
- an old towel and wash cloth, some rags
- snake
- mouthpiece brush
- valve casing brush
- valve oil
- slide grease

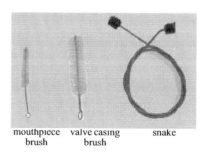

mouthpiece   valve casing   snake
brush   brush

1. Spread the towel in the bottom of the tub. The towel will protect both the tub from getting scratched and your trumpet (especially the valves) from sloshing around and getting damaged. Fill the tub with soap and water to a level that will cover your trumpet. *DO NOT USE HOT WATER!!!* This will strip the lacquer from your trumpet! The temperature of the water should be neither hot nor cold to the touch.

2. As the tub fills, place your trumpet on the counter next to the sink and pull the tuning slide. Clean it with the soap and wash cloth. Run water through the slide as you clean the inside with the snake. When you're done, place the tuning slide in the tub.

3. Repeat step #2 with all the slides. As the tub fills, check the tub water level frequently!

4. Pull the first valve. Clean the holes in the valves with the valve casing brush. Be careful not to scratch the valve with the metal tip of the brush. Place the valve in the tub with the slides. Repeat with the other two valves.

5. Clean the valve casings with the valve casing brush. Don't scratch them!

6. Run the snake through the lead pipe of the trumpet, and all other pipes. Rinse with running water. Be sure to get the tubes between the valves, too. Lots of gunk is hiding there. Also run the snake backwards through the horn from the bell end into the first valve casing.

7. Run the valve casing brush through each of the valve casings again. Rinse with running water.

8. Place the valveless, slideless trumpet into the soapy water.

9. Let the trumpet soak for 15 to 20 minutes. This will free up any crustiness there might be in the horn.

10. Drain the tub and run the snake through the slides and trumpet again as you rinse it with clean, cool water.

11. Dry off your horn and place all the parts on a counter. Be careful with the valves.

> To remove hard green crusty stuff from the inside of your horn, use vinegar. This also works for clogged water keys.

All Together Now

There are a few tips to follow when putting your horn back together to help keep things clean and in the right place. The first of these is that it's important your horn is completely dry. It's best to let it dry overnight. Water on or in the horn will interfere with the slide grease and valve oil. The lubricants won't bond to the metal as well if the metal is wet. If you're in a hurry, a hair dryer works real well, but watch out! The brass gets hot.

Grease with Ease

Greasing your slides is the messiest part of the job. Follow these tips and you'll keep the goop to a minimum. Have a rag handy because no matter how careful you are there will be some leftover grease you'll need to wipe up.

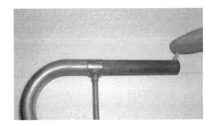

Place just a little grease all the way around the farthest end of the unlacquered part of the slide. Work just one side of the slide in and out of the horn until it's well-greased. Wipe up any extra grease and then do the same with the

---

other side of the slide. Wipe up again and put the whole thing back on the horn. A final grease wipe-up may be needed. Repeat with each slide.

Replacing The Valves

The only tricky part about putting the valves back in your horn is getting the valve in the correct place. A very funny thing to watch is a trumpet player who tries to blow through a horn which has the valves in the wrong slot. Absolutely *no* air goes through the horn, the player's face turns bright red and they make a sound like pphhhhhht! when the air shoots out past the sides of their chops.

Screw on the caps that go on the bottom of the valve casings. Don't tighten them too much or they'll be tough to get off.

Put the valve halfway in the correct slot with the valve number facing the mouthpiece. This is important because you want to minimize any twisting of the valve in its case. Turning the valve around in the valve casing can result in horizontal scratches which will stop oil from coating the entire valve and may also cause the valve to stick.

Dribble valve oil on the lower half of the valve, six to eight drops, then slide the valve the rest of the way in and give it a little twist to be sure it's locked into place. Screw down the cap, then do the same thing with the other two valves.

oil goes here   *not* here

On most trumpets each valve is stamped with its number. Valves are numbered from the mouthpiece toward the bell, so the valve closest to the mouthpiece is number one, and the valve closest to the bell is valve number three. Valve two is always easy to find because it's in the middle. In addition to helping you put the right valve in the right slot, the number will also help you position the valve correctly in its slot.

The number *usually* faces the mouthpiece. If you put your valve in as mentioned and can't blow any air through the horn, twist the valve until it locks into place. Once the valve is locked into place, pull it out again and memorize where the number faces so you won't have to twist the valve next time you clean or remove your valves.

That's it! Below is a list of things mentioned in the chapter you'll need to keep your horn clean and happy.

Cleaning Supplies

Nearly all music stores sell cleaning kits which have everything you need for your instrument, including snakes, mouthpiece and valve casing brushes, greases and oils. Below are some more specific guides about the best supplies to have.

- soft cloth: the only thing to remember here is that you don't want an abrasive polishing cloth. You're just trying to wipe away the oils from your hands. If a cloth is abrasive, it'll wear away the lacquer on your horn. Music stores have what you're looking for.
- valve oil: the best oils are those that are clear and don't smell at all. It's pretty nasty to put the horn up to your mouth and get a big whiff of oily fumes. It's probably not good to breathe such fumes either. Good brands are *Al Cass Fast*, or *Ultra-Pure Professional Valve Oil* made at 352 Mt. Union Ave.; Philomath, OR 97370 (www.ultrapureoils.com).

- slide grease: lanolin works well, as does pretty much any commercially available grease sold at your local music store. In a pinch Vaseline and a little valve oil works, too.
- brushes: mouthpiece brush and valve casing brush.
- snake: a snake with plastic over the metal will protect your horn from scratches a little, but any snake will serve your purposes well. Don't get a trombone snake as the brushes will be a little too big for trumpet.

Up Next

That's it for Part II. There were a *lot* of techniques and information in this Part and it's a great idea to do a review from time to time to check in and see if you're doing everything you can to be a great player. I hope all that information is sticking in your head.

Part III coming up also has a lot of information. You'll learn about special sounds on the trumpet, mutes, how to transpose, trumpet method books and songs, gear to help you play smarter, performance tips, a chapter with brief biographies of great trumpet players past and present, and even a chapter on the didgeridoo, an ancient Australian type of trumpet that is fun and pretty easy to play.

The first chapter in Part III is a fun one in which you'll learn about many special effects used on trumpet including vibrato, trills, alternate fingerings, shakes, mordents, scoops, falls, doits, the growl, flutter tongue, and the ever-popular horse whinny. Good stuff!

But first, a few jokes on the next page.

Clean Trumpet Jokes

We are at our best when we can laugh at ourselves. There are thousands of jokes out there. Here are some of the funnier ones I've come across that aren't too mean....

- How many trumpet players does it take to change a light bulb?
    Five. One to change the bulb and four to contemplate how Louis Armstrong would have done it.

- Do you play the *Trumpet Voluntary*?
    No, my parents made me do it.

- What would a trumpet player do if she won a million dollars?
    Continue to play gigs until the money ran out.

- How are trumpeters like pirates?
    They are both murder on the high Cs.

- What's the difference between a trumpet player and a large pizza?
    A large pizza can feed a family of four.

- How many trumpet players does it take to change a light bulb?
    One, but he'll do it too loudly.

- How many trumpet players does it take to change a light bulb?
    12: One to screw it in and 11 to stand around and say, "I could do that better."

- Did you hear about the French horn player who locked his keys in the car?
    It took an hour to get the trumpet player out.

- How many trumpet players does it take to change a light bulb?
    One. He holds the light bulb and the entire world revolves around him.

- How many 2nd trumpet players does it take to change a light bulb?
    None. They don't go up that high.

- How do you get a trumpet player to play *fff*?
    Mark *mp* on the part.

- There are two trumpet players sitting in a car. Who is driving?
    The policeman.

- Discord: Not to be confused with *datcord*.
- Crescendo: A reminder to the performer that he has been playing too loudly.
- Accidentals: Wrong notes.
- Allegro: Leg fertilizer.
- Conductor: A musician who is adept at following many people at the same time.

Part III
Tricks and Treats

What You'll Learn In This Part

- Trumpet Sound Effects
- Trumpet Repertoire
- Transposing for Trumpet
- Mutes
- Sound Equipment
- Performing
- Trumpet All-Stars

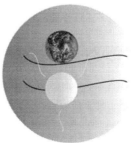

SolUt Press

Musician-friendly Resources.
www.Sol-Ut.com

Chapter 15
TRUMPET SOUND EFFECTS

One doesn't discover new lands without consenting to lose sight of the shore for a very long time.

~ Andre Gide (1869-1951)

In This Chapter

- Vibrato
- Alternate Fingerings
- Scoops, Doits and Falls
- Half-valve Technique
- Flutter Tongue
- The Growl
- Trills
- Shakes
- Other Ornaments

Terms to Know

glissando: A smooth and continuous change from one note to another. Done on trumpet with the half-valve technique.

slide: Another name for *glissando*. Also a name for part of the trombone.

trill: Changing quickly from one note to another note, usually above the primary note.

scoop: A short glissando into a note from below.

doit: A short rising glissando after a note.

ornament: Melodic embellishment. Ornaments may be written in or improvised by the performer. Ornaments covered in this chapter are vibrato, trills, turns, and shakes.

Make Your Trumpet Talk

This chapter is all about sounds on the trumpet that aren't what you might expect. Most of them aren't something you'd use in a symphony, wind ensemble, or marching band, but you can use them in jazz, especially in a small jazz combo or an improvised solo. The major exception to this general rule is the vibrato and the horse whinny at the end of the Christmas song *Sleigh Ride*.

Embellishing melodies is something that musicians have probably always done. In the Baroque period, musicians were expected to add their own flourishes to melodies. The modern practice of making these "novelty" sounds originated with jazz in New Orleans. Joe "King" Oliver, the mentor of Louis Armstrong, was one of the most famous early jazz trumpet players known for making these sounds through his horn. King Oliver would often play with a handkerchief over his valves to hide what he was doing so others couldn't copy him easily.

These sounds are fun to make and folks seem to like them as long as they're not overdone. Some techniques, like the vibrato, are absolutely essential to learn no matter what style you play. A good rule with these effects is "a little goes a long way." These tricks are no substitute for good technique and if you use ornaments in a solo, think of them as spice. Too much pepper in a dish ruins the taste.

The Vibrato

Vibrato is a type of ***ornament***, something added to music to make it more beautiful. Vibrato is an ornament that is so important it gets a section all its own. Vibrato is used in all genres of music with almost all instruments. Tasteful vibrato can make a sound much more beautiful.

Vibrato is a slight raising and lowering of the pitch of a sustained note and can happen quickly or slowly. If you've seen a violinist play, did you notice how her left hand moved back and forth during a long note? This is vibrato. When we play a long sustained tone we vary the pitch by a tiny amount up and down to give the note more shape and beauty. An added bonus is that a good vibrato can hide any slight intonation problems.

Vibrato has two aspects: amplitude, which refers to how wide the vibrato is (think of an opera singer for an example of a wide vibrato), and frequency, which refers to how fast the vibrato is (think of a classical violinist for an example of a fast vibrato).

There are three ways to perform vibrato on trumpet: with your airstream, with your jaw, and with your hand. It's much easier to do the vibrato with your hand, so we'll cover that one first. After we cover all three techniques for vibrato I'll tell you in more detail exactly how vibrato is used and give you exercises to get you working on your own vibrato.

The Hand Vibrato

Most of us have greater control over our hand than we do over the muscles that control breathing and that's the reason the hand vibrato is easier to perform. This is the vibrato technique that many players use because it's the easiest and you can achieve almost immediate results. Harry James and Rafael Méndez used this type of vibrato.

Play a second-line G and sustain it for one full breath. While the note sounds, use your right hand and *very gently* rock the trumpet forward and back about once a second. This will increase and decrease the pressure against the lips which will give you a nice oscillation of the pitch. The pitch will rise when you increase pressure to your lips and fall when the pressure is released.

This should be a subtle effect, so don't use too much pressure. The motion of your hand is so slight that it's hard to see. Vary the speed at which you move the trumpet back and forth against your chops. In a little bit you'll learn exactly how fast or slow to do your vibrato. For now, simply experiment with different speeds from slow to fast.

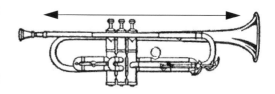

The Jaw Vibrato

Jaw vibrato is done with, you guessed it, the jaw. Hold the G as before and make a slight chewing motion with your front teeth, but don't bring your teeth all the way together. You should hear a wavering of the pitch. Many players advocate the jaw vibrato because it doesn't involve putting added pressure on the embouchure. The jaw vibrato is perhaps the most common used vibrato technique in the United States.

The Airstream Vibrato

The airstream vibrato is the type that a singer or a good flute player uses as well as some trumpet players. In one way this is a better type of vibrato for us trumpet players because it doesn't involve adding pressure to the lips, something we should always be conscious of. Although it's a little harder than the hand vibrato, it's still not a very difficult technique. Try it and see which one you like better, or which one sounds better.

To get a vibrato with your air, play the second-line G  and as you sustain the note, give your air a little push faster about once a second. Use the muscles of your diaphragm and stomach to give the air these pulses. Did it work for you? Keep trying until you can vary the speed of the vibrato from slow to fast.

Vibrato Exercises

There are many different styles of vibrato. A trumpet player in a mariachi band will use a much wider and faster vibrato than a symphony trumpet player (as long as the symphony player isn't playing a mariachi number), so the style of vibrato may vary depending on the type of music you're playing. As with any trumpet technique, your best course of action is to listen to accomplished players and imitate what you hear. Your best teachers are in your recorded music collection.

That being said, there are some basic traits to vibrato you should know. Generally speaking, a long tone will start out with a straight tone (no vibrato) and the vibrato will be added after a beat or so, and the waves of the vibrato will gradually speed up as the end of the note is reached. It's much better to hear this than to have it explained. Go listen to your recordings and see if you can pick out the vibrato. It's there, I guarantee it.

To gain control over your vibrato, you'll be methodical about it by doing the following exercises. The notes you see are connected with a tie. Usually this means the notes are connected without any audible break between the notes. In this case however, you'll use a pulse of air, pull the horn gently against your chops, or move your jaw with the rhythm is shown.

Example 15.1 Vibrato exercise #1. Only the G is shown here. Practice vibrato with all fingerings in all registers.

p = pull horn *gently* towards chops, raise jaw, or push air with abdomen

r = relax (no pressure), or jaw down, or no pushing of air

For each exercise, choose a different note on each repeat. Repeat several times.

Vibrato in the Real World

The above exercises are strictly rhythmic and very even (at least they *should* be). When you actually start using vibrato to shape a note, the speed of the vibrato usually changes over the course of the note. Though there may be variations in certain styles like the mariachi, for the most part the vibrato will start slowly and speed up smoothly and gradually. This is one of the reasons you should practice vibrato at all speeds in the above exercises.

For a really long note the vibrato may start slowly, speed up and then slow down again. Use of vibrato is a matter of personal taste. It's a good idea to listen to your favorite players and hear how they use vibrato. Experiment for yourself to discover what pleases your ears, then do it!

Below are a couple exercises to help you get the feel of speeding up and slowing down your vibrato. Although the exercises will be in a strict tempo, when you use the vibrato on a long note in a performance, you don't need to be so strict with the rhythms. In fact, if you *are* strict with the rhythm of your vibrato, it may sound a little corny. Use your judgement and your ears.

Example 15.2 Vibrato exercise number 2. Be sure to choose a tempo fast enough to allow you to get through the exercise in one breath. Do this exercise on all notes in your range.

Ceasura or Grand Pause: a break in the rhythm. Use the space to take a good breath before the whole note.

Hold this note out for one full breath and use the vibrato skills you've been practicing. (straight tone, gradual increase of vibrato speed, then slowly back to straight tone.

Example 15.3 Vibrato speed-change exercise number 3. Do this exercise on all notes in your range.

Hold this note out for one full breath and use the vibrato skills you've been practicing.

Alternate Fingerings

One of the easiest trumpet tricks is to use an alternate fingering. Alternate fingerings are fingerings other than the most common one. For example, the E in the fourth space is one of the most expressive notes on trumpet because it has more valve combinations than any other note. The usual fingering is open. That E can also be played with 3rd valve, 1st and 2nd valve, and all three valves. A list of alternate fingerings is below and you can find more in the fingering chart at the back of the book.

Alternate fingerings are used to do a one-note trill or for doing some intricate rhythms on the same note. A good use of this can be heard in the second chorus of Lee Morgan's solo during the tune *The Sidewinder* on the album *The Best of Lee Morgan* by Blue Note Records. In fact, Lee Morgan used this device a lot. Also hear Nat Adderly use it on his tune Work Song on the album *The Best of Cannonball Adderly, the Capitol Years.* Check it out.

Alternate fingerings can also be used to make a passage easier to finger or to tune "problem" notes.

A good way to practice alternate fingerings is to do them in strict rhythmic patterns as well as the "flail away" type of trill. Below you'll see the note, its fingerings and a sample rhythm to practice with each set of fingerings. You'll find some fingerings are more difficult than others, and some are nearly impossible at a fast tempo. Practice all variations for those notes with more than one alternate fingering.

At first, don't use your tongue at all on this exercise. Just work the valves and get the patterns as precise and rhythmic as you can. When you've got the pattern down, try using your tongue on some of the notes. For example, tongue the first note of every measure for the whole exercise. Then tongue every beat. Then every other beat. Then try tonguing randomly. Invent variations.

Fingerings are shown as valve number: 0, 1, 2, 12, 23, etc. Below the rhythm for this exercise are the notes with their alternate fingering. If the sixteenth note triplets in the rhythm below look intimidating to you (the second-to-the-last measure), just put six notes evenly in one beat and you'll be correct. For a variation, play the exercise backwards. Enjoy!

Example 15.4 Use the same rhythm for each of the notes below. Don't use your tongue. Slam your valves down. Start slowly and use a metronome. Listen to example 15.4 at www.sol-ut.com.

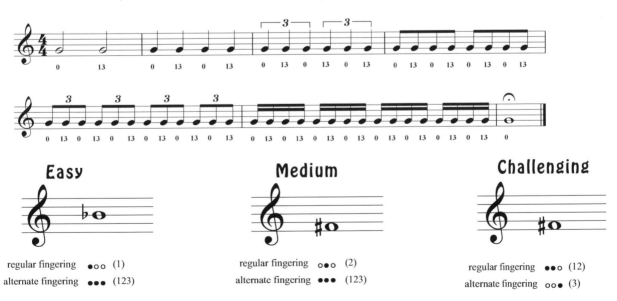

Example 15.5 Alternate fingerings cont'd. Start slowly. Pound down those valves in perfect time! Use a metronome. As you go higher in the range, notes have more and more possible valve combinations. Discover on your own the possibilities for notes above the high B♭.

Easy

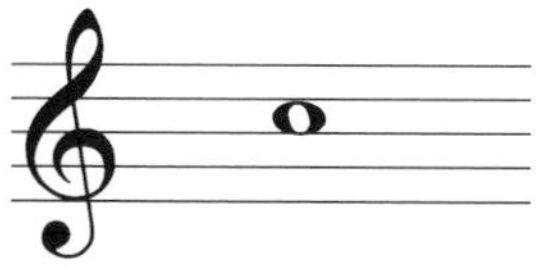

regular fingering ooo (0)
alternate fingering oo● (23)

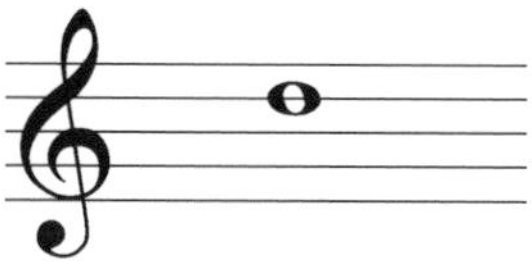

regular fingering ●oo (1)
alternate fingering ●o● (13)

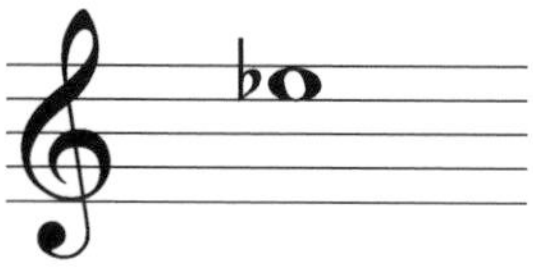

regular fingering o●o (2)
alternate fingering o●● (23)

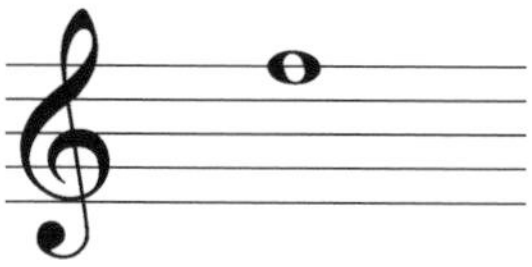

regular fingering ●oo (1)
alternate fingering ●o● (13)

Medium

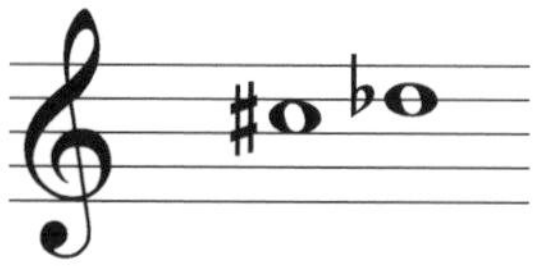

regular fingering ●●o (12)
alternate fingerings ●●● (123)
oo● (3)

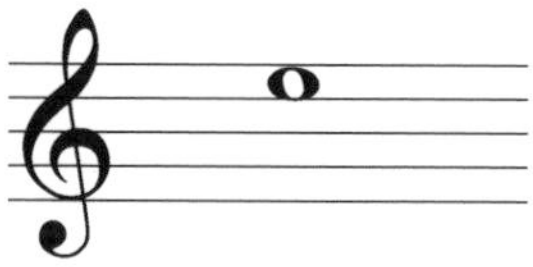

regular fingering ooo (0)
alternate fingerings oo● (3)
●●o (12)
●●● (123)

regular fingering o●o (2)
alternate fingerings o●● (23)
●●● (123)

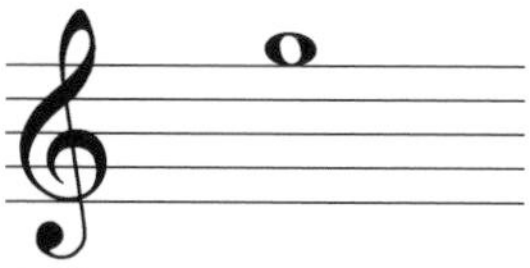

regular fingering ooo (0)
alternate fingerings ●o● (13)
oo● (3)

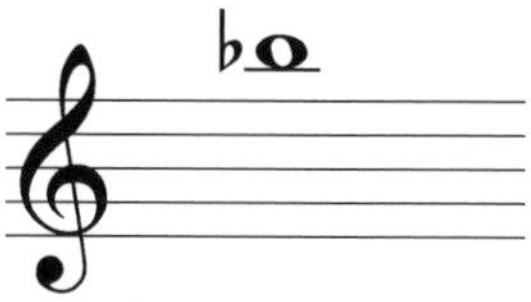

regular fingering ●oo (1)
alternate fingerings ooo (0)
●●● (123)

Challenging

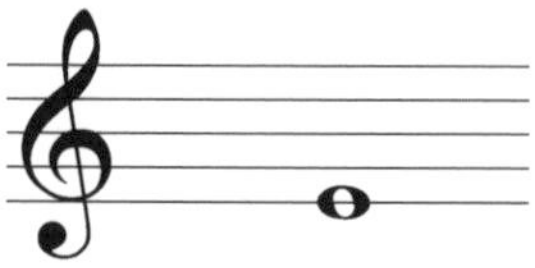

regular fingering ●●o (12)
alternate fingering oo● (3)

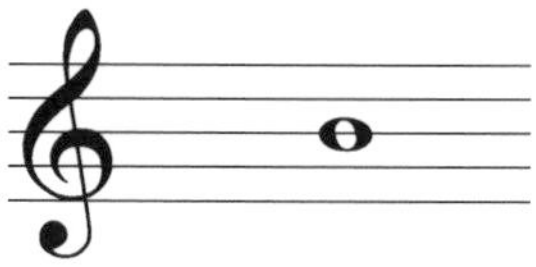

regular fingering o●o (2)
alternate fingering ●o● (13)

regular fingering o●● (23)
alternate fingerings ●oo (1)
●●● (123)

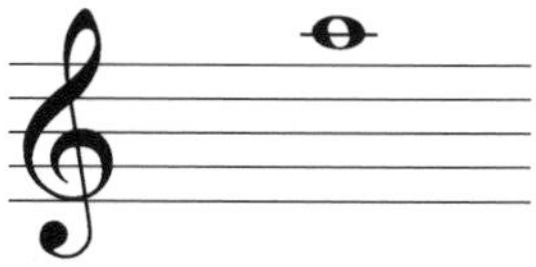

regular fingering ●●o (12)
alternate fingerings oo● (3)
o●o (2)

Trumpet Sound Effects

Scoops, Doits, Falls, and the Horse Whinny

All of those strange words in the title of this section use the same technique, the *half-valve*. Just like the name implies, to do it you push the valve or valves down halfway and play. It's that simple. Try it.

One of the best ways to get your trumpet talking is to use the half-valve technique. You've probably already done this accidentally when not pounding your valves down or maybe when a valve is stuck or slow coming up. Done accidentally it's not a good thing because most of the time you want note changes to be clean, but the half-valve technique is a great thing to do now and then on purpose. It's a neat sound.

One of the terms you'll see used in this section is *glissando*. That means a long smooth slide from one note to another, either upwards or downwards. In fact, slide is another name for glissando. Think of a trombone playing a low note with the slide (different use of the word) fully extended. With a continuous sound, the slide is pulled in. The sound rises smoothly upwards. A downward slide on trombone sounds like a dive-bombing plane. Two other instruments that can easily produce a smooth glissando are voice and violin. On trumpet, a glissando is done with the half-valve.

trombone slide

The half-valve technique bypasses the horn's ability to "lock in" to the pitches of the overtone series. This allows you to make a smooth glissando from a low note to a high note or vice versa. You can do a glissando with just one valve halfway down, two valves halfway down, or all three.

With all of these half-valve techniques, you've got to use a *lot* of air to make the sound stand out. Half-valve notes are much quieter than a regularly fingered note, so to make them heard you really have to blow!

Try the following. Start at a low pitch with all three valves halfway down. Make the sound go steadily upwards as far as you can, then come back down. Keep your air moving. Try it with only the first valve halfway down, then only the second valve halfway down, 1st and 2nd, 2nd and 3rd, 1st and 3rd, etc. This is the basis of all the specific techniques we'll get to next.

Just like with any special technique, a little goes a long way. Be wary of over-using this or any special technique because overuse makes the effect less dramatic.

The Scoop

Try this. Play an F (1st valve) and go to a G (open) but let your first valve come up *very* slowly. Blow steadily through the change. Did you hear that wonderful smear from the F to the G? Try it again and emphasize the smear by blowing a little harder when the valve is between notes. You can help the smear by bending the pitch with your chops as you make the change.

When you use this half-valve trick just before a note, it's called a *scoop*. Scoops are a great way to ease into a pitch and are an effective device to use while playing a melody or improvising a solo. You can do a scoop with one valve halfway down before a note, two valves halfway down, or all three halfway down. As you approach where the note falls in the rhythm, gradually let your valves come up. A scoop doesn't change the rhythm of the note at all, so you've got to start the scoop a little bit early (half of a beat or less). Starting before the note in this way doesn't alter the rhythmic placement of the scooped note. Here's what a scoop looks like written down.

Example 15.6 In this example, the note to be scooped is on beat 4, so the scoop starts just *before* beat 4. This way once you do get to beat 4, the note is there, just as it should be. To hear example 15.5, go to www.sol-ut.com.

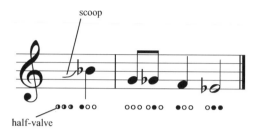

The Doit

This is an onomonapoetic word. That means it's a word that represents a sound, like *meow*. It's pronounced *doyt* and is one syllable. A doit is also an upwards glissando, but happens after a note. Usually there is a rest after the note to give the doit some breathing space.

A doit continues upward in pitch after the note is played and can be a quick little upward sound or can last several beats as a long glissando. It's up to the performer or group leader how long the doit should be. Doits are often seen after high notes. It adds a dramatic effect when the high note is taken higher still with the doit. Here's what a doit looks like.

Example 15.7 A doit from low and high B♭. To hear this example, go to www.sol-ut.com.

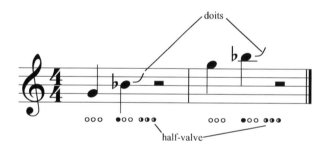

The Rip

This is also an upwards type of glissando but is more rough-sounding and does *not* use the half valve technique. Rips are a little tougher to perform because they take more air and more lip strength. A rip

can be performed with any valve combination including open, but is easiest when done using all three valves down. During the rip press all three valves down and blow through all the partials until you get to the target note where you quickly revert to the correct fingering for the target note.

The Fall

A fall is the opposite of the scoop and doit. A fall occurs after a note and is a downward glissando. As with the doit, there is usually a rest after the fall and the length of the glissando is up to the performer or leader. For obvious reasons, the fall usually happens after notes higher in the trumpet range.

There are two types of fall, the smooth one with the half-valve, and a louder, rougher one. For the smooth fall, use the half-valve technique and *really blow* through the fall to make it heard. For the rougher fall you have a few options. One is to simply leave the valves as they are and fall off the note, also blowing hard all the way down through your range. This is difficult to do if you're not used to it. For the other option, when you fall off the note, quickly finger all three valves randomly and blow really hard. This will make the fall a little smoother than the first option and still be plenty loud. A third option is to push all three valves down as you fall off the note and again, really blow. This is like a rip in reverse. Experiment with these falls to hear the difference.

The length of the fall is decided by the performer or leader. Here's what the fall looks like written down.

Example 15.8 A fall from G. Try all three types of fall techniques described above.

The Horse Whinny

One of the fun and funnier uses of the half valve technique is to do a horse whinny. It appears near the end of the Christmas song *Sleigh Ride*. Push all three valves halfway down. You must blow hard to make the sound loud enough to be heard.

Start on a relatively low note, around second line G. Do a quick scoop up to a high G and fall off the note as soon as you start it while shaking the horn back and forth against your chops all the way down to a low pitch, around low C. Don't shake the horn too hard or you'll damage your lips. Use your ears to hear if you've got the sound right. If it sounds like a horse, you're all set. If not, try again 'til you get it.

Check out the Chapter 15 sound clip on www.sol-ut.com.

The Growl and Flutter-Tonguing

When playing the blues, or playing with a plunger (not the one in the bathroom), growling through your horn is a great effect, especially if you're playing some "dirty" blues number. This technique is also used in some modern pieces to create a brash, in-your-face kind of sound.

The growl and flutter tongue are used sparingly and usually only for one or *maybe* two notes in a musical phrase. Use your judgement. Listen to other trumpet players and remember this is just a general guideline. I heard a live concert by Wynton and Branford Marsalis on NPR the other night and Wynton took at least a full chorus using a growl the entire time. It was a startling and masterful use of this technique. Another master of the growl and plunger combination is Cootie Williams, trumpeter for Duke Ellington. His version of Caravan is about the coolest thing I've heard!

Though you can interchange the growl and the flutter tongue, they have a slightly different sound. Try them both and see which you prefer. Learn them both and you'll be able to choose the right sound for the right tune. You can't learn enough technique.

The Growl

The growl is the easier of these two sound effects. To do it you simply growl back in your throat as you play. Before trying it on the horn, do it without the horn. The sound you're listening for should be a rough, rumbly sound, like you're clearing your throat.

When doing a growl, we naturally use the *aahh* shape inside the mouth. This may make it a tough to play a note higher in your range. While you're making the sound, practice changing the shape of the inside of your mouth with the *aahh* and *eee* vowel shapes (for more info about this, see "Lip Slurs: Going Up!" on page 104). If you're having trouble with holding a note, try to make your oral cavity (the inside of your mouth) smaller.

Start on a second-line G or lower to try this effect, then gradually use higher and higher notes. Get yourself a plunger and use that with the growl as well. For more info on how to use a plunger, see "The Plunger" on page 178.

The Flutter Tongue

This is one case where a loose tongue is a good thing. It takes a loose tongue and steady air flow to master this technique. The tip of your tongue will hit the edge of your soft palate (that flat place just behind your teeth) very rapidly when you do the flutter tongue. Placement of the tongue is crucial; too far back and it won't work; too close to the teeth and it won't work. Looseness of the tongue is also critical. If it's not relaxed, the tongue won't move rapidly. Air flow is important to keep the tongue moving rapidly. Move that air!

If you can't get your tongue to flutter immediately, try this: with a steady air flow, touch your tongue to the middle of the roof of your mouth and gradually move it forward in your mouth toward your teeth. Think of saying "brrrrrrrr," as if you were cold, then gradually move the tongue forward. Keep the tongue as loose and relaxed as you can. You should find the sweet spot where the tongue flutters easiest. If that doesn't work, try making a purring sound like a happy cat. If you can't get it, don't be discouraged, just keep trying until you can do it.

Ornaments Aren't Just for Christmas

For a long, long time musicians have taken a given melody and added things to it to make the melody more personal, more intricate, or more interesting. *Ornaments* is the collective name of those melodic embellishments. There are a bunch of them, including trills, turns, grace notes, mordents, and lip trills (also known as shakes).

When these ornaments are written in the music you don't need to worry about when to use them. But, depending on the musical setting, all of these ornaments can be used at any time. If you're sitting third chair in a symphony orchestra, you should probably stick to what's written and not improvise your own ornamentation of the melody (if you even have the melody).

However, if you're playing lead in a jazz band, a small jazz combo, or are performing a solo, you can insert ornaments wherever you think they sound good. As with anything extra, use good taste. Listen to other trumpet players and musicians on other instruments to hear what professionals do.

Trills

 Trills are a fairly common ornament in classical music, especially baroque music, and are an interesting effect. A trill is a rapid change from one note to the next higher note in the key signature and you can see how trills are written to the left. You may see the squiggly line or just the "*tr*" in a piece of music. They mean the same thing.

The trill on the *A* shown above would be played by moving rapidly between the *A* and the next higher note, the *B*. Sometimes the trill is *started* on the higher note.

Trills often begin slowly, speed up to as fast as you can do the trill, then slow down again before ending on the principal tone of the trill (the written note). Here's an example of where you might find a trill in a piece of  music. Two good source for listening to trills are the second movement of the Hummel trumpet concerto and the melody of *Ceora* a tune by Lee Morgan.

Mordents

A mordent is a rapid *single* alternation between the written note and its upper neighbor (upper mordent) or its lower neighbor (lower mordent). Here's an example of each. Sound clips for all of these techniques can be found at www.sol-ut.com.

Turns

Another common ornament is the *turn*, which "turns" around the principal note. Turns are indicated with this symbol: ∾. Turns are performed by playing the principal note (the one written), rising up to the upper neighbor tone (the note just above the principal), back to the principal, down to the lower neighbor tone (the note just below the principal) and then back to the principal note again. It's probably more difficult to read that than it is to look at the musical notation, so here you go.

this turn, when written out, looks like this:

Turns are a very effective ornament when used sparingly and in the right places. The final movement of the Hummel trumpet concerto has enough turns to satisfy anyone. Give it a listen and then go practice turns. Turns aren't limited to classical music and you'll hear all the Masters use this device in their treatment of a melody. Incorporate the turn into your musical tool kit.

Grace Notes

Grace notes are also known as *acciaccatura* and are easy to do. A grace note is a quick note before the principal note. Grace notes are usually performed right on the beat designated for the note, unlike the scoops above which started before the note. Grace notes are shown in written music by writing a very small note just

grace notes/acciaccatura

before the principal note. Grace notes are usually only a half or whole step away from the principal note.

In a jazz setting, this type of ornament is done spontaneously.

It's probably safe to say that grace notes are more common than every other ornament except vibrato. They're a neat little effect. Practice some right now.

Appoggiatura

The appoggiatura is similar to the grace note, but longer. The term is based on the Italian word *appoggiarae* which means "to lean." The appoggiatura is more significant melodically because it's length is half of the note which follows it.

The appoggiatura looks very similar to the grace note, but if you look closely, that teeny little note does not have a slash like the grace note does. Here's a written example.

appoggiatura

Trumpet Sound Effects

The Shake or Lip Trill

This type of ornament is simply a lip slur on steroids. The shake has been used in jazz for quite a while and can be an exciting addition when used in the right place. As with all of these other ornaments, too much use ruins the dramatic effect. Use all ornaments sparingly. Listen to your favorite players to get an idea of when to use the shake. Louis Armstrong is a master of many things, the shake included. Go listen to him.

The shake happens in the upper register of trumpet, usually above the staff. The partials are closer together in the high range and this makes shakes easiest to perform from 4th line D on up into the range. A shake is often not notated in the music, but is up to the performer to insert where and when it's appropriate. Listen to Jazzology play *Mambo Influenciado* to hear a shake used in a melody. You can download the short excerpt for free from www.sol-ut.com.

The way to practice the shake is to first practice lip slurs lower in the range. Start on F# on the first space (use the 123 valve combination) and work up through all seven valve combinations. Use a metronome and gradually increase the speed until you can do four notes per beat at mm=120. You should be using the ah-ee vowel shapes inside your mouth. Something like ta-ee-ya-ee, for every beat of the metronome. Air support is crucial. Blow through the notes.

Once you can get the speed of the low notes up to four notes per click at mm=120 you're ready to take the shake above the staff. Start on the top line F# (123) and continue on up the valve combinations just as you did an octave lower. A slight amount of pressure in and out may help the shake up high, but be careful not to overuse mouthpiece pressure. Use your air speed instead.

The Best Sources for Learning Cool Sounds

All this information is great and should be helpful to you, but the very best way to learn cool, funny or strange sounds on your horn is to experiment on your own. Use your creativity and imagination to think up different ways you can use that hunk of brass to make a sound nobody's heard before.

In addition to that, listen to all the trumpet players you can find, either live (definitely the best way) or on recordings. This is your very best source for discovering what trumpet sounds are out there. Listening is the best education you can give yourself on how to use those sounds tastefully. Good luck!

Up Next

There are a whole bunch of things you can, and should, stick in the end of your horn to change its sound. They're called *mutes* and will be covered fully in the next chapter. You'll learn what mutes are, how and when to use them, and how to keep them out from under foot when you play. Mutes are a fun way to get even more cool sounds from you horn.

CHAPTER 16

MUTES & DAMPFERS & PLUNGERS, OH MY!

If you shoot at mimes, should you use a silencer?

~ Steven Wright (1955-)

In This Chapter

- What are Mutes?
- Mute in Other Languages
- Basic Mute Use
- Types of Mutes

Terms to Know

mute: A device to alter the sound of a brass instrument. Placed in the bell of the instrument.

closed: term used with a plunger mute to indicate the plunger covers the bell of the horn. Shown with the "+" symbol.

open: Remove mute. May be used with any mute. With the plunger mute, this is shown with the symbol "O."

back pressure: the resistance of air blown through a pipe. With a mute inserted, back pressure is usually greater.

What is a Mute?

Mutes are very interesting to those who aren't musicians. Of all the questions and comments I get after a gig, the most common by far is about "those things you stick in the end of your trumpet." People like to call it a "muffler" or a "silencer" and either of those is probably a better name, because nobody has ever guessed the real term, *mute*.

A mute is something you stick into the bell of your horn to change the sound of the horn. Mutes can make your sound bright and harsh or mellow and soft, and there are even mutes that block almost all sound, a boon to a trumpet player's family members.

Here are the names of the most-used mutes: practice, straight, cup, Harmon, Wah-wah, plunger, and bucket. These types of mutes can be used effectively in many musical settings. We'll go over all of the mutes below. But first a few names for mutes for mutes in foreign languages and some other basic details.

A Mute By Any Other Name...

Mutes are known by different names in other languages. In Italian mutes are called *sordinos*. Because most musical terms are in Italian, you'll see this one a lot. When you're supposed to put the mute in you'll see *con sordino* (with mute) and when you take it out you'll see *senza sordino* (without mute).

In German mutes are known as a *dämpfers*. In a piece by a German composer like Wagner, you'd see *mit dämpfer* (with mute) when the mute should be put in, and *ohne dämpfer* (without mute) when the mute is to be taken out. Let's not leave out the French. *Avec sourdine* means "with mute," and *sans sourdine* means "without mute. In English you'd see *with mute* and *without mute*, but you probably guessed that already. You may also see the word *open* when the mute is to be removed.

Mutes and Intonation

When playing with a mute one of your chief concerns is intonation. High quality mutes are usually pretty well in tune, but even the best mutes will need some tweaking to get them perfectly in tune. A mute will usually make your tone higher, or sharp. This involves either pulling out your tuning slide or filing down the cork on the mute.

How to Put in Your Mute: Avoid the Accidental Mute Solo

If you've ever used a mute, you've probably had a *mute solo*, which is an accidental solo. This will happen when the entire group is quiet so that your mute solo can be heard and appreciated by all. It happens when your mute falls out of your bell and clatters around on the floor for several minutes. The embarrassment will pass and is harmless, but the damage you may do to your mute might seriously alter its intonation and harm its smooth good looks.

There are steps you can take to avoid the shame of an inadvertent mute solo and damage to your mute. Before you put the mute in your horn, turn the horn around and give a hot breath of air (haah) into the bell. This will lay down a thin film of condensation which will help your mute stick inside the bell. After the breath, immediately put your mute in snugly and give it a little twist to seat it tightly. That should do it.

The Practice Mute or the Whisper Mute

A Dennis Wick practice mute. Good for its small size.

This type of mute is a great help for trumpet players who must practice in an environment where making a lot of sound isn't an option. This could be a hotel room, a crowded apartment building or even late at night in your house. With this mute the sound of the trumpet is all but silenced. You can still hear it, but it's pretty quiet.

The reason this mute is quiet is that little of the air is escaping. A practice mute has cork all the way around to seal off the air escaping from the horn and this causes a lot of *back pressure*. Blowing with a practice mute in your horn is tougher because of all that resistance.

Yamaha makes a practice mute using their Silent Brass System. It allows you to hear yourself better while playing with the mute in, includes a reverb function to enhance your sound, and allows you to pipe in a CD or MP3 player so you can play along. I just got one and love it! It is very free-blowing for a practice mute, and the ability to practice anywhere, any time is invaluable. This is only one of several similar type mutes on the market that allow you to hear yourself. Check out the others online.

Silent Brass System by Yamaha

If you have the option of practicing without a mute in, by all means do it. It's much better to practice without a mute in your horn. Practice mutes are for when you have no other options but still need to get some time in on the horn without making enemies. Occasionally a whisper will be called for in a piece for an ultra-soft effect.

The Straight Mute

A Dennis Wick
straight mute

The straight mute is the most frequently used mute in classical and band music. Often in these styles of music the type of mute isn't specified, you'll just see *con sordino* or something similar. If this is the case, you can bet that it's a straight mute that is being called for. If something other than a straight mute is to be used your director will tell you.

The straight mute gives the trumpet a much brighter and more piercing tone. These mutes come in a bewildering array. Some are made entirely of copper, some have copper bottoms (for a darker sound), some are stone-lined, and some are plastic. They all play a little sharp and below you'll learn how to fix this.

A copper-bottom
straight mute by
Jo-Ral

Your best course of action is to go to your local music store and try them all out. Choose the one with the sound you like best, or the sound that you may need for a song or recording. There is no rule that says you can only have one straight mute. Buy as many as you think you need.

extra cork is
available if
you get file-
happy

It's the cork that allows the mute to stick inside your bell. Most straight mutes come with too much cork on them. You're supposed to file or sand the cork down to the proper height so the mute is in tune with your horn. Be careful when you do this! If you file too much cork you have to buy more cork and glue it on, a time-consuming task. To avoid this, *only file a little bit at a time* and *check it with your tuner* after each filing. Most mutes have several pieces of cork around the mute. Be sure to file each cork equally. Take your time and you'll have no problems.

The Wah-wah, or Harmon Mute

stem

The original
Harmon mute,
made by Harmon.

The Harmon mute is one of the most interesting sounding mutes you can stick in your horn. It's a fairly quiet mute, but if you really push some air through the horn you'll get a great sizzle from it. This is a mute Miles Davis used a lot and if you're looking for a great example, listen to Miles' version of *Autumn Leaves*, and *Love for Sale* on the album *Somethin' Else*. Two classic examples of masterful Harmon mute work.

The Harmon mute has two distinct sounds. Changing the sound of the Harmon mute involves the stem. With the stem in, this mute is known as a wah-wah mute because of the sound you can make with it. With the stem in, the Harmon mute gets a brighter "old-timey" sound. The great thing about using the stem is that as you play, if you take your left hand and put it over the cup of the stem, then take it off, you change the quality of sound. With the stem in you can make your trumpet talk. It's a great effect and people really like it.

Without the stem, the Harmon mute creates a dark, full tone that is very dramatic. Even when you're red in the face from blowing hard through this mute, it's still fairly quiet. For this reason, players often use a microphone with the Harmon mute. If you do use a microphone, you'll need to put the mute right on the mic but be careful not to hit the mic with the mute. Use your hand to feel the distance.

Jo-Ral's Bubble mute produces more *buzz* than other Harmon mutes.

the Mu-Shew

Bobby Shew, master trumpeter, has designed this harmon mute for the soloist. It gets a warmer, darker sound, but still has the *buzz* and should be used with a mic.

The Cup Mute

Mutec's version of the cup mute. This cup is made of copper.

The cup mute is another popular mute and it should be obvious how it gets its name. The cup mute gives the trumpet a soft, almost hollow tone. This can make your trumpet sound more intimate, help it to blend in better with other instruments, or simply give you a quieter sound for a small dinner club.

You often find cup mutes used in jazz bands, swing bands, musicals or in a small jazz combo.

Jo-Ral offers an adjustable cup mute for changing sound quality.

The Plunger

Dennis Wick's version of the plunger

This is another fun mute and is popular with people both because of the sound it can get and the fact that it's a tool used in the bathroom. The plunger is another great way to make your trumpet talk. Learn how to do this in detail with *Plunger Techniques*, a book by Al Grey.

Shown here are two commercial versions of the plunger. For an equally great sound at a *much* cheaper cost, you can use an actual rubber plunger. Be sure to get the smaller sink plunger. Check your local music store or you local plumbing supply store.

To work this mute, hold it in your left hand while you hold the horn with your right. You finally get to use the pinky-finger hook as it's meant to be used! Hold the plunger in your left hand and cover the bell with it. Does it make the pitch go higher or lower? When you use the plunger, you don't need to put it all the way over the bell. This will actually change the pitch of your note up a half step. Your aim is to change the note just a little. Play a long note and fan the plunger on an off the bell. Experiment with the types of sound you can get. Make your trumpet talk.

Hume and Berg's plunger mute has a handle

A regular sink-size plunger available from any hardware store.

Another great effect often heard with the plunger is the growl or the flutter tongue. To find out how to do this fun and interesting technique, see "The Growl and Flutter-Tonguing" on page 170. This is a great mute to use on blues tunes when you solo, or for the entire trumpet section in a swing band. Fun stuff!

Many players who use the sink plunger cut a hole in the top of the dome where the stick would go and place a nickel in the neck at an angle. This gives the sound more sizzle and even if it didn't get a better sound, it's a cool thing to do.

For some great recordings of plunger use, listen to Bubber Miley play the melody on *East St. Louis Toodle-oo* by Duke Ellington, or Cootie Williams, also playing with Ellington's band on *Caravan*. Another impressive use of the plunger can be heard on Wynton Marsalis's tune *The Seductress* from the album *Standard Time vol. 3*. Is that a trumpet or a voice?

Plunger mutes can be played open or closed and this is shown with a + (closed), or O (open) symbol above the note, like so:

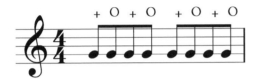

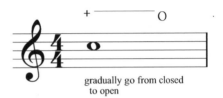

gradually go from closed to open

The Bucket Mute

Jo-Ral's version of the bucket mute. A great sounding mute.

The bucket mute also creates a great sound. It's got a cavernous sort of sound to it, a lot like playing into a bucket. Go figure.

Jo-Ral's mute at left goes in the end of the bell like most other mutes and the HB mute on the right clips on the end of your bell. Though the Jo-Ral is quite a bit more expensive, the ease of use and sound quality make it a good choice if you're in the market for a bucket mute.

Hume and Berg's bucket mute

Other Mutes

There are other mutes out there and don't be afraid to invent your own. Maybe you'll come up with a new one that will sound cool. Below are a few more mutes that are less common, but still used, especially the derby mute. Check out a big band to see that one in action, especially the Lincoln Center Jazz Orchestra, the Basie Big Band, and a few others.

A derby mute by Hume and Berg (this would be used when you see the direction "in hat" in your music.

A Walt Johnson "Gatsby" mute, also known as a solotone mute. This mutes gets an "old-timey" sound.

A Buzz-Wow mute by Hume and Berg

Mute Holders

Bill Pfund's mute holder

Now instead of stumbling over all those mutes you've got on the floor, you can get a mute holder to put them in. Not only will these mute holders get your mutes out from under foot, they'll be easier to reach during a performance. Here are a few versions available to you.

Manhassett's mute holder

Jo-Ral's mute holder

Up Next

There are many, many different types of trumpets out there. You've probably seen cornets, but have you see a Flumpet, a flügelhorn, a Firebird, or a piccolo trumpet? The next chapter will introduce you to the many different trumpets available to you. Collect the whole set!

CHAPTER 17

SO MANY TRUMPETS, SO LITTLE TIME

If you wish in this world to advance, your merits you're bound to enhance; you must stir it and stump it, and blow your own trumpet, or trust me, you haven't a chance.

~ W. S. Gilbert (1836-1911)

In This Chapter

- Flügelhorn
- C trumpet
- E♭ trumpet
- D trumpet
- Piccolo trumpet
- Other trumpets

Terms to Know

piston valve: A type of valve that uses up and down motion of a cylindrical tube to divert air to the appropriate slide.

rotary valve: A type of valve that uses rotating motion of a cylindrical tube to divert air to the appropriate slide.

overtone series: Also known as the *harmonic series*. Tones above a fundamental pitch which are related to the fundamental. As you blow harder/faster through a tube, you'll play successively higher tones. These are the tones in the overtone series.

Superbone: A slide trombone with valves.

A Trumpet for Every Occasion

The B♭ trumpet is far and away the most common trumpet in the world, but there are many others which you can and should explore. Some trumpets, like the flügelhorn, have a special sound that works well with certain tunes. Others, like the C and E♭ trumpets, are pitched in a certain key to make playing a piece easier. And of course there is the piccolo trumpet, an instrument whose range is an octave above that of regular trumpets.

All of these horns have specific uses and also particular challenges that are slightly different than the B♭ trumpet. It's good to know what you're getting yourself into, so this chapter will cover the basics of all these types of trumpet and then some. Here we go!

Cornet

Cornet
(Bach Stradivarius 184ML)

This is the most common type of trumpet after the B♭ trumpet. The cornet is also in the key of B♭ but has a more mellow tone than the trumpet because it has a conical bore, like the French Horn. A conical bore, means the tubing of the instrument is cone shaped, like so: 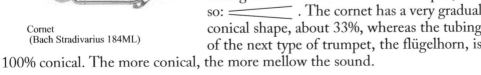 . The cornet has a very gradual conical shape, about 33%, whereas the tubing of the next type of trumpet, the flügelhorn, is 100% conical. The more conical, the more mellow the sound.

Cornet (Holton B♭)

Cornet music used to be very popular, especially in the heyday of the concert band in the late 1800s through the early 1900s. The influence of the cornet can still be seen today in every school band across the country. Most band music has both cornet and trumpet parts, but it's rare for a band to actually use cornets for the cornet parts. Trumpets are ubiquitous these days.

Flügelhorn

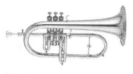

Flügelhorn
(Leblanc F357 Arturo Sandoval model)

4-valve Flügelhorn
(Getzen Eterna 896S)

This is a beautiful sounding instrument and though it has been used in classical music it's primarily a jazz instrument. The flügelhorn is a conical bore instrument like the cornet and French horn. Instruments with a conical bore have a mellow tone and the flügelhorn is no exception.

This horn is used often for ballads and softer tunes because the flügelhorn isn't as loud an instrument as the trumpet, though it can still play pretty loud. Often in a jazz band setting, a tune will call for the entire trumpet section to use flügelhorn.

Phat Boy Flügel
(Taylor)

Flügelhorns come in both a three-valve and four-valve version. Because they are notoriously out of tune in their extreme low and high registers, a fourth valve can be used to correct these troubles with pitch.

Some famous and gifted flügelhorn players are: Art Farmer, Hugh Masakela, and Chuck Mangione. Art Farmer played a hybrid horn made by Dave Monette, called a Flumpet. The Flumpet has qualities of both the flügelhorn and trumpet.

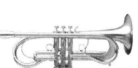

Flumpet
(Dave Monette)

The C Trumpet

C Trumpet
(Monette Raja)

After the B♭ trumpet, the C trumpet is probably the most commonly used trumpet in orchestral music. Many orchestral trumpet parts are written in C, and if you don't like transposing by sight, you can just buy yourself a C trumpet.

The C trumpet is shorter than the B♭ trumpet, shorter by the length of the first valve slide. This makes the C trumpet higher by a whole step. Consider buying a C trumpet if you're serious about playing classical music.

C trumpet
(Bach Stradivarius)

The Eb/D Trumpets

Two trumpets for the price of one. These horns usually have interchangeable lead pipes and/or bells to convert between Eb and D trumpet.

These trumpets aren't used nearly as much as the first three horns. These horns are notoriously difficult to play in tune, but are useful when playing a piece that requires and Eb or D transposition. The Eb trumpet is often used for both the Haydn and Hummel trumpet concerti, both of which are in Eb.

The Eb trumpet sounds a perfect fourth higher than the Bb trumpet. The D trumpet is a major third higher than the Bb trumpet.

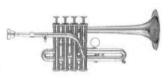

D/Eb trumpet
(LeBlanc T353)

The Piccolo Trumpet

This is the highest sounding trumpet, but don't get your hopes up for playing an easy double-high C. The difficulties in range with this instrument are the same as with a normal, Bb trumpet.

Piccolo trumpets come in both Bb and A versions, often with interchangeable bells and/or lead pipes, so that one horn can do double duty. Piccolo trumpets are also used exclusively in classical music. Maurice André pioneered the use of piccolo trumpet as a solo instrument.

piccolo trumpet
(Getzen custom 3916)

The Pocket Trumpet

pocket trumpet
(Amati)

Going on a road trip? Backpacking through Europe? Well, don't forget to take your pocket trumpet. These little trumpets sound exactly like a Bb trumpet but the tubing is wrapped much more tightly, making them more compact. Pocket trumpets are more for convenience than anything else. If you have access to a full-sized horn, you'll find it plays better and sounds better than the pocket trumpet, but a full sized horn doesn't fit well into a suitcase or backpack, or a large pocket. Free jazz pioneer Don Cherry usually played a pocket trumpet.

Rotary Valve Trumpet

rotary valve trumpet
NY Bach

The trumpets you are probably most familiar with have piston valves, valves that work up and down like the pistons in your car's engine. A rotary valve trumpet has valves which move the air stream by rotation instead of moving up and down. French horns and some tubas use rotary valves. Rotary valves need more maintenance than piston valves.

1890 rotary valve trumpet
(Austro-Hungarian)

Modern orchestras in Germany and Austria still use rotary valve trumpets. In this country they're being used more frequently now in the works of Austro-German Classical and Romantic composers from Mozart to Mahler. Some feel that the warmer tone quality of the rotary valve trumpet is more similar in sound to the natural trumpet used in the Classical and early Romantic periods. For the later Romantic period in the late 19th and early 20th centuries, the rotary valve trumpet was the trumpet then in use. To preserve the authentic sound, rotary valve trumpets are still used for these pieces.

closeups of rotary valves

These images have been generously donated by Roy Hempley, Doug Lehrer and the Conn-Selmer Corporation.

Heraldic Trumpets

These are fun trumpets and are usually in the key of B♭ or C but can also be found in the key of G, A, and others. Banners can be hung from the bell for an added effect, though this makes the horn much more difficult to hold up for long periods. These horns are shaped for visual effect and not playability. They're fun to play and add a certain pomp and circumstance to special occasions.

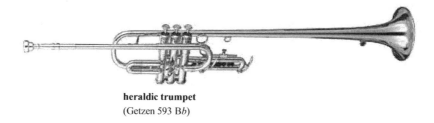

heraldic trumpet
(Getzen 593 B♭)

A Trumpet You Can't Have: The Firebird

This is a trumpet developed and played by Maynard Ferguson in the 1970s. It's a trumpet with a little bitty trombone-like slide attached. Originally, the slide had less positions than a trombone slide (7), but apparently in 2000 Maynard toured with a 7-position Firebird. If you know a trumpet manufacturer, or someone who is good at tinkering with things, you might talk them into making you one. Otherwise, you're out of luck. There are only a couple of these horns in existence.

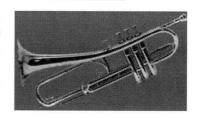

Satish is the name of the artist pictured at left playing a Firebird. He's a New York musician who plays with the group Indofunk. You can check out videos featuring these instruments at www.AllAboutTrumpet/ST/extras.html

Do you like the idea of playing with a slide? Well, all hope is not lost. You can find yourself a soprano trombone, a much easier task than trying to locate a Firebird. Miraphone makes a pretty good one, like the one pictured to the right.

Soprano trombones have the same range as trumpet, but changing notes is a little tricky if you've never used a slide before. Any beginning trombone book will help you start to figure out where the slide positions are. The tone of this instrument is mellow and warm, much like a flügelhorn. Playing this itty bitty trombone will take a good ear if you want to play in tune. It's a fun instrument and is always a hit visually. It's so little!

soprano trombone
(Miraphone)

If It's Got Valves, You Can (probably) Play It

There's no reason you have to stick with only trumpets. Once you understand the fingering on trumpet you can transfer that knowledge to any instrument that uses three (or four) valves. Your options are: mellophone, Sousaphone, tuba, baritone, euphonium, valve trombone, French horn, and an instrument with one of the greatest names, the Superbone (this is a valve trombone with a working slide). Maynard Ferguson often played a Superbone. It was probably developed right alongside the Firebird.

Holton Superbone

Euphonium
(Jupiter 470S)

French Horn
(Holton Farkas H281)

Sousaphone
(Amati ASH260)

Tuba
(Besson Sovereign 993-1-0)

Mellophone
(Blessing M100)

Natural Trumpets

Natural trumpets have no valves and in some ways are more difficult to play, especially if you're doing a piece like the Brandenburg Concerto. Natural trumpets are restricted to the notes in the overtone series. In order to get a scale, you must play high in the instrument's range.

Some natural trumpets are below. You can make your own natural trumpet with any length of tubing (yes, even a length of garden hose) and a mouthpiece. The pitch of a trumpet is a factor of tube length. Go experiment!

bugle

over-the-shoulder
Rhein Horn

double-belled ceramic bugle/
euphonium

to buy such instruments, go to
http://members.aceweb.com/clay/

garden hose trumpet

for instructions on how to make one, go to: http://www.mudcat.org/kids/blowers.cfm

or

http://www.philtulga.com/HomemadeMusic.html

didgeridoo
learn more about this fascinating natural trumpet from Australia in Chapter 23

Up Next

So all you have is your trusty B♭ trumpet and you've got a piece of music that calls for an E♭ trumpet? Not to worry. You can transpose the part in your head (after some practice, of course). The next chapter is all about transposition: reading one pitch and playing a different pitch. Sound confusing? Better read the next chapter.

CHAPTER 18

THE TRANSPOSING TRUMPETER

Be the change you wish to see in the world.

~ Mohandas Ghandi

In This Chapter

- What is Transposing
- B*b* Instruments
- C Instruments
- The C Transposition
- E*b*, F, D, A*b* and E
  Transpositions

Terms to Know

transpose: Changing a piece of music from one key to another, keeping the relationship between pitches exactly the same.

fake book: a book of standard tunes containing only the melody and the chords. Originally used only for jazz, but there are many types of fake books now available.

C instrument: instruments which use concert pitch and need not be concerned with transposing. Some are: piano, guitar, bass, flute, oboe, trombone, tuba, and bagpipes.

B*b* instrument: an instrument one whole step above concert pitch. Some are: trumpet, clarinet, treble clef baritone, and tenor sax.

Trumpet is a Bb Instrument

If you've ever tried playing with a piano player or an alto sax player and used the same music, you probably noticed that things didn't sound quite right. This is because the music for these three instruments is written in different keys. Play a C on piano and it will sound like a D on trumpet or like an A on alto saxophone. Sound confusing? It is, but there's hope. You'll make sense out of it soon. Read on.

Instruments like piano, bass, guitar, trombone, flute, oboe and violin (there are many others) are C instruments. This means that their note C is just that, a C. I know this seems weird, but stay with me. A trumpet is what is called a B*b* instrument. Some other B*b* instruments are clarinet, bass clarinet, tenor Saxophone, soprano Saxophone and treble clef baritone. The lowest open note on trumpet is written as C, first leger line below the staff. The exact same *pitch* on piano is B*b*. This is why trumpet is called a B*b* instrument. Here's a piano keyboard to help you with this concept.

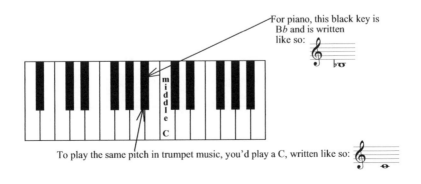

For piano, this black key is B*b* and is written like so:

To play the same pitch in trumpet music, you'd play a C, written like so:

You might be asking, "Wouldn't it be easier if every instrument just used the same notes as piano?" Well, *I* think it would be easier, or at least less confusing, but that's what we've been given to deal with so there's nothing to do but try to understand how it works.

If you're reading music for a C instrument, you have to adjust the notes you play on trumpet to get the right pitch. This is called *transposing*. It's a great skill to have and takes a little time to acquire, but learning to transpose is well worth the effort. If you plan on playing in a symphony, transposing to many different keys is a requirement. If you teach, you'll need to transpose in order to play duets with Saxophone, French horn, and bass clef players. If you want to play jazz in a small combo using a fake book (a fake book is a book of standard tunes with only the melody and chords), you can read from a C fake book which piano and bass players will have. If you sit down to jam with some guitar players or singer-songwriters, you'll have to transpose to get yourself into their key.

Even if you never find yourself in any of these situations, learning to transpose is an excellent exercise for your brain and a good workout for your music-reading skills. Some transpositions are more common than others. We'll cover them in the most useful order.

The C Transposition

This is the most valuable and most used transposition for trumpet players. Using this transposition will allow you to jam with guitar, keyboard, and bass players, play the trumpet parts of many symphonies, play music from a piano part, play from a C fake book, and play the part of any C instrument in treble clef (you may have to transpose piccolo and flute parts down an octave).

As I showed you on the piano keyboard above, the piano's B♭ 𝄞 is the same pitch as the trumpet's C 𝄞 . What is the interval between these two notes? How far apart are they as written? The trumpet note is written two half steps (or one whole step) *higher* than the piano note. (If the concept of intervals like half steps and whole steps is new or unfamiliar to you, brush up on your music theory. Go online to *www.sol-ut.com* to look at a free copy of *Basic Music Theory: How to Read, Write and Understand Written Music*. Part V deals with intervals.)

If the trumpet's written note is a whole step higher than the note for piano (a C instrument) then you now know how to transpose from one to the other. When looking at a part written for a C instrument, all the notes *you* play on trumpet need to be a whole step higher. Here's a simple example and a practical example of what I'm talking about. Looking at a piano keyboard will help you visualize this.

Example 18.1 A simple quarter and half note melody. Each note of the transposed part (as well as the key signature) is up one whole step from the original.

Part for C instrument

transposed for B♭ trumpet

Example 18.2 This trumpet part is an excerpt from *Ride of the Valkyries* by Richard Wagner. An excellent recording of this piece is done by the Cleveland Orchestra, directed by George Szell. Check it out!

The Part as Written:

Tromp. in C

p   mf

The Part as Transposed for Bb Trumpet:

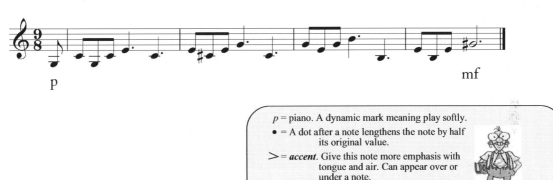

p   mf

p = piano. A dynamic mark meaning play softly.

● = A dot after a note lengthens the note by half its original value.

> = *accent*. Give this note more emphasis with tongue and air. Can appear over or under a note.

mf = mezzo forte. A dynamic marking meaning play at medium loud volume.

If you have a C part that needs to be transposed you have a couple options. You can go through the entire part and write it out a whole step higher. This can be a long process, but it's a great way to get your transposing chops in shape. A better and faster way is to do the C transposition on the fly as you read through the part. This takes a little more practice and will be very slow at first, but the more you do it, the quicker you'll get. To practice the C transposition, pick a piece of simple music and read through it slowly, changing the part in your head before you play the note. Jazz tunes are a great source of short tunes to practice transposing. For a list of tunes, see "Essential Jazz Standards" on page 200.

Using C Transposition to Jam

When you get together with piano, guitar and/or bass players to make sound, be aware that all those instruments are in C, so to sound like you know what you're doing, you have to transpose. This is a little simpler than transposing a written melody on the fly because you'll be dealing with keys (scales) more than individual notes. For example, if a guitar player is playing in the key of C, you'll be playing in the key of D. This means that to get the cool-sounding notes, you'll be using your D scales (major, minor, pentatonic, blues, whatever sounds like it fits).

The tricky part about playing with string players is that they are often in sharp keys. For example, a lot of songs on guitar are in the key of E. A whole step up from E is F#, which isn't a key that trumpet players are particularly fond of. That's only because it's unfamiliar. If you plan on playing with string players, start practicing these keys now. Here are the C transpositions for each of the keys. Notice that when you transpose keys, you're adding two sharps. The most common keys used by guitar players are in bold. Major keys are the letter on the left, and relative minor keys are on the right.

Part to Be Transposed (in C)	B♭ Trumpet Key
C (no sharps or flats) Amin	D (2 sharps) Bmin
G (1 sharp) Emin	A (3 sharps) F#min
D (2 sharps) Bmin	E (4 sharps) C#min
A (3 sharps) F#min	B (4 sharps) G#/A♭min
E (4 sharps) C#min	F# (6 sharps) D#/E♭min
F (1 flat) Dmin	G (1 sharp) Emin
B♭ (2 flats) Gmin	C (no sharps/flats) Amin
E♭ (3 flats) Cmin	F (1 flat) Dmin
A♭ (4 flats) Fmin	B♭ (2 flats) Gmin
D♭ (5 flats) B♭min	E♭ (3 flats) Cmin
G♭ (6 flats) E♭min	A♭ (4 flats) Fmin
C♭ (7 flats) A♭min	D♭ (5 flats) B♭min

There is information below about the flats and sharps contained in each of the 12 keys. Start learning this information as soon as you can. You won't regret it!

To practice these keys, start with the Major scale. Learn it up and down and with as many patterns as you can.

Learn the blues scale for the keys as soon as possible. The blues scale is very common because it sounds so cool. People like it. Start with the 5 most common keys, then learn the other 7.

Don't neglect the minor scales in these keys either. Check out the index in the back of the book for most of the scales you'll need. Start practicing them now!

The Other Transpositions

Unless you're playing symphonic music, you probably won't have much use for the following transpositions. If you do plan on playing in an orchestra, learning these transpositions is mandatory. We'll take care of the more common transpositions first.

Theoretically, you can transpose a part to *any* of the other 11 keys. You may be relieved to find out that there are only five or six transpositions that are commonly used. After the C transpositions, the next most common are the E♭ and F transposition. After you master those you can tackle the less frequently seen transpositions like A♭, D, E, and A.

The Eb Transposition

Keep in mind that trumpet is a B♭ instrument. This will help you find out how far away each transposition is from the written note. When we did the C transposition we figured that C was a whole step above B♭, and so all the notes were transposed up a whole step, right? Well, you apply that same principle to the E♭ transposition. What is the interval between B♭ (the trumpet's key) and E♭? You should come up with 5 half steps, or a perfect 4th. Use your keyboard to help visualize this concept.

Another way of finding a perfect fourth is to go up the major scale which begins on your starting note. Stop on the 4th note of the major scale and you have a perfect fourth. This requires you to know your major scales, which is a great idea. If you go up the B♭ Major scale and stop on the fourth note what do you get? I hope you came up with E♭. Examples are always the best way to understand a concept, so here are a few on the next page.

The Transposing Trumpeter

Example 18.3 A simple E♭ transposition and below it a practical example from the Hummel trumpet concerto.

trumpet in E♭   transposed for B♭ trumpet

Opening statement in the
Concerto for Trumpet in E♭ by
Johann Hummel as written for
the E♭ trumpet.

Opening statement in the
Concerto for Trumpet in E♭ by
Hummel. Transposed for the
B♭ trumpet.

The E♭ transposition may take more time to get under your fingers than the C transposition did, but stick with it. As before, you could write out the transposition into E♭ (this is good practice anyway), or just learn to transpose by sight.

When learning to transpose by sight, go slowly and be aware of what key you're playing in. With an E♭ transposition, you're adding one flat to the original key signature. Here's a table with the E♭ transpositions and their respective keys transposed to B♭ trumpet keys. Major keys are on the left, and the relative minor keys are on the right.

Key of Part to be Transposed (in E♭)	Key Transposed for B♭ Trumpet
C (no sharps or flats) Amin	F (1 flat) Dmin
F (1 flat) Dmin	B♭ (2 flats) Gmin
B♭ (2 flats) Gmin	E♭ (3 flats) Cmin
E♭ (3 flats) Cmin	A♭ (4 flats) Fmin
A♭ (4 flats) Fmin	D♭ (5 flats) B♭min
D♭ (5 flats) B♭min	G♭ (6 flats) E♭min
G♭ (6 flats) E♭min	C♭ (7 flats) A♭min
G (1 sharp) A♭min	C (no sharps or flats) Amin
D (2 sharps) Bmin	G (1 sharp) Emin
A (3 sharps) F#min	D (2 sharps) Bmin
E (4 sharps) C#min	A (3 sharps) F#min
B (5 sharps) G#/A♭min	E (4 sharps) C#min
F# (6 sharps) D#/E♭min	B (5 sharps) G#/A♭min
C# (7 sharps) A#/B♭min	F# (6 sharps) D#/E♭min

Order of Flats

The order of flats in a key signature is something you should memorize as soon as possible. The order of flats is BEADGCF. When written in a key signature, flats must be written on a specific line or space. A key signature with all 7 flats looks like this:

Order of Sharps

The order of the sharps in a key signature is the order of flats backwards, or FCGDAEB. If you memorize the flat order, you've also memorized the sharp order. Here's a key signature with all 7 sharps.

F Transposition

Okay, by now you should know the drill. What is the interval between B♭ and F? To find out, go up the B♭ Major scale until you get to the F. It's the 5th note, so an F transposition means you play the note a perfect 5th above the written note. Remember to go slowly as you learn to read by sight in F. Whenever you transpose, it's wise to know what key you'll be playing in. For the F transposition, add one sharp to the key signature. Some examples:

Example 18.4 A simple F transposition and below it another example from Wagner's *Ride of the Valkyries*.

Key of Part to be Transposed (in F)	Key Transposed for B♭ Trumpet
C (no sharps or flats) Amin	G (1 sharp) Emin
F (1 flat) Dmin	C (no sharps or flats) Amin
B♭ (2 flats) Gmin	F (1 flat) Dmin
E♭ (3 flats) Cmin	B♭ (2 flats) Gmin
A♭ (4 flats) Fmin	E♭ (3 flats) Cmin
D♭ (5 flats) B♭	A♭ (4 flats) Fmin
G♭ (6 flats) E♭min	D♭ (5 flats) B♭min
C♭ (7 flats) A♭min	G♭ (6 flats) E♭min
G (1 sharp) Emin	D (2 sharps) Bmin
D (2 sharps) Bmin	A (3 sharps) F#min
A (3 sharps) F#min	E (4 sharps) C#min
E (4 sharps) C#min	B (5 sharps) G#/A♭min
B (5 sharps) G#/A♭min	F# (6 sharps) D#/E♭min
F# (6 sharps) D#/E♭min	C# (7 sharps) A#/B♭min

Order of Flats

Why is this sidebar repeated? Because the order of flats in a key signature is something you should memorize as soon as possible. Use a mnemonic device to remember the order: the word *BEAD* plus *Greatest Common Factor* works. Make up your own using the letters BEADGCF.

Order of Sharps

There are two things to learn with the order of sharps and flats. Not only the order they appear, but where they're written on the staff in the key signature. Study these key signatures to memorize where they go.

D Transposition

The D transposition is a good one to know because with it you can create harmony parts on the spot. Harmony parts are often a third above or below the main melody, and this is the interval you'll use for the D transposition. More on this below after you get the information about the transposition. As with the others, figure out the interval between B♭ and D. What did you get? It should be 4 half steps, or 2 whole steps, or a Major 3rd. Here are the examples of D transposition.

Example 18.5 A simple example of D transposition and a practical example, again from *Ride of the Valkyries*.

trumpet in D

transposed for B♭ trumpet

tromp. in D (from *Ride of the Valkyries* by Richard Wagner)

transposed for B♭ trumpet

When transposing the D trumpet parts, you change keys by adding 4 sharps. This causes some difficulty when transposing from a key with 4 or more sharps because you end up with a need for double-sharps (they raise a note a whole step). Technically, you should use the double-sharps, but it's easier to think in a flat key. For example, when transposing from the key of E (four sharps), you'd use the G# Major scale which contains an F double-sharp. Instead of using this unwieldy scale, you can think in the key of A♭, which only has 4 flats. If you've memorized your major scales and the order of sharps and flats, this will help you make these transitions more easily.

Key of Part to be Transposed to D	Key Transposed for B♭ Trumpet
C (no sharps or flats) Amin	E (4 sharps) C#min
F (1 flat) Dmin	A (3 sharps) F#min
B♭ (2 flats) Gmin	D (2 sharps) Bmin
E♭ (3 flats) Cmin	G (1 sharp) Emin
A♭ (4 flats) Fmin	C (no sharps or flats) Amin
D♭ (5 flats) B♭min	F (1 flat) Dmin
G♭ (6 flats) E♭min	B♭ (2 flats) Gmin
C♭ (7 flats) A♭min	E♭ (3 flats) Cmin
G (1 sharp) Emin	B (5 sharps) G#/A♭min
D (2 sharps) Bmin	F# (6 sharps) D#/E♭min
A (3 sharps) F#min	C# (7 sharps) A#/B♭min
E (4 sharps) C#min	think in Ab (4 flats)
B (5 sharps)	think in E♭ (3 flats)
F# (6 sharps)	think in B♭ (2 flats)

The Ab Transposition

You won't see this one too often unless you're playing a C trumpet (a type of trumpet that plays in the key of C) and reading the music for a Bb trumpet. Basically, it's the C transposition reversed. Instead of transposing up a whole step, you'll transpose *down* a whole step.

Use the same process to find the right interval to transpose. The Ab is a whole step *below* the Bb, so you'd transpose down one whole step. Here are the examples:

Example 18.6 The Ab transposition.

For the Ab transposition, add two flats to the original key signature to get the key signature you'll use for the transposition.

Key of Part to be Transposed to Ab	Key Transposed for Bb Trumpet
C (no sharps or flats) Amin	Bb (2 flats) Gmin
F (1 flat) Dmin	Eb (3 flats) Cmin
Bb (2 flats) Gmin	Ab (4 flats) Fmin
Eb (3 flats) Cmin	Db (5 flats) Bbmin
Ab (4 flats) Fmin	Gb (6 flats) Ebmin
Db (5 flats) Bbmin	Cb (7 flats) Abmin
G (1 sharp) Emin	F (1 flat) Dmin
D (2 sharps) Bmin	C (no sharps or flats) Amin
A (3 sharps) F#min	G (1 sharp) Emin
E (4 sharps) C#min	D (2 sharps) Bmin
B (5 sharps) G#min	A (3 sharps) F#min
F# (6 sharps) D#min	E (4 sharps) C#min
C# (7 sharps) A#min	B (5 sharps) G#min

Order of Flats

Write in all 7 flats in the correct order below. Try to do it without looking back, but if you must, go ahead.

Order of Sharps

Write in all 7 flats in the correct order below. Try to do it without looking back, but if you must, go ahead.

The E Transposition

This is a transposition you won't see too often, but it does exist in symphony pieces, like our old favorite, Wagner's *Ride of the Valkyries*. The E transposition is a little challenging because we're going up three whole steps, an interval we don't use very often. This interval is called a *tritone* because of those three whole steps. On the next page is a basic example of an E transposition.

Example 18.7 The E transposition.

trumpet in E

transposed for Bb trumpet

A tritone can be explained either as a diminished 5th or an augmented 4th. Don't worry if this means nothing to you, but if it means nothing, get busy with your music theory. What it means for the key signatures below is that usually you add 6 flats to a key signature. Where this is impractical (any key with 2 or more flats), you add 6 sharps to the key. Sound confusing? Although there is a rhyme and reason to these key signature changes, at first it's easiest if you just memorize them. If you want the rhyme and reason, study your music theory. Here are the keys transposed. As before, the major key is the letter on the left, and the relative minor key is on the right.

Key of Part to be Transposed to E	Key Transposed for Bb Trumpet
C (no sharps or flats) Amin	Gb (6 flats) Ebmin
F (1 flat) Dmin	Cb (7 flats) Abmin
Bb (2 flats) Gmin	E (4 sharps) C#min
Eb (3 flats) Cmin	A (3 sharps) F#min
Ab (4 flats) Fmin	D (2 sharps) Bmin
Db (5 flats) Bbmin	G (1 sharp) Emin
G (1 sharp) Emin	Db (5 flats) Bbmin
D (2 sharps) Bmin	Ab (4 flats) Fmin
A (3 sharps) F#min	Eb (3 flats) Cmin
E (4 sharps) C#min	Bb (2 flats) Gmin
B (5 sharps) G#min	F (1 flat) Dmin
F# (6 sharps) D#min	C (no sharps or flats) Amin
C# (7 sharps) A#min	G (1 sharp) Emin

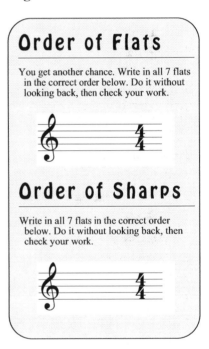

Order of Flats

You get another chance. Write in all 7 flats in the correct order below. Do it without looking back, then check your work.

Order of Sharps

Write in all 7 flats in the correct order below. Do it without looking back, then check your work.

Still More Transposition

Yes, there are more transpositions, but by now, you should have a pretty clear idea of what's involved and you should be able to figure out for yourself how to do them. What would you do for an A transposition? Answer: go down a half step. How about a G transposition? Can you read and play from the bass clef staff? (Hint: it's very much like an Eb transposition). Always try to push the boundary of your knowledge and ability. It's the only way to grow as a musician and as a human being.

Transposing in Foreign Languages

If you're interested in playing symphony music, you need to know how transpositions are identified in other languages. Did you ever see *The Sound of Music*? Remember the song that goes, "Do, a deer, a female deer, Re, a drop of golden sun...." Well, this little ditty is teaching you solfege, a system for singing written music. The notes of the solfege scale are Do (or Ut), Re, Mi, Fa, Sol, La, Ti, Do. These terms are used in many European languages to identify notes of the scale. You'll often encounter these terms when a transposition is called for.

English	French	Italian	German
B♭ Piccolo Trumpet	Petite Trompette en Si♭	Ottavino Tromba in Si♭	Kleine Trompete in B
F Trumpet	Trompette en Fa	Tromba in Fa	Trompete in F
E♭ Trumpet	Trompette en Mi♭	Tromba in Mi♭	Trompete in Es
D Trumpet	Trompette en Re	Tromba in Re	Trompete in D
C Trumpet	Trompette en Ut	Tromba in Do	Trompete in C
B♭ Trumpet	Trompette en Si♭	Tromba in Si♭	Trompete in B
A Trumpet	Trompette en La	Tromba in La	Trompete in A

How to Practice Transpositions

A good way to practice transposing is to get a compilation of orchestral excerpts and find pieces with the type of transpositions you want to practice. It may sound intimidating, but there are orchestral excerpts that range from simple to complex. Start with the simple ones. That way you're doing double-duty: practicing your transpositions and getting in practice on orchestral excerpts at the same time. There are several compilations of orchestral repertoire available.

The main thing to remember when practicing transpositions is to take it slow and give yourself a lot of time to wrap your brain around the concept of reading a note on the page and playing a note that's different from what you see. Many people have mastered this skill, and you can, too. Remember it takes time to be able to transpose immediately at a fast tempo. Keep at it! Below are some sources for further study.

Title	Author	Publisher
Have Trumpet Will Transpose	Broiles	Chas. Colin
Duets for Two Transposing Trumpeters	Telemann	Balquid
100 Etudes (difficult)	Sachse	International
Orchestra Musician's CD-Rom Library	http://www.orchmusiclibrary.com/	

What's Up Next

There is so much music for trumpet in the world that it's difficult and maybe even a little intimidating to find what you need. Not to worry, the next chapter covers written music for trumpet. You'll find sources for method books, etude books, solos, jazz tunes, symphony excerpts, duets, trios and brass ensembles. Get ready to dig in!

CHAPTER 19
TRUMPET MUSIC

What we play is life.

~ Louis Armstrong

In This Chapter

- Making Sense of Your Choices
- Method Book Repertoire
- Classical Symphony Repertoire
- Classical Solo Repertoire
- Jazz Repertoire

Terms to Know

repertoire: a collection of works that an artist can perform.

étude (AY-tude): A short piece of music studied to improve technique.

fake book: A book which includes a song's melody and chords. There are fake books of jazz tunes, Christmas tunes, Latin tunes, Christian tunes, and on and on.

Un-Boggling Your Mind

There is a lot of written music out there for a trumpet player. Making a selection can be the most confusing part of the process. Know what your goals are, what kind of music moves you, and try to be open to other styles. One of the wonderful things about music is the way styles can mix together. What you study in one style you can use in another, often with interesting and new effects. Sample everything you can.

The following lists are far from complete. Instead of trying to include everything, I've limited choices to the most useful, popular, beautiful and fun. Don't worry, it's still a very long list.

Be sure to talk with your teacher about what books and music will best suit your ability and focus.

Where to start?

Method books will be covered first, as they should be used by trumpet players of any and every style. Method books cover everything from tone production (lip slurs, pedal tones, high notes) to scale theory, to improvisation and beyond. I'll give you a run-down of each of the most popular and useful books.

Etude books are a great source of short pieces, from easy to difficult. Etudes use techniques you've learned in method books. Trumpet teachers usually have a few they like to use. Ask your teacher which ones he or she uses. Below is a list of the more popular etude books.

Jazz repertoire is great stuff to learn because it will open up possibilities to perform with thousands of other musicians who know the same tunes. Jazz tunes everyone knows are called *standards* and are fun and fairly easy to learn and memorize. Find sources for standards and the names some of the most popular ones below, graded from easy to difficult.

Classical solo repertoire are tried-and-true pieces composed for trumpet and they range from easy to very difficult, from slow and lyrical to fast and rhythmic and most include piano accompaniment. These are graded from 1-5, with 1 being the easiest and 5 being the most difficult.

Classical symphonic repertoire are pieces of music performed by symphonies, and more importantly, the pieces that are used to audition trumpet players. If you want to play in a symphony, you must know these pieces well and be able to play them artistically.

Essential Method Books

Keep in mind these are just a few of the *many* books available and are a good place to start. Highly recommended books are in bold. Find many of these titles and more at www.somusic.com. For more trumpet web sites, check out the links on this book's "extras" page at www.sol-ut.com.

Method Book Title	Author	Publisher/Distributor	Topics Covered
27 Groups of Exercises for Cornet or Trumpet	Earl Irons	Southern Music Co. www.southernmusic.com	lip slurs
A Physical Approach to Playing the Trumpet	Lynn K. Asper	Wave Song Press www.trumpetbook.com	training physical reflexes for trumpet playing
Advanced Lip Flexibilites	Charles Colin	Charles Colin Music www.charlescolin.com	warm-ups, lip slurs, flexibility
Chops	Bill Spilka	Charles Colin	
Systematic Approach to Daily Practice	Claude Gordon	(Carl Fischer)	
Chord Studies for Trumpet	Raymond Kotwica, Joseph Viola	Hal Leonard	
Complete Conservatory Method	J. Arban	Carl Fischer www.carlfischer.com	scale studies, chord studies, lip drills, double- triple- tonguing, etudes, duets
Daily Drills and Technical Studies	Max Schlossberg	M. Baron	warm-ups, lip drills, technical studies
Developing Technique	Kenneth Baird	Kenneth Baird Music Publications	warm-up, flexibility, major, minor, chromatics
Exercises and Etudes for Jazz and Classical Players	Bobby Shew	JA Jazz	
Extensions for the Trumpet Player	Allan Colin	JA Jazz	
Grand Method	St. Jacome	Carl Fischer www.carlfischer.com	scale studies, chord studies, lip drills, tonguing, etudes, duets
How to Play and Improvise	J. Abersold	JA Jazz, Inc. www.jajazz.com	beginning jazz improvisation
How to Play High Notes, Low Notes, and All Those In Between	John Haynie	Charles Colin Music www.charlescolin.com	

Method Book Title	Author	Publisher/Distributor	Topics Covered
Jazz Conception for Trumpet	Jim Snidero	Advance Music	
Jazz Trumpet Tech #1, Vol 1, 2	Toni D'Aveni	Hal Leonard	
Jazz Trumpet Techniques	John McNeil	Warner Brothers	
Lip Flexibility	Smith	Carl Fischer www.carlfischer.com	slurs, flexibility studies
Method for Trumpet, Book 1	Anthony Plog	Balquidder music www.somusic.com	
Musical Calisthenics for Brass	Carmine Caruso	Hal Leonard www.halleonard.com	range, endurance, attack, breath control, intervals
Physical Approach to Elementary Brass Playing	Gordon	Carl Fischer www.carlfischer.com	getting started with correct habits
Playing Technique & Performance Studies for Trumpet, vol.2 (basic),vol.3(advanced)	Arturo Sandoval	Hal Leonard	
Prelude to Brass Playing	Rafael Mendez	Carl Fischer	
Reading Key Jazz Rhythms	Fred Lipsius	JA Jazz	
Setting Up Drills	Herbert L. Clarke	Carl Fischer	warm-up exercises
Super Chops	Jerome Callet	www.super-chops.com	tongue-controlled embouchure
Systematic Approach to Daily Practice	Claude Gordon		range,
Technical Drills for the Jazz/Commercial Trumpet Player	Randall Reyman	Kendor Music, Inc.	
Technical Studies	Herbert L. Clarke	Carl Fischer www.carlfischer.com	scale studies/patterns
Technical Studies for the Modern Trumpet Player	Pat Harbison	JA Jazz	
The Art of Jazz Trumpet vol. 1 & 2	John McNeil	Gerard & Sarzin	
The Cat Anderson Trumpet Method	Cat Anderson	Alfred www.alfred.com	
The Original Louis Maggio System for Brass	Carlton McBeth		range,
The Secret of Technique Preservation	Williams	Chas. Colin/ www.somusic.com	
The Vizzutti Trumpet Methods (vol. 1-3)	Allen Vizzutti	www.somusic.com	vol. 1: Technique vol. 2: Harmonic vol. 3: Melodic
Trumpet Routines	William Vacchiano		warm-ups, lip drills, technical studies
Warm-ups Plus Studies	James Stamp	Editions Bim www.editions-bim.com	warm-ups, pedal tones, range exercises, pitch-bending etc.

Essential Etude Books

Again, just a small sample of what's available. Be sure to check with your teacher before buying any of these, and if possible, purchase them from your local music store so you can open them up and get an idea of what's inside and how it fits with your skill level. Feel free to look around for other books, too. Don't rule out books for other instruments.

Level	Book Title	Author	Publisher/Distributor
1	1st Book of Practical Studies	Robert Getchell	Warner Bros.
1-2	24 Melodic Studies	Boehm	International
1-2	First Tunes and Studios	Wiggins	Oxford
1-4	Abersold Jazz Books: Maiden Voyage (vol. 54), and Killer Joe (vol. 70) or any other that interests you	Jamey Abersold www.jajazz.com	JA Jazz
2-4	Jazz and Latin Duets	Fritz Pauer	JA Jazz
3-4	40 Studies	Wurm, ed. Voison	International Music Co.
3-4	Characteristic Studies	Clarke	Carl Fischer
3-4	Lyrical Studies for Trumpet	Concone	Brass Press
3-4	Orchestral and Last Etudes	V. Brandt	MCA
3-4	Practical Studies	Goldman	Carl Fischer
4	Etudes Transcendantes	Theo Charlier	A. Leduc
3-4	Courting the Upper Register	Michael Stewart	Michael Stewart
	Lyrical Etudes for Trumpet	Phis Snedecor	
	Legato Etudes for Trumpet	John Shoemaker	
	Duets for Trumpet	Bob Martin	Hal Leonard

Essential Jazz Standards

I've limited this list to 40 tunes. Memorize the melodies. If you really want to learn them well, memorize the chords, too. To truly learn them, you must do them in all keys. This will prepare you for any playing situation. These tunes will give you a great basic start on a jazz vocabulary and will enable you to play with almost all jazz musicians.

Included is an example of a great recording of the tune. Though I've included a lot of trumpet versions, there are also versions on other instruments. Listening to other instruments will give you fresh ideas and approaches to performing the tunes on trumpet. Be on the lookout for other treatments of the same song to hear what is possible, which is anything. Sometimes the tunes are changed radically!

Most jazz standards can be found in what are called *Fake Books*, which contain the bare bones of hundreds of tunes. There are many of them out there, so be sure you know what the book contains before you buy it. Some of the best are the *Real Book* (RB1, 2, or 3) and *New Real Book* (NRB 1,2 or

3) series by Sher Publishing, Hal Leonard's *Real Jazz Classics Fake Book* (HLJC), and the Jamey Abersold (JA) books which have the added benefit of recorded accompaniment and scale suggestions.

Song Title	Difficulty (1-5)	Composer	Great Recording, Artist (Label)	Where to Find It
All Blues	1	Miles Davis	*Kind of Blue*, Miles Davis (Columbia)	JA50, HLJC
Autumn Leaves	2	Johnny Mercer	*Somethin' Else*, Cannonball Adderly, Miles Davis (Blue Note)	NRB1, JA20/44/54
Blue Monk	2	Thelonius Monk	Nights of Ballads and Blues, McCoy Tyner (Impulse)	
Caravan	3	Duke Ellington	*The Artistry of Freddie Hubbard*, Freddie Hubbard (MCA/Impulse)	NRB3, JA59
Cherokee	3	Ray Noble	Clifford Brown and Max Roach, Clifford Brown (Verve)	NRB2, JA15/61
Con Alma	2	Dizzy Gillespie	Dizzy's Diamonds, Dizzy Gillespie (Verve)	HLJC
Girl from Ipanema, The	2	Jobim	Getz/Gilberto, Stan Getz and Joao Gilberto (Verve)	
Green Dolphin Street	3	Bronislaw Kaper	Live at the Plugged Nickel, Vol. I, Miles Davis (Columbia)	NRB3, JA34/59, HLJC
I've Got Rhythm	2	Gershwin	Mr. Wilson and Mr. Gershwin, Teddy Wilson (Sony)	JA51
It Don't Mean a Thing (If it Ain't Got That Swing)	2	Duke Ellington	Thelonius Monk Plays Ellington, Thelonius Monk (Riverside)	NRB2, JA59
Jordu	4	Clifford Brown	Clifford Brown and Max Roach, Clifford Brown (Verve)	NRB2, JA53
Lullaby of Birdland	3	George Shearing	*Birdland '53*, Bud Powell (Fresh Sound)	JA40, HLJC
Misty	2	Errol Garner	*The Original Misty*, Errol Garner (Mercury)	NRB1, JA41/49
Over the Rainbow	2	Harold Arlen	The Amazing Bud Powell vol. 1, Bud Powell (Blue Note)	NRB3, JA34
Salt Peanuts	4	Dizzy Gillespie	Steamin', Miles Davis (Prestige)	HLJC
So What	1	Miles Davis	*Kind of Blue*, Miles Davis (Columbia)	HLJC, JA50
Summertime	2	Gershwin	*The Artistry of Freddie Hubbard*, Freddie Hubbard (MCA/Impulse)	JA25/54
Take Five	4	Paul Desmond	*The Essential Dave Brubeck*, Dave Brubeck et. al. (Legacy)	HLJC
Watermelon Man	1	Herbie Hancock	Takin' Off, Herbie Hancock (Blue Note)	HLJC, JA11/54
Well, You Needn't	3	Thelonius Monk	The Best of Miles Davis, Miles Davis (Blue Note)	NRB1, JA56, HLJC
Take the A Train	2	Duke Ellington		RB1, NRB1
Sandu	3	Clifford Brown		NRB1, RB2
Birk's Works	2	Dizzy Gillespie		RB2

Song Title	Difficulty (1-5)	Composer	Great Recording, Artist (Label)	Where to Find It
Sweet Georgia Brown	3			RB2,
Killer Joe	1	Benny Golson		RB2, NRB2
Doxy	2	Sonny Rollins		RB2
Now's the Time	1	Charlie Parker		RB2
Work Song	2	Nat Adderly	Best of Cannonball Adderly	RB2,

Jazz Trumpet Solo Transcriptions

An essential part of a jazz player's education is the study of what other players have improvised. It's best to transcribe these solos yourself, because this will train your ear-finger coordination. It's a long process but is the best things you could do to understand improvisation. Lucky for you, others have paved the way and done the homework for you. Below is a long list of solo transcriptions. Don't let this make you lazy and neglect your own transcription endeavors. Transcribing a tune is one of the best things you can do to train your ears and your brain. Do it.

Book Title	Artist	Author/Publisher
15 Transcribed Trumpet Solos	Abersold	JA Jazz
A Jazz Master	Armstrong, Louis	Warner Brothers
Great Trumpet Solos of Louis Armstrong	Armstrong, Louis	Ecklund, P. / Hal Leonard
Solos (11 Transcribed Solos)	Baker, Chet	JA Jazz
Solos (13 Transcribed Solos)	Baker, Chet	JA Jazz
Chet Baker: Trumpet Artistry	Baker, Chet	Bastion, J. / JA Jazz
Chet Baker's Greatest Scat Solos	Baker, Chet	Bastion, J. / JA Jazz
Bix Beiderbecke Great Cornet Solos	Beiderbecke, Bix	Ecklund, P. / JA Jazz
Randy Brecker Artist Transcriptions	Brecker, Randy	Davison, M. / Hal Leonard
Clifford Brown Styles & Analysis	Brown, Clifford	Baker, D. / JA Jazz
Clifford Brown: Solo Patterns Study	Brown, Clifford	Cervantes & Ruiz / Charles Colin
Clifford Brown Complete Transcriptions	Brown, Clifford	Hal Leonard
Clifford Brown Trumpet Solos	Brown, Clifford	Slone, K. / Warner Brothers
Kind of Blue	Davis Miles	Hal Leonard
The Jazz Style of Miles Davis	Davis, Miles	Baker, D. / Warner Bros
Kinda Blue Complete Transcriptions	Davis, Miles	Hal Leonard Publications
Originals	Davis, Miles	Hal Leonard
Standards	Davis, Miles	Hal Leonard
Miles Davis Standards, vol. 1	Davis, Miles	JA Jazz
The Artistry of Roy Eldridge	Eldridge, Roy	Stewart, T. / JA Jazz

Book Title	Artist	Author/Publisher
Artist Transcriptions	Hubbard, Freddie	Hal Leonard
Ballads	Marsalis, Wynton	Warner Bros.
Standards	Marsalis, Wynton	Warner Bros.
Blue Mitchell Solos	Mitchell, Blue	Bunnell, J / Hal Leonard
The Jazz Style of Fats Navarro	Navarro, Fats	Baker, D. / Warner Brothers
Greatest Hits of Woody Shaw	Shaw, Woody	Warner Brothers
Bobby Shew Solos	Shew, Bobby	JA Jazz
Allen Vizzutti: Play-Along Solos, (book, CD)	Vizzutti, Allen	Hal Leonard
Jazz Trumpet 2		Brown, John R. / International
20 Authentic Bebop Solos (book and CD)		Harbison, P / JA Jazz
Jazz Trumpet Transcriptions		Harrell, T. / Hal Leonard
Jazz Solos for Trumpet vol. 1		Jarvis, J / Kendor
Then and Now		Rodney, R. / Charles Colin
28 Modern Jaz Trumpet Solos (Books 1 & 2)		Slone, K. / Warner Brothers
Trumpet Solos for the Performing Artists (book, CD)		Vizzutti, A. / JA Jazz

Jazz Books

If you plan on playing jazz, this means studying jazz. Here are some good books to get you into the swing of things.

Book Title	Author (Publisher)	Concepts Addressed
Inside Improvisation (Series of 6 books)	Jerry Bergonzi (Advance Music)	melodic structures, pentatonics, jazz line, melodic rhythm, intervals, jazz language
How to Improvise	Hal Crook (Advance Music)	like the title says....
The Jazz Theory Book	James Levine (Sher)	chord structure, scale structure, discography, practicing scales, much more. An essential book.
Clifford Brown Complete Transcriptions	Marc Lewis (Jamey Abersold Jazz: www.jazzbooks.com)	transcriptions of Clifford Brown's astounding improvisations. Lots of material to practice here. Great idea resource.
II-V-I (vol.)	Jamey Abersold (Jamey Abersold Jazz: www.jazzbooks.com)	covers many versions of the most common chord progression in jazz.
Gettin' It Together (vol.)	Jamey Abersold (Jamey Abersold Jazz: www.jazzbooks.com)	

Classical Solo and Small Group Repertoire

This is such an incomplete list! There are thousands of possibilities out there, and these are just a few of the standards. They are graded 1-6, with 1 being the easiest and 6 the most challenging. Consult your teacher before buying, and when you do buy a piece, try to buy it from your local music store. They can order any or all of these titles and it keeps money in your community.

The Essential Trumpet Concerto Collection

These concertos are considered necessary by most players and teachers. If you're interested in classical music, these concertos are the pinnacle of solo trumpet work. They are challenging, beautiful pieces of music and if you're interested, you should start studying them now. You don't need to tackle the whole concerto. Pick just one movement, one you like. Often the slower movements will be less challenging technically but will challenge you to be expressive. Remember, one of the best ways to study these pieces is to *listen* to them. Many recorded versions exist. For recording suggestions, see "Solo Classical Trumpet" on page 20.

Solo Repertoire List

Level	Title	Composer	Publisher/Distributor
1-2	Carnival of Venice	J. Arban	Carl Fischer
	Concert Piece No. 1	Brandt/Voison	International Music Co.
	The Best of Herbert L. Clarke —The Bride of the Waves —The Debutante —From the Shores of the Mighty Pacific —The Harp That Once Thro' Tara's Halls —The Maid of the Mist —Sounds from the Hudson —The Southern Cross	Herbert Clarke	Warner Bros.
	Sonata No. 8	Corelli	CPP/Belwin
	Sonata	Dello-Joio	Associated Music Publishers
	Legende	Enesco	International Music Company
	Concert Etude	Goedicke	MCA/Hal Leonard
	Song of the Pines The Grand Canyon	Irons	Southern Music Co.
	Jota	Mendez	Carl Fischer
	The Hollow Men	Persichetti	Elkan Vogel
	Ode For Trumpet	Reed	Southern Music Co.
	Sonata No. 17	Scarlatti/Voison	International Music Company
	Three Bagatelles	Tull	Boosey Hawkes
	Allegro	Vivaldi/Fitzgerald	CPP/Belwin

Level	Title	Composer	Publisher/Distributor
3-4	Tarantelle	Barrow	CPP/Belwin
	The Maid With the Flaxen Hair	Debussy/Jenkins	RBC Publications
	Carnival Petite	Cimera	Belwin
	Indispensible Folio —Forest Echo —Fox Hunt —Holiday Medley —Moonlight Serenade —Polish Dance —School Musician —Spinning Wheel —The Envoy —Valse Caprice —Whistlin' Pete	Endresen	Rubank
	Gavotte, Op. 10, No. 3	Elgar	Medici Music Press
	Conversation for Cornet	Grundman	Boosey Hawkes
	Gaelic Suite	Fitzgerald	Theodore Presser
	Aria and Allegro	Haydn/Voxman	Rubank
	Suite	Nelhybel	General Music
	Little Purcell Suite	Purcell/Dishinger	Medici Music Press
	Fanfare and Lament	Smedvig	Shawnee Press
	Concert and Contest Collection —Air Gai —Andante and Allegro —Elegie —Orientale —Premier Solo de Concours —Romance in E*b* —Sarabande and Gavota —Serenade	ed. Voxman	Rubank
5-6	May Song	Beethoven/Dishinger	Medici Music Press
	Amourette	Burke	Carl Fischer
	Medici Masterworks Vol. 1 —Ayre —The St. Catherine Rigaudon —Tambourin from Pieces de Clavecin —Courante —Gavotte —La Voltigeuse	Dishinger	Medici Music Press
	Master Solo Collection —Andantino —Menuet and Ballo —Baroque Suite —Aria —Sarabande and Gigue —Largo and Allegro —Proclamation, Serenade and Frolic —So Soft the Silver Sound and Clear	Getchell	Hal Leonard

Level	Title	Composer	Publisher/Distributor
	Concert Solo Suite	McKay	Carl Fischer
	Your Ring on My Finger	Schumann/Dishinger	Medici Music Press
	Tchaikovsky Suite No. 2	Tchaikovsky/Balasanian	Southern Music Co.
	Parable	Persichetti	
	second suite for trumpet	Presser	
	Flight of the Bumblebee	Nikolai Rimsky-Korsakov	
	Litany of Breath	David Sampson	
6	Concerto for Trumpet in E♭	Franz Josef Haydn	Boosey & Hawkes or Robert King
	Concerto for Trumpet	Johann Nepomuk Hummel	Boosey & Hawkes or Robert King
	Honnegger		
	Mendez	Raphael Mendez	
	Sonata for Trumpet	Paul Hindemith	
	Concerto	Artunian	

Trumpet Duets, Trios and Quartets

Level	Title	Composer	Publisher/Distributor
Duets			
N/A	Bach for Two Trumpets	Bach/Hering	Carl Fischer
N/A	Dialogue	Eugene Bozza	A. Leduc
N/A	12 Concert Duets	Cox-Simon	Rubank
N/A	3 Fanfares	Bernard Fitzgerald	Presser
N/A	10 Concert Duets	Anthony Plog	Western International
N/A	Contemporary Music for 2 Trumpets	Plog, ed.	Wimbledon
Trios			
1-2	Fanfare for St. Edmundsbury	Britten	Boosey Hawkes
	The Earle of Oxford's March	Byrd/Dishinger	Medici Music Press
	Six Pieces d'Audition	Defaye	A. Leduc
	Echo Waltz	Goldman	Carl Fischer
	The Three Stars	Staigers	Carl Fischer
	Suite for Three Trumpets	Tomasi	A. Leduc
3-4	Chiapanecas	arr. Mendez	Carl Fischer
	The Magic Trumpet	Burke	Carl Fischer
	Whip-Poor-Wills	VanderCook	Rubank
5-6	Hail the Conquering Hero	Handel/Milford	A. Leduc

Level	Title	Composer	Publisher/Distributor
	Three Dances	Mattheson/Voxman	Southern Music Co.
Quartets			
1-2	Jesu, Joy of Man's Desiring	Bach/Thurston	Southern Music Co.
	Scherzino	Fitzgerald	Carl Fischer
	The Rushin' Trumpeters	Gillis	Belwin
	Festival Prelude	Johnson	Belwin
3-4	Kyrie in F	Bach/Dishinger	Medici Music Press
	March and Chorale	Dillon	Boosey Hawkes
	Io Pur Respiro	Gesualdo/Dishinger	Medici Music Press
	American Panorama	McKay	Carl Fischer
	Fanfare and Allegro	Ostransky	Rubank
	Sonatina for Four Trumpets	Simpson	Carl Fischer
5-6	Quartet Repertoire	Anon.	Rubank
	Prelude	Fitzgerald	Carl Fischer
	Trumpet Symphony	Holmes arr.	Rubank
	Musette	Bach/Dishinger	Medici Music Press

Symphony Excerpts

Below is a list of pieces asked for in symphony auditions, arranged by how often they are asked for. This is a truly extensive list of tunes and it will take time for you to master them if that is your goal. Be absolutely sure to listen to as many different recordings of these pieces as you can find. You will learn something with each conductor's interpretation of the music.

Title	Composer
Brandenburg Concerto No. 2	Bach
Mass in B Minor	Bach
Concerto for Orchestra	Bartok
Leonore Overture No. 2 & 3	Beethoven
Symphonies 7, 9	Beethoven
Carmen Suite No. 1	Bizet
Outdoor Overture	Copland
Quiet City	Copland
La Mer (1st cornet part)	Debussy
Nocturnes (*fetes* mvmt.)	Debussy
An American in Paris	Gershwin
Concerto in F	Gershwin
Concerto in F	Gershwin

Title	Composer
The Messiah (The Trumpet Shall Sound)	Handel
Symphonies No. 2, 3, 5,7	Mahler
Fingal's Cave	Mendelssohn
Pictures at an Exhibition	Moussorgsky
Alborada del Gracioso	Ravel
Pines of Rome	Respighi
Scheherezade	Rimsky-Korsakov
Symphony 5	Shastakovitch
Bourgeois Gentilhomme	Strauss
Ein Heldenleben	Strauss
Symphonia Domestica	Strauss
Til Eulenspiegel	Strauss
L'Histoire du Soldat	Stravinsky
Petrouchka	Stravinsky
The Rite of Spring	Stravinsky
Requiem	Verdi
Siegfreid Idyll	Wagner
Siegfreid's Funeral Music	Wagner

Orchestral Excerpt Collections

These are usually the best way to practice auditions. The most important trumpet parts are distilled from the orchestral repertoire. The down side to this is that during a real audition, you'll have the actual part in front of you and will be asked to play *anything* from the part. Because some of these books are excerpts, the entire part isn't included and you may find yourself sight-reading. If you have an audition, it's best to get an actual part so there are no surprises.

To avoid this, get the trumpet version of the *Orchestra Musician's CD-Rom Library* below. It includes the entire part and the files are printable. By far the best resource for orchestral music. Each disc has about 90 orchestra parts.

Title	Publisher
Orchestra Musician's CD-Rom Library	http://www.orchmusiclibrary.com/

Books!

Below is a list of helpful books that may or may not be directly related to trumpet. Making music is all about awareness. The more you know, the more you understand about sound and how to buzz your lips to get that sound, the better your sound will be. Buy the books, read them, put them away, go about your practice for a few months, then read them again. I re-read many of these books, either to try and understand them better, or to refresh my memory. Some of the concepts and ideas expressed within the books will take more than one reading before they are fully understood and become part of your wisdom. Don't give up. Anything will reveal itself to you if you keep at it!

Book Title	Author (Publisher)	Concepts Addressed
Hearing and Writing Music	Ron Gorow (September Publishing) www.rongorow.com	ear training, writing music, writing what you hear, writing down musical ideas
The Art of Brass Playing	Philip Farkas	just about everything you need
The Inner Game of Music	W. Timothy Gallwey	a book designed to help musicians overcome obstacles, help improve concentration, and reduce nervousness.
Keys to Natural Performance for Brass Players	Robert D. Weast (The Brass World)	musicality, repetition, strength and endurance, awareness, warm up and much more.
Brass Playing is No Harder Than Deep Breathing	Claude Gordon, (www.claudegordonmusic.com)	a master player and teacher addresses the thing that will help your playing more than any other: breathing.
Essentials of Brass Playing	Fred Fox (Warner Bros.)	an explicit, logical approach to important basic factors that contribute to superior brass instrument performance.
Indirect Procedures: A Musician's Guite to the Alexander Technique	Pedro de Alcantara (Oxford University Press)	Alexander technique
The Whole Musician: A Multi-Sensory Guide to Practice, Performance, and Pedgogy	Susan Bruckner (Effey Street Press)	like the title says. I don't think the smell of performance, practice, etc. is covered.
The Art of Practicing: A Guide to Making Music From the Heart	Madeline Bruser (Bell Tower)	practice technique.
Playing in the Zone	Andrew Cooper (Shambala)	concentration and focus while performing
Arnold Jacobs: Song and Wind	Brian Fredriksen (Windsong Press)	the teachings of brass legend Arnold Jacobs
Zen in the Art of Archery	Eugen Herrigel (Vintage)	concentration, focus, Zen
The Augmented Encyclopedia of the Pivot System	Donald Reinhardt (Charles Colin)	classification of the Pivot system
A Soprano on Her Head	Eloise Ristad (Real People)	Reflections on performance and life

Book Title	Author (Publisher)	Concepts Addressed
Awaken the Giant Within	Anthony Robbins (Fireside)	self-confidence, mastery
Effortless Mastery: Liberating the Master Musician Within	Kenny Werner (Jamey Abersold Jazz)	self-confidence, mastery, meditation

Up Next

Believe it or not, this is not a complete list of trumpet music. Keep on the lookout for more music! If sheet music wasn't enough for you to keep track of, there are all kinds of accessories you can (and sometimes should) own. Things like microphones, metronomes, cases, gig bags, stands and recording equipment will be covered in the next chapter. There's always more *stuff* to buy, and we trumpet players are usually pretty gadget-friendly.

CHAPTER 20
GEAR TO GRIND THROUGH

The notes are in the horn. Find them.

~ Charles Mingus

In This Chapter

- Tuners
- Metronomes
- Microphones
- Recording Devices
- Cases
- Electronic Effects

Terms to Know

MM: Maelzel's Metronome, or Metronome Marking. Used to indicate tempo. MM=120 is the same as 120 beats per minute.

bpm: Beats per minute.

cent: A measurement of sound. There are 100 cents in a half step.

XLR: An audio cable used to connect microphones to audio devices. It has 3 pins and provides balanced input.

track: A distinct selection of music from a recording.

effects pedal: A device used to shape amplified sound. The effect is turned on and off via a foot pedal.

Why Do I Need More Stuff?

Some of the items in this Chapter are certainly not necessary. Keep in mind that the most important thing in this adventure of yours is making music. For that, all you need is your horn. You don't even need a case. Charlie Parker often carried his alto saxophone around in a paper bag.

That being said however, there are some big benefits with a lot of this stuff, and some of the benefits are so incredibly important and helpful that you really should get the thing. I'll let you know if an item is a "must have."

Metronome: Your Rhythmic Best Friend

This is the first gadget you absolutely must have. This tool is crucial if you want to be the best player you can be. The metronome will not only help you stay steady, but will also be a useful tool in achieving the fastest possible tempos for your exercises or performance pieces. Get one and use it early and often. You won't regret it. There are a bewildering number of varieties. Here are a few of the best ones available. Before you decide, consider getting a combination tuner/metronome. See some options for those after this section.

MM=120 means you set your metronome to 120 and it will click merrily away at 120 *beats per minute (bpm)*. The MM stands for Mazel's Metronome, or Metronome Marking.

Be sure to look for a metronome with a headphone jack. Trumpet is often loud enough to drown out the click, especially with the pendulum metronomes.

Pendulum Metronome: Metronomes don't get any more low-tech than this, and if you don't want to buy and throw away batteries, or read a user's manual, this is the metronome for you. A weight slides up and down the moving arm. The higher the weight, the slower the tempo. Metronome markings are read just above the weight position. Simple and easy to use. Just wind it up, set your tempo and go. The only down side is that this type of metronome is pretty quiet and the sound of your horn may drown it out.

Taktell mini ($30)

Boss Dr. Beat 88: Incorporates enhanced memory and beat combination functions. It memorizes tempo, beat, and rhythm level settings, performs time signatures up to 15 beats per measure, features independent slider based control of desired volumes and has a tap function so you can tap in a tempo. Has a large value dial and custom LCD for easy user interface. ($150)

Boss Dr. Beat 12: You can carry this credit card-sized metronome in your pocket! Features a mode with combined beats (2+3, 3+4, and so forth), tap tempo, tune mode with chromatic tuning and fine-pitch adjustment, timer mode with 60-minute timer in one-minute increments, stopwatch function, and headphone jack. ($60)

Yamaha Clickstation: The Yamaha Clickstation features a small, round vibrating pad that pulsates with the beat, allowing the user to feel the beat as well as hear it. It can subdivide the beat, has a volume adjustment and 86 user memory locations. A 10-key pad and jog dial helps when entering rhythm and tempo information and accessing Clickstation functions. Other features include a backlit display, MIDI-in jack, and a trigger input that allows it to be connected to a Yamaha DTX pad to start or stop the metronome. ($120)

Qwik-Time QT-3 Quartz: Features a speaker that projects clear clicks that cut through the music. More than 200 speed settings, A440 tuning tone, low-battery indicator, and an earphone jack. Measures 3-1/2" x 2-1/2". ($15)

Korg MM-2: This micro metronome slips over the ear and offers 39 tempo steps in a 40-208 BPM range. It will give you 0, 2, 3, 4, 5, 6, 7 beats per measure, and has 8th note, triplet, and 16th note settings. An easy-to-adjust volume control together with the ear pad reduce sound leakage. The ear hook fits on either ear. Includes interchangeable silver and black faceplates plus a lithium battery. ($25)

Korg MM-1 MetroGnome: If the metronome above wasn't small enough for you, here's something that will take up even less precious space in your case but will be easily misplaced.($25)

Tuners for In-tune Tunes

A tuner is the next *must-have* and if you don't have one, consider a combination metronome/tuner. You'll only need one gadget and one set of batteries.

If you want to learn exactly how in tune your horn is, you need a tuner. This device will show you exactly which notes are out of tune on your horn and how much correction each problem note needs. For more information on this, see "Out of Tune Notes on Trumpet" on page 120. Intonation problems can also be an indication of some other deficiency in your playing which need fixing. Get a tuner from your local music store and practice with it.

Korg CA-30: This is a chromatic tuner with a range from C1-C8 (lower and higher than you'll need for trumpet). A calibration function lets you specify concert pitch and it will produce a reference tone on an internal speaker. Auto power off and low energy draw means you don't have to buy batteries very often. ($19.95)

Arion UM-70: This chromatic tuner has a mode for C, F, Bb, and Eb scales (I'm assuming they're major scales). Metronome functions are suitable for a range of musical styles. Tempo and beat can be finely adjusted and rhythms are easily selected. It has an earphone jack and a clip-on pickup, something most other metronomes don't supply. ($10)

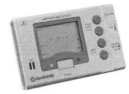

Korg MT 9000: Metronome/tuner. This gadget will subdivide the beat in many different patterns from sixteenth notes to swing, will click in meters up to 7 beats long, has an analog arm that sweeps back and forth, has volume control and an earphone jack. Tuner can be calibrated and also has an analog arm to show pitch level. It also has a jack for guitar. ($30)

Boss TU-80: This reliable tuner includes a handy, built-in metronome with 7 rhythms and 10 beats plus an animated LCD display. Has multiple features and an ultra-wide tuning range of almost 8 octaves (yeah, you wish you had an 8 octave range!). The TU-80 supports chromatic tuning. Something called the *Accu-Pitch* function sounds a tone when pitch is correct. A *Reference Tone Play* function makes it easy to verify tuning by ear, and it tunes down to 5 flats. The ultra-thin body slides easily into a guitar case, gig bag, backpack, or pocket. ($28.99)

V-SAM: This is a Virtual Strobe tuner, audio tone generator, and metronome in a fairly compact format. Strobe tuners are very accurate. I've never used this particular tuner and can't vouch for the accuracy of a "virtual strobe," but I bet it's pretty accurate. It automatically detects notes accurately to 1/1000th of a semitone. The high-output tone generator within V-SAM offers 10 octaves of audible tones, adjustable in 0.1 cent increments. Its audio/visual metronome allows tap or dial-in tempo, adjustable beats per measure, beat subdivisions, and a stopwatch function. ($249)

Microphones

Trumpet is one of the loudest acoustic instruments on the planet and most performance situations won't require you to make your horn even louder. However, if you're playing for large audiences, or are playing with a harmon mute and need a little more volume, you'll need a microphone and something to amplify the sound. In addition, if you plan on recording yourself for any reason, a microphone of some sort is a must. There are two basic types of microphones: condenser mics and dynamic mics.

Dynamic Microphone

Dynamic mics don't need a power source. The vibrations of the source (your horn) are sensed by the mic and the vibrations are turned into a signal that is sent to the sound board. Pretty simple.

Sure SM58: Legendary for its ability to withstand abuse that would destroy any other mic. World-renowned for its distinctive upper-midrange presence peak that ensures a lively sound. Perfectly fits the hand, balanced for total comfort during long gigs. Frequency response is a smooth, vocal-tailored 50Hz-15kHz, and the price is a bargain considering its life expectancy. ($100)

Condenser Microphones

Condenser mics need a power source. This usually is supplied by batteries, or what is called *phantom power*, which is a power source sent through a cord to the mic. The power is sent to the diaphragm within the mic that vibrates when sound waves are present. Because the diaphragm is powered, it reacts with much more sensitivity to sound.

Sure SM57: One of the most popular professional instrument/vocal mics of all time. This dynamic mic is reliable and natural-sounding. Durable design stands up to road travel and abuse. Perfect at home or in the studio, too. Its wide frequency response (40Hz-15kHz) and tight cardioid polar pattern are ideal for close-in miking. ($70)

Clip-on and Wireless Microphones

All of the above microphones will require a mic stand and cord. Here are a couple alternatives that do away with the microphone stand and cords as well.

LCM-77: This is the microphone developed in close association with Miles Davis and allows space between the bell and the mic so you can fit a mute in the horn easily. This mic is used and endorsed by Chris Botti, who, in addition to his own recordings, performs and records with Sting.

Applied Microphone Technology Roam 1: If you want to do without wires altogether, this is a great option. Not only is it wireless, but the mic is in a shock mount to avoid the noise you make when pounding down your valves. And as you can see, there's still room for a mute. ($580)

Microphone Stands, Cords, and Adapters

A regular mic won't do you much good without the cord that goes with it or a stand to hold it. So here are all those little details. In addition, you may need an adapter to convert an XLR cord used by most microphones to 1/4" which is useful if the mic is to be run into an amp, a sound board, or a recording device which doesn't have XLR inputs.

Here is a close-up of the XLR-type attachment used in microphone cords. The female end goes to the microphone and the male end connects to the sound amplification/recording device. To the right is a Planet Waves adapter that will convert the male end of an XLR mic cord to a 1/4" jack, like the size used in guitar amplifiers. I use one of these to convert XLR to 1/4" so I can mic my harmon-muted trumpet and send it through a small amp.

To the right is a picture of a basic mic stand and a boom mic stand to which you attach your mic and its cord. Though the boom stand is nice and a little more versatile, the basic stand is really all you'll need, and it has a smaller footprint so people will be less likely to trip over it. When playing into a mic, be sure to set it at a height which allows you to maintain good posture. If you've got the money, you may want to get a clip-on mic that clips to your bell so you can avoid a mic stand altogether.

If you get a small recording device, often they use 1/8" mic inputs, so you may need another adapter, from 1/4" to 1/8", like the one shown here made by Planet Waves.

Recording Devices

One of the best ways to improve all aspects of your playing is to record yourself and listen to what you're working on. The recording machine tells no lies. You have a few options for recording devices and there are advantages and disadvantages to each.

Cassette Recorder

The major benefit of using a tape recorder is that they're cheap and pretty easy to find. Cassette tapes are also cheap and easy to find. The down side to these devices is that the sound quality may not be great and finding a passage you recorded earlier can be difficult. Shown here is a Sony TCM929 which sells for about $25. Visit a few garage sales and you'll probably find something much cheaper which may work just as well.

Mini Disc Recorder

Sony HI MD: This amazingly tiny device will hold up to 45 *hours* of recorded music as well as pictures and text and it's also an FM/AM/TV/Weatherband receiver. Its batter will last up to 14 hours. These are great little devices. If you're serious about your music, consider getting one. I've got one and will never go back to a tape recorder. The greatest thing about these little gadgets is that you can advance to a track quickly and easily. Trying to search through a cassette tape for a particular recording can drive you bug-nuts. ($250)

Multi-Track Recorder

Korg Pandora PXR4: But why stop there? For another fifty bucks you can get a device that will allow you record multiple *tracks*. This means you can record the first trumpet part of a quartet, then go back and do the second, third and fourth parts as well. Put it all together, hit play and you're playing a quartet with yourself. These are also great for writing songs and figuring out harmony parts. There is also a function which lets you slow down a recording so you can learn a particularly tricky or fast lick from a tune you're trying to transcribe. A fun little device that will entertain you for hours and hours. ($300)

Online Free Recording

Audacity: If you've got a computer and an internet connection, forget all of the recording options above and go get the Audacity program. It's a *fantastic* recording program that does much much more than record audio. You can use it to slow down recordings (mp3 or other formats), and a whole slew of other options. I've got several tutorials on my YouTube channel which, by the way, also has a bunch of trumpet video lessons for you to peruse. If you have a computer, get Audacity! ($FREE)

Cases

There are a whole lot of ways to put dings in your horn and almost as many ways to protect it. Here are some of your case options. If your horn didn't come with a case, you'll probably want one. If you aren't satisfied with the case you have because it's too heavy, too small, or not cool enough, here are some options for you.

The Torpedo Bag: this case will withstand 400 pounds of pressure and can be worn like a backpack. Its design makes it low-profile and easy to store in the overhead compartment of an airplane or just about anywhere else. Also available is a bag for mutes, or a music pouch, both of which will strap to the case and are easily detachable. This is a great little case that is very sturdy. ($160)

BAM Trekker Backpack Case: A high-end backpack case with waterproof cover. Comfortable backpack straps tucked into the case for convenience and a shoulder strap with pad. Has an expandable sheet music pocket, an accessory pocket and an additional waterproof polyamid cover for heavy rain. ($320)

Gator Lightweight Case: If you want a lighter case, but don't want to risk the lesser protection of a gig bag, this is the case for you. They're constructed from dense foam and the exterior is covered in heavy nylon fabric. To insure your instrument doesn't get scratched, the interior is covered in soft plush. The cases have external pockets for gear, shoulder straps with D rings, and detachable external elastic straps for carrying jackets or a music stand. ($40)

Gig Backpack: The modern Cordura-style exterior and high-density foam interior protect your instrument. Backpack straps adjust to any body size. Roomy compartments hold your accessories. This case is a free-standing design with a rigid bottom insert. Four different colors. ($50)

Reunion Blues Gig Bag: an excellent, sturdy gig bag made of leather with a shoulder strap and outer pocket for accessories. I used one of these for many, many years until I bought another horn that wouldn't fit the bag. An excellent case. ($125)

Wolfpack Quad Case: When you have a C, D, B♭ and piccolo trumpet to take to the gig, you'll want a multi-horn case. The one to the right holds 4 trumpets, but there are others for two trumpets, trumpet and flügelhorn, and three-horn bags. I haven't seen one that will hold five trumpets but it wouldn't surprise me if one is out there somewhere.

Electronic Effects

Miles Davis began experimenting with electronic effects for his trumpet sound in the sixties. There are so many different effects that there isn't enough space to list them all here, but I'll give you a few of the more interesting and/or useful ones.

In order to use these effects, your trumpet sound must be amplified through a sound system. To modify the trumpet sound, these devices (called *effects pedals*) are put between the microphone and the amplifier. They can be turned on and off with the tap of a foot. Guitar players use these gadgets all the time, but who says they should have all the fun?

For the most part, all the pedals look the same except for the color. They are all adjustable to control how much of the effect you want to use, and some have equalizers built in. They range from $50-$200 depending on the brand and the effect you want. To the right is a sample pedal made by Ibanez.

Pre-Amp: this isn't an effect, but is a way to gain more control over your amplified sound. The line from your microphone goes to this little box (usually clipped to your belt or stand) and then from the pre-amp to the house sound system. It's good to do this for a couple reasons. Imagine you just played a tune with open horn, no mutes. The next tune uses a harmon mute and you need a boost of power to make that harmon sound louder. With a pre-amp clipped to your pants, you can just twist a little dial. Otherwise, if you even have a sound technician, they have to boost your power and probably will either forget about you or do it incorrectly.

Reverb: This can be one of the most useful effects, especially if you're playing in an acoustically "dead" room. The sound is muffled, absorbed by walls, carpet, draperies, people, or any other sound-gobbling substance. Reverb is used to simulate the acoustical effect of rooms and enclosed buildings. In a room, for instance, sound is reflected off the ceiling, walls and the floor. The sound heard at any given time is the sum of the sound from the source as well as the reflected sound. Reverb adds a slight echo to the sound and can make the sound more "live." Settings can be changed to fit the room you're in or the sound you want.

Chorus: The chorus effect gives the impression that more than one instrument or voice playing. It got its name because it makes the recording of a vocal track sound like it was sung by two or more people singing in chorus. This is done by adding a delayed signal (echo) to the original input. The delay of this echo is varied continuously between a minimum delay and maximum delay at a certain rate.

Flange: The flange effect is like the chorus effect on steroids. Flanging also uses an echo of the original input to get its sound, but it's a little more dramatic than the chorus effect. It has a swirling, whooshing, pulsating sound that is pretty cool. Before the digital effect was invented, flanging was created by sound engineers who put their finger onto the tape reel's flange, thus slowing it down. Two identical recordings are played back simultaneously, and one is slowed down slightly to give the flanging effect.

Distortion: this pedal will add signal noise to your sound, not something that many trumpet players have messed around with to my knowledge, but it might be fun. Guitars use this effect a lot, especially the harder edged, heavier rock and rollers and metal heads. A powerful effect.

Wah Wah Pedal (parameteric equalization): This is an interesting effect you've probably heard. Guitars use the wah-wah pedal to make the guitar "talk" and it's a cool, funky sound. I've experimented a little with one of these and it's a pretty fun device. Instead of spending a hundred and ten bucks, you can get this same effect from a Harmon mute with the stem in or a plunger.

Boomerang 4MB Phrase Sampler: This cool device allows you to layer parts in forward or reverse, create loops up to 4 minutes long, and play reverse leads. Features 2 independent loops, each with 7 decay rates (including no decay). It will transpose your sound down a 2nd, 4th, 5th, 7th, and an octave. It's got a foot roller volume control and the record button can be turned on or off during playback. ($430)

Up Next

You don't need any of these gadgets to get out there and play music for people. In fact, all this stuff might just get in the way of your progress because you spend all your time reading manuals, looking for the right cord, or the batteries of your tuner just went out, or who knows what.

Though there are many players in the world who play only for their own enjoyment, there is something special about going out and sharing your music with others. It's fun, challenging and rewarding. Getting out there to play for people can be intimidating, but there are ways around all these challenges. Learn about what you need to do to perform in the next chapter.

Chapter 21
The Practice of Performance

The struggle is not with the instrument, it is with ourselves.

~ Vincent Cichowicz, trumpet master and teacher

In This Chapter

- Why Perform?
- Performance Anxiety
- Combatting Performance Anxiety
- Preparing for Performance
- Stage Craft 101
- Finding Performance Venues

Terms to Know

open mic (pronounced "mike" as in microphone): A venue where amateur musicians can get up and play for an audience. Often professionals use this venue to try out new songs.

busking: Playing in the street (or anywhere) for tips. Leave your case open and folks will put money in it.

seed change: Money you put in your case or tip jar to show people that they can (and should) give you money for playing.

set list: The list of tunes in the order you'll play them for the gig.

yogic breathing: A breathing technique of yoga used to calm the body and mind. Especially useful before a gig.

Why Perform?

Louis Armstrong, one of the godfathers of modern popular music and unrivaled innovator of trumpet once said, "... the music ain't worth nothin' if you can't lay it on the public." Music is meant to be shared. Music is a great and beautiful thing that can bring a group of strangers together in ways that doesn't compare to anything else in life.

Once you've experienced the thrill of getting up before an audience and *nailing* a performance, you'll always want more. When you practice a song and get it into your soul, performing can become a mystical experience, and for some an ecstatic trance. I've talked with musicians who experience a sort of out-of-body state when the playing is especially good, and this feel translates to the audience. Music is magic.

I doubt there is anyone on the planet who truly wants less music in their life. We have a need for music, which for some of us is a true hunger. Get out there and play for the people! We all need more live music in our life whether we realize it or not.

All that hippy-dippy stuff aside (don't snicker—it's important hippy-dippy stuff), performing is a great way to face and conquer fears, to take your playing to the next level, to entertain people, to make friends, and a whole slew of other things.

Let's take a look at some practical concerns that can get in the way of that great performance. The first of these, and something a lot of us suffer from, is performance anxiety. You know, that tightening of the shoulders, the queasy stomach, shallow breathing, sweat, and an allegro heartbeat. I've been playing a long time and still get nervous before I play. With practice, a case of nerves is easy to deal with and you can even harness all that nervous energy to give your performances more zing.

Performance Anxiety

Most of us get nervous before we play. It's a normal reaction, but let's look at some causes of all these butterflies. A few possibilities are:

- **Fear of Failure**: None of us wants to fail. We attach a lot of our self-worth to succeeding and it's the *attachment* to success as self-worth that makes failure so scary. In some ways this attachment is good because it helps to push us towards Mastery. But too much attachment to success can really get in the way. You can still want success but not be attached to it. Adopt this mantra: "Your opinion of me is none of my business." Focus on the music and all will be well.

- **Limited Performing Experience**: If you're new to this, performing can be scary and nerve-wracking simply because it's unfamiliar. Why is everybody staring at me!? Being under a microscope and in the spotlight is a strange place to be and it takes time to get used to it. You won't get used to it just by thinking about it, though that will help some. You've got to get up there! I recently adjudicated a high school solo/ensemble festival and of all the brass players that played, only one or two had *ever* performed their prepared piece before the festival. The more you play for people, the easier it will be to get up there, even if your nervousness never goes away. Just do it!

- **Music is Not Sufficiently Learned**: This one is entirely preventable. Be sure you prepare beyond what you think you need for a performance. When you perform under scrutiny, often the performance you give will be under the level you can play alone in the practice room. The greater level of stress is the culprit. Many musicians over-prepare as a way of compensating for this.

- **Size of the Crowd**: Sometimes the size of crowd can be intimidating. This can mean different things for everyone. If you rarely play in front of people, six might seem like a crowd. If you've had more experience, the number rises, and for some reason the more people, the more nervous we can get. Don't think of it as 500 people hearing your music, but as one person hearing your music (500 times).

- **Members of Crowd**: Say Wynton Marsalis, Brian Lynch, Charlie Schlueter, and Bud Herseth are in the audience listening. God help you. It doesn't have to be Master musicians in the audience that get you all worked up. It could be your boyfriend in the audience, or the cool girl you've seen around and want to meet, or it could be your parents coming to hear you perform, or that record company executive carrying a multi-million-dollar contract in her briefcase for you to sign if she likes your playing. Don't focus on the audience members, focus on making the best music you can. The audience members can take care of themselves just fine. It's the music that needs your attention the most.

- **Not Wanting to Be a Show-off**: What? Isn't that a contradiction? A shy trumpet player? Yes, there are actually trumpet players out there who are shy, and you just might be one of them. Getting up to play trumpet is not something shy people will be very comfortable with. I can say this with authority because I'm one of them. Tell yourself it's okay to show off a little. You might even like it. Better yet, make it about the music and not about showing off. Get on up there and face your fears! Cultivate a sense of bold humility.

Combatting Performance Anxiety

Look at the above list and find the one and only item that you can practice in the practice room. What is it? The only thing you really have immediate control over is preparing the music you are to perform. This doesn't mean just getting the notes to come out your bell. It means you must find a way to connect emotionally with the music. It also means listening to the piece performed by as many players as you can, either live or on recordings. It means you have to record yourself (video and audio) and be very critical of what you see and hear so you can fix those things that need fixing. It means performing the piece several times for smaller audiences before the major performance. It means over-preparing the music so that when you get on up there you *know* without a doubt that you've got all the preparation you need and then some. This will help your confidence more than anything else you can do. Practice smart. As for the other aspects of performance anxiety, there are many techniques that will help minimize your nervousness.

Realistic Expectation and Repertoire Choice

Set a realistic expectation when choosing what to perform. Be sure your choice of music is within your ability to perform well. This includes the amount of time you have to practice the music before the performance date. If you only have a month or two, don't choose a major piece like the Hummel or Haydn Trumpet Concerto. You need time to learn the music and additional time to live with it before the performance.

Practice Performing

This one is often skipped. If you're preparing a piece for an important audition or festival, it's *crucial* that you get up to play it for people long before the day of the festival/audition arrives. The playing of a piece in the practice room and the playing of a piece for an audience, even an audience of one, are two *very* different experiences. If you have limited performing experience, performance practice is even more important. Your concentration will probably not be at its peak if you're not used to playing for an audience.

This doesn't mean you have to rent out Carnegie Hall and sell tickets. Play for your loved ones, play for your friends, stand up and play in your band class, go out on the street corner and blow your horn at passing traffic, stand on a rooftop and play for the pigeons, go play at a local coffee shop, or play at your school during lunch. These are only a few options. Think up some more. The point is to get out there and do it. It's best if you can perform in the space where your big performance will be taking place. Get yourself used to being in the spotlight and you'll be much more comfortable when that important performance comes around.

Focus on the Now

If you stay in the present you'll eliminate much of the anxiety available to you. Stay in the present and focus on what you're performing. Avoid thinking of the difficult passage coming up, or the little mistake that just went by. Charles Schlueter said, "There is no anxiety in the present. Anxiety is either in the past, worrying about what was just played, or in the future, worrying about what you are about to play." Stay in the moment. Focus on the music you are making right *now*.

Avoid Inner Dialogue and Replace Negative Thoughts

Inner dialogue is your monkey mind chattering on about unimportant things, and this distracts you from making beautiful music. Immerse yourself in the music and strive to turn off that inner voice. If the voice won't shut up, simply ignore it and focus on your breathing. Just like with annoying people, the voice will stop if you ignore it long enough. Meditation also helps quiet the mind.

Negative thoughts often go right along with that inner dialogue. Negative thoughts will suck the juice right out of you. On the other hand, positive thoughts will juice you up, and be a positive influence on your playing and maybe even your life. Practice replacing negative thoughts with positive ones whenever you play music, or whenever you have *any* negative thoughts. Your life will change.

Anxiety and Breathing

When we're anxious or nervous our breathing changes. We often tend to breathe more shallowly and less often when we're very nervous. In a performance situation or any nerve-wracking situation, this type of breathing doesn't help us relax at all. There is a relatively easy way to combat this through controlled breathing.

Normally you breathe about 15 times per minute. If you slow down your breathing to an easy six breaths per minute, you'll get total relaxation of the body. A relaxed body means a relaxed mind. Six breaths per minute is an easy a five-second inhale and a five-second exhale. For the inhale, your lungs should be as full as they can comfortably be by the time the five second point is reached. *Without stopping the flow* immediately reverse direction for the exhale and by the five-second mark, your lungs should be as empty as is comfortable.

Sit in a relaxed position and try this type of breathing for five minutes. It sounds easy enough, doesn't it? Try to stick with it for the entire five minutes. You may be surprised to discover how difficult this actually is to do. Take the time to relax. It will help not only your playing, but will improve your life, too. Do it as a warm-up routine in addition to before a performance. You'll get a better practice session if you do.

Once you've mastered six breaths per minute, stretch the time longer for each breath. Shoot for one breath per minute; a thirty-second inhale and a thirty-second exhale. Feel yourself relax.

Another variation which will deepen relaxation further is to make the exhale longer than the inhale. A five-second inhale and a ten-second exhale is a good place to start. This will stimulate your parasympathetic nervous system and will slow down internal functions like heartbeat. Try it.

These exercises are great any time but are especially effective if practiced regularly. Use this breathing technique for five or ten minutes before your performance and you'll feel more relaxed and in control. Of course, you can't control your breath in this way all the time, but you'll find that as you practice these techniques, your breathing will be slower even when you're not paying attention to the breath.

Progressive Muscle Relaxation

This is a technique developed in 1939 by Edmund Jacobson and involves tensing muscles, then relaxing them and becoming aware of the sensation of relaxation. It's easy to do. Inhale and squeeze the particular group of muscles as hard as you can for about ten seconds, then exhale as you relax and let the tension ease out of the muscles. Stay relaxed for about 20 seconds before moving on to the next muscle group. After a while you'll be able to recognize and relax any muscles in your body which are tense.

Here are the muscle groups you should work through. Start with your feet and work up to the crown of your head.

1 right foot	6 entire left leg and foot	11 left forearm and hand
2 right lower leg and foot	7 right hand	12 entire left arm
3 entire right leg and foot	8 right forearm and hand	13 abdomen
4 left foot	9 entire right arm	14 chest
5 left lower leg and foot	10 left hand	15 neck and shoulders
		16 face and scalp

The Alexander Technique

The Alexander Technique is used by actors, musicians, and athletes around the world to improve their performance. The Alexander Technique was developed by the Shakespearean actor F. M. Alexander in the late 1800s. Alexander experienced voice loss which threatened his acting career. He studied the reasons behind the loss of his voice and eventually discovered that a slight change of his head and neck position solved his problem. This lead to even more study of head and neck position which has created the Alexander Technique as we know it today.

Incorrect head position creates an imbalance in your body which your muscles will automatically correct. This leads to unnecessary tension, and that tension will come out in your sound. Excess tension will negatively affect your range, speed, and endurance. The Alexander Technique is one way to avoid this excess tension. You can probably find a teacher in your area. Look in the yellow pages or ask musicians, actors and athletes in your area. Studying with an Alexander Method teacher is a great investment if you're serious about improving your playing.

There is No Such Thing as a Wrong Note

Miles Davis said, "Do not fear mistakes. There are none."

Barney McClure is a wonderful jazz pianist and author of an excellent book on improvising called *There is No Such Thing as a Wrong Note: I was only trying something*. The title of the book says it all. When you're performing, especially when you're improvising, there is no such thing as an incorrect note. But here's where it gets tricky. If you're performing a solo and hit a note that you "think" is a wrong note, the audience will perceive it that way also, especially if you make a nasty face when you hit the "wrong" note. However, if you play the same note with intent, or if you hit the note unintentionally and *embrace* its dissonance, the audience will also embrace the note. This is a concept that is strange but true.

A friend told me a story about going to hear Dizzy Gillespie play. Dizzy made his entrance for a solo and hit a "wrong" note. Instead of backing off and avoiding that note, he built his entire solo around that "wrong" note and by the end of the solo, that "wrong" note was the coolest one he could've played. I seriously wonder if the note was actually a mistake. Knowing Dizzy's ability and incredible knowledge, it wouldn't surprise me if that "wrong" note was the one he intended to play all along.

Those who perform classical music in which it's important to play precisely what's on the page may argue that *no such thing as a wrong note* doesn't apply to them. They are right in that there is a difference between improvisation and performing another composer's ideas. What is important is that the performer is involved in the music and doesn't let incidental, insignificant mistakes mar the intent and emotional spirit of the music.

Don't get me wrong. You should be ever-vigilant and continually strive for perfection even if you may never reach it. In Count Basie's band, Lester Young used to keep a little bell on his stand and when someone played a wrong note he'd ring the bell and Jo Jones would sometimes echo it on the rod of his cymbal stand.

Strive for perfection but don't let any *kacks* or *clams* distract you from making beautiful music. Once you perceive a mistake, it's already in the past and that's where it needs to stay. You don't need to drag that mistake back into the present and brood about it. It won't do anybody any good. Let the mistakes go and focus on the music.

How to Prepare for a Performance

Preparing correctly for a performance can make all the difference not only in the performance itself, but in how you feel going into it, during it, and after it. Aside from the usual things like knowing the music you'll be playing, there are a few things to keep in mind which may help.

Practice, Practice, Practice, Listen, Listen, Listen

Yeah, I know it's obvious, but it's got to be said. Be sure your music is prepared and polished at *least* two weeks before the big day. If you have a couple weeks between the completion of your study and the major performance, you can use that time to relax and be confident about your preparation and to practice performing. If you're still practicing the day or even the week before a big performance, it may be too late. Do your work early so it has time to take hold in your little gray cells, and in your soul.

I've seen many students at important solo/ensemble festivals perform their pieces and it's quite obvious they have *never* listened to the piece before, even something as ubiquitous as the Haydn or Hummel trumpet concerto. Part of your practice regime should include listening; not only listening to the piece you're working on, but listening to trumpet players playing other music, too. These sounds and techniques for shaping melody will get into your blood and your heart if you listen, and this will come out in your music. For suggestions, see "Some Listening Tips" on page 17.

Stage Craft 101

If you're not used to getting up in front of people there are a few things to keep in mind to make your performance more polished and professional. Getting up to play music involves more than simply blowing your notes and then sitting back down. When you perform, you enter a relationship with the audience and it's up to you to shape and nurture that relationship. If you take care of this important aspect of your performance, your audience will like you no matter what comes out the end of your horn. Well, if you *really* kack it up, you'll have to be very charming and/or funny for your audience to love you, but you get the point, right?

Set Up Early

Until you get that big-time recording contract complete with *roadies* (people who cart your sound equipment around), you'll be setting up your own stands, mutes, microphones and sound equipment. Most musicians function best when relaxed. You'll be much more relaxed if you arrive to your gig early, set up all your equipment, then take fifteen or twenty minutes to relax, warm up, have a glass of juice and a snack or just sit and whistle. If you feel rushed or flustered, your music will reflect this. Some venues have their own sound equipment and sound technician. Check beforehand so you don't haul all your heavy gear for nothing.

Look Sharp, not Flat

Your appearance has an immediate impact on your audience and tells them how much you care about being up there. Well, really, it means how much you care about how you *look* when you're up there, which is pretty close to the same thing. There is a reason lawyers tell their clients to dress nicely when they go to court. It makes a better impression.

Jazz musicians have a tradition of looking sharp as a razor, dressed to the nines. Classical musicians usually wear a tuxedo or at least all black and shiny shoes. There are certainly exceptions to this general rule and it's truly the music that is most important, but looking great doesn't hurt any and it's fun to get all decked out. Even if it means wearing a tie.

I detest ties and will not wear one if there is any way I can escape the noose. You don't have to wear a tie to look great, but some performing situations demand it. When you *do* wear a tie to perform, be sure it's loose enough that it doesn't constrict your throat because your breathing is more important than your suave good looks.

You're On the Air!

From the minute you step out into view, you're the center of attention. It sounds strange, but try not to forget this. Don't pick your nose, scratch your butt, pace around, or any other of those fidgety things you might do when you're nervous. Before you step into the light, breathe deeply, shrug your shoulders a few times, maybe stretch a little to relieve tension, then get on out there and look confident even if you feel like a bug under a microscope.

Talk to the Audience

Yes, that's right, talk to the audience. Be sure to look everyone in the eye, welcome them, tell them who you are and why you're there. Thank them for coming to listen to you, introduce any band members or accompanists that may be playing with you, and tell the audience what you're going to play. Interaction with the audience is very important and will have an effect on how your performance is perceived.

You don't have to do this right away. Sometimes it's more effective to come out and burn through a few tunes before you say anything. After all, they're coming to hear you play, not speak. Use your judgement.

Do your research about the pieces you'll be playing. Most pieces of music have stories behind them, either directly relating to the piece itself or perhaps to the composer, or some musical luminary who has performed the piece in the past. If it's a good story, tell it. But don't tell too many.

You don't want to over-do the talking thing because too much talking might annoy the audience. They're sitting there looking at you because they want to hear music. There are exceptions, however. I've been to several Leo Kottke concerts and he often talks for several minutes, telling some hilarious story or other, and that kind of talking is actually part of his performance which his fans have come to expect. It's up to you.

Acknowledge the Audience

When you finish your piece and the audience claps, look them all in the eye and say, "Thank you," nod, or take a little bow. It's important and your audience will feel slightly robbed if you don't thank them for their applause. And it should be a genuine thank you. After all, without an audience, you wouldn't be up there getting paid (possibly) to make sound. Show your appreciation for the audience's appreciation.

There are musicians who are exceptions to this rule. Miles Davis is the first who comes to mind. To combat his shyness, he affected an air of disdain, even contempt, for the audience, and rarely spoke, especially after throat surgery made his voice soft and scratchy. But remember, this is Miles we're talking about. If *you* are that good, your music will speak for itself too, but it won't hurt you any to be friendly.

Even Miles' treatment of the audience was an interaction, and however abusive it may have sometimes been, he was acknowledging the audience in his own weird way. Above all, you should be true to yourself, you should be real. Fake and smarmy words aren't appreciated by anybody.

Thank the audience for their attention and they'll be happier no matter what you played.

Tip Jar

People truly appreciate live music, no matter where it is you're performing. Even if you're a beginner and struggling with the instrument, people appreciate your struggle and your bravery in getting up there to play in public. They will give you money if there is a place to put it. This is why you should put out a tip jar when you play.

When you put the tip jar up, you must also put in some *seed change*. This is some coins and a dollar or two of your own that you put in the jar or your open case to show people that it's okay to give you money and that others already have done so (even if it's you who did it).

Know What You're Going to Do

This seems like common sense, but I've seen a lot of performances (and been part of a few) in which the leader doesn't have a set list and the band or accompanist doesn't know what is to be played next. When this happens there is a lot of shuffling of papers, and you'll often hear, "I don't know, what do *you* want to play?" and the whole time the audience sits there twiddling their collective thumbs as they try not to be embarrassed for you.

Make a *set list* if you have more than two or three songs to play and be sure everyone organizes their music in that order. If you take this simple precaution, things will flow much more smoothly onstage and you'll look like the professional you are.

If you're playing with an accompanist, rehearse how you'll walk on and off stage, practice introducing yourself and your accompanist, and don't forget to practice the bow. Be sure to acknowledge your accompanist when your piece is over. Practice how you'll exit the stage. People notice such things and you should, too.

Have Fun!

Sometimes in our quest to make the greatest music we are able to make it's easy to forget this important aspect of performance. There is a reason it's called *playing* music. An audience likes to see someone having a great time. Even if the music isn't really hot, if the musicians are obviously enjoying themselves the audience will, too. And really, music should be a fun and joyous thing. You can be deadly serious about your music and still have a great time. You might find that the more fun you're having, the better the music is. Give it a try!

Find Performance Venues

If you've been pursuing live music to listen to in your area, you probably already know where people play. If you haven't, get yourself out there and listen to what music others are creating. What are you waiting for?

Whether or not you want to get paid will affect your choices. If you're new to performing, open mics are your best option for playing with a supportive and encouraging audience. Find the open mics near you. Unless you live in a *very* small community, there is probably an open mic in your area. If there isn't, why don't you start one?

If you live in the right climate and community, you can always play in the street for tips. This is called *busking*. In the New York City subway there are busking musicians of all colors and styles. A woman playing gorgeously on violin had a good amount of money in her case and was sawing away when a commuter stopped to talk to her. "Your sound and technique are *so* beautiful," the commuter said, "you should be playing professionally." The violinist smiled and said, "I'm a member of the New

York Symphony. This is where I practice," and went back to playing. Busking is a great way to get paid for your practice time.

The style of music you play will also determine your performing options. Folks at the local pub might not want to hear the entire Hummel trumpet concerto (or any classical music), but then again, you never know. It doesn't hurt to ask. Classical music venues you might look into are cafes, art galleries and museums. Many cities have monthly art walks which are well-attended.

In high school in rural Alaska I was a member of a brass quartet. We worked up a few sets of material and got a gig playing during the summer at one of the local stores. For two or three hours of playing, each of us got twenty-five bucks. Pretty good cash for a high school kid back then. Getting paid to play music is like receiving a wonderful gift. Keep an eye out for likely stores in your area and maybe you can strike up a deal with the owner or manager. People love live music and it's a great feeling to share it.

If you're in a small jazz combo or maybe a bluegrass group, you can look into the above options as well as bars and lounges. If you're not of an appropriate age to play such places, often you can get a special waiver to play music or you can have a guardian with you. The only drag about playing such venues is that many of them are smoking establishments, and not only does this make your clothes and hair smell bad, it's not very good for your lungs either. Look for smoke-free venues.

Playing for people will take your music to greater heights and will help you focus like nothing else will. Get on up there and blow it!

Sources for Further Study

Book/Article Title	Author (Publisher)
Effortless Mastery: Liberating the Master Musician Within	Kenny Werner (Jamey Abersold Jazz)
Musical Performance: Learning Theory and Pedagogy	Daniel Kohut (Prentice Hall)
Performance Power	Irmtraud Tarr Krüger (Summit Books)
Performing Your Best: A Guide to Psychological Skills for Achievers	Tom Kubistant (Life Enhancement)
The C Zone: Peak Performance Under Pressure	Robert Kriegel and Marilyn Harris Kriegel (Anchor/ Doubleday)
The Inner Game of Music	Barry Green (Doubleday)
The Alexander Technique: How to Use Your Body Without Stress	Wilfred Barlow (Healing Arts Press)
Indirect Procedures: A Musician's Guide to the Alexander Technique	Pedro de Alcantara (Oxford University Press)
Psycho-Psybernetics	Maxwell Maltz (Pocket)
Maximum Performance	L. Morehouse and L. Gross (Magilla, Inc.)

Up Next

The next chapter is all about trumpet stars of the past and present. The musicians I chose to include are Trumpet players of great artistry and vision who have contributed to our musical heritage in some significant way. You should know the names and sounds of the players who have come before you. They are also your teachers whether you know it or not.

CHAPTER 22

TRUMPET ALL-STARS

Be humble, for the worst thing in the world is of the same stuff as you.
Be confident, for the stars are of the same stuff as you.

~ Nicholai Velimirovic

In This Chapter

- Cornet Masters
- Orchestral Masters
- Classical Solo Masters
- Jazz Masters
- Present-day Luminaries

Terms to Know

All the "terms" you should really know in this chapter are actually names. In here you'll find the most fantastic trumpet players who have ever lived. Check them out on:

pandora.com: On this site you can listen for free and create "stations" that play similar songs. A great way to discover new music and musicians.

last.fm: another "radio station" on the net. You can find music in all different styles. Great site.

accujazz.com: A site devoted to jazz music. Superbly organized.

The Best of the Best

In this chapter you may find all the teachers you need. One of the very best ways to educate yourself is to listen, listen, listen, and then listen some more. With the exception of many of the early Masters, all of these players have laid down a lot of tracks on a lot of albums. Buy them, listen to them, learn the music if you like it. Play with your favorite recordings no matter what style or what instruments are used.

The trumpet players in this chapter will be broken down by styles and also by instrument. Choosing which players to include was difficult, and in order to keep this chapter shorter than it threatens to be, I've included only the most well-known or most deserving (in my opinion of course) players. My humblest apologies to you if I've left out one of your favorite players. Let me know who he or she is. It could be I don't know of them and I always love discovering a new player's approach to music. I'd appreciate it if you'd E-mail me information from www.sol-ut.com.

The Cornet Masters of Band Music

In the late 1800s and early 1900s, bands like John Phillip Sousa's were incredibly popular. They specialized in concert marches but played a wide variety of other light classical and original music. Remember there were no radio broadcasts until after 1920 and at the time only relatively wealthy people had record players.

The primary instrument at the time was the cornet and there were many virtuosi. Here are a few in rough chronological order.

Jean Baptiste Arban (1825-1899)

Yes, this is the J.B. Arban who wrote the Arban book, the "bible" for trumpet players around the world. Nobody alive today has heard Mr. Arban, because he was born in France in 1825, and after what must have been a whole lot of practice, he had a great career as a cornet soloist. Then he became a professor at the Paris Conservatory at age 32. Three years later he produced his "Cornet Method," the standard text for all brass players from cornet to tuba for the next 144 years, and it's a good bet the book will be used for a long time to come. If you don't have one, go get one.

Herbert L. Clarke (1867-1945)

Mr. Clarke was born in Massachusetts and is the author of the excellent book *Technical Studies*, which you should own. Clarke was the greatest cornet player of the early 20th century and possibly the most famous that ever played. He got that fame from his position as the cornet soloist for John Philip Sousa's band. A few recordings exist of Clark playing solos like his composition "Shores of the Mighty Pacific" and "Bride of the Waves." Even though the earliest of these recordings dates to 1904 and are of poor quality, you'll hear a player of masterful virtuosity, technique and artistry.

James Shepherd

Shepherd was the principal cornet player for the brass band Black Dyke and had great tone and flawless technique. It has been said that Shepherd revolutionized the art of cornet playing and serves as a bridge between the great players of the post war period and the modern superstars of today. Listen to him play with Black Dyke on their album *High Peak*. Shepherd also recorded with his own group Versatile Brass and produced definitive versions of the classic cornet solos *Cleopatra* and *Pandora*. Look for him. Listen to him!

Wynton Marsalis (1961-)

I'll say more about Wynton under the Jazz trumpet heading. The reason he's here under cornet players is that when he chooses to pick up the cornet, the results are amazing. Get a copy of his album *Carnival* and you will understand. A Master, undoubtedly.

Orchestral Trumpet Masters

These are the men and women few people outside the trumpet world are aware of. There are some incredible players in the orchestral tradition and there are hundreds of great recordings available of these people making music. Here are just a few. Also check out Philip Smith (NY Philharmonic), Craig Morris (Chicago Symphony), Glen Fischthal (San Francisco Symphony), Michael Sachs (Cleveland Orchestra), Paul Beniston (London Philharmonic), and Steven Hendrickson (National Symphony)

Adolph "Bud" Herseth (1921-)

Undoubtedly the orchestral trumpet player's trumpeter. His reign at the helm of the Chicago Symphony trumpet section is legendary and long. He played with the Chicago Symphony for 53 years! He retired in 2001 at age 80.

Herseth got his first trumpet at age seven from his dad who was a band teacher and got to play in the local town band when he was 8, a concert that turned him on to music. Part of Herseth's success is his ability to project emotion and story with any music he plays. He has often demonstrated this by playing a passage with no particular concept in mind and though the notes were flawless, the music was lifeless. He would then play the same passage again but with a story or an image or an emotion in mind and the music came alive.

Musicians who influenced Herseth are varied and range from trumpeters like Louis Davidson, Harry Glantz, Maurice Andrè and Maynard Ferguson, to vocalists like Swedish tenor Jussli Bjoerling and Frank Sinatra.

If you're interested in playing orchestral music you must listen to Mr. Herseth. Get just about any recording done by the Chicago Symphony before 2001 and you'll hear him. Be sure to choose music that has trumpet parts.

Roger Voisin

Roger Voisin began studying trumpet with his father, Boston Symphony Orchestra trumpeter René Voisin. Roger himself joined the Boston Symphony at the age of 17 and became principal trumpet in 1952. In 1950, he was named chair of the New England Conservatory brass and percussion department and remained at the Conservatory as its principal trumpet teacher for nearly 30 years. Mr. Voisin remains an active voice at the Boston Symphony and is on the faculty of the Tanglewood Music Center.

Mr. Voison is responsible for countless arrangements and publications of classical trumpet music. Voison retired in 1998 after seventy years of performing and teaching.

William Vacchiano

Mr. Vacchiano first began playing with the New York Philharmonic in 1935 and played for 38 years, taking the principal trumpet chair in 1942. He has played under Stravinsky, Barbirolli, Rodzinski, Stokowski, Szell, and Bernstein. Known for his impeccable technique, beautiful tone and graceful legato, Vacchiano was largely responsible for the widespread modern practice of using trumpets in various keys to fit the instrument to the music more closely. He has published numerous trumpet method books and designed his own line of trumpet mouthpieces.

Just as important as his impressive orchestral contribution is Mr. Vacchiano's teaching. He began teaching professionally in 1935, taught at the Julliard School of Music for 67 years and to this day students travel from all over the world to study with him in New York. His more well-known students include Wynton Marsalis, Gerard Schwarz and current Julliard faculty member and New York Philharmonic's principal trumpet, Philip Smith.

Charles Schlueter

Charles Schlueter has been principal trumpet of the Boston Symphony Orchestra since 1981. Prior to his appointment in Boston, he held the same position in the Minnesota Orchestra, the Milwaukee Symphony, and the Kansas City Philharmonic. He was also associate principal trumpet in the Cleveland Orchestra under George Szell. Schlueter has taught and performed around the world.

Mr. Schlueter founded the non-profit organization, Charles Schlueter Foundation, Inc., in 2001 to encourage communication among brass players and to advance the artistic level of performance, teaching and literature associated with brass instruments. Its mission is to foster the enjoyment of music, promote music education, and assist in the training of talented young brass performers. The Foundation strives to promote music as an essential part of school curriculums and to understand and demonstrate how music serves as a means of communication across a range of cultures throughout the world.

Susan Slaughter

Susan Slaughter joined the Saint Louis Symphony Orchestra in 1969 and four years later became the first woman ever to be named principal trumpet of a major symphony orchestra. A graduate of Indiana University, she received their coveted performer's certificate in recognition of outstanding musical performance. Ms. Slaughter has studied with Herbert Müeller, Bernard Adelstein, Arnold Jacobs, Robert Nagel, Claude Gordon and Laurie Frink.

At the invitation of baseball commissioner Fay Vincent, Ms. Slaughter performed the National Anthem for game three of the 1991 World Series. She has served on the board of directors of the International Trumpet Guild and in 1992 Ms. Slaughter founded the International Women's Brass Conference, an organization dedicated to provide opportunities and recognition for women brass musicians. In 1996, she founded Monarch Brass, an all women's brass ensemble which has toured in the U.S. and Europe.

Classical Soloists

Most of the above-mentioned orchestral musicians also give frequent performances as a solo instrument. Below are some people who are well known for their solo trumpet playing ability.

Maurice André (1933-)

Maurice André was the son of a miner who was an amateur trumpeter who taught Maurice the rudiments of trumpet playing at age twelve. After four years of study, Maurice's teacher knew the lad had talent and suggested he study at the Paris Conservatory. Because Maurice showed potential but lacked money, he joined the military and was allowed to attend the Paris Conservatory for free.

When he was 30, in 1963, Mr. André began his astounding solo career. He had played trumpet in several orchestras up until this time. When he started to perform as a trumpet soloist the trumpet was not considered a solo instrument like violin or oboe. There was very little music for trumpet available. In addition, Mr. André also began using the piccolo trumpet for which there were few solo transcriptions. Today there are more than 130 transcriptions for piccolo trumpet and countless solo trumpet pieces.

Very important to André's solo career was his wife, Liliane, who became his manager and companion on his tours all over the world. In a 1978 interview he said he had done 220 concerts that year, and an average of 180 each year prior to that. That's more than 2,000 concerts!

In addition to his intense touring, he has recorded over 300 albums. This man with superb technique, gorgeous tone and wonderfully emotional playing did more for solo classical trumpet than any other person in the 20th century.

Alison Balsom (1978-)

Alison Balsom is an exciting young trumpet player who has been playing professionally since 2001, with a debut album out in 2002 with the EMI Classics label. She won an award for he tone quality in the 4th *Maurice André International Trumpet Competition*. In 2006, Alison won 'Young British Classical Performer' at the 2006 Classical BRIT Awards (similar to the Grammy Award) and was awarded the 'Classic FM Listeners' Choice Award' at the Classic FM Gramophone Awards. She won 'Female Artist of the Year' at the 2009 Classical BRIT Awards. *Caprice*, Her third album, was released in September 2006 and won Balsom the *Solo CD of the Year*, given by Brass Band World magazine. If all that wasn't enough, Alison is a professor of trumpet at the Guildhall School of Music and Drama and is the principal trumpeter in the London Chamber Orchestra.

Jazz Trumpet Masters

Again, there are so many that it's tough to pick which ones to include. Players included here are not just great players, but were selected because of major contributions to music, trumpet playing, and improvement of life in general. Other players you should explore are Lee Morgan, Blue Mitchell, Kenny Dorham, Booker Little, Bobby Hackett, Charlie Shavers, Harry James, Doc Severinsen, Art Farmer, Freddie Hubbard, Clark Terry, Chet Baker, Claudio Roditi, Marvin Stamm, Conte Candoli, Woody Shaw, Al Hirt, Maynard Ferguson, Don Cherry, Lester Bowie, Roy Hargrove, Tom Harrell, Dave Douglas, Brian Lynch, and Ryan Kisor. I could go on and on. Sorry if I left out your favorite player.

Buddy Bolden (1877-1931)

Even though Bolden played cornet, he's included here because of his importance to jazz. In 1895 Buddy Bolden formed his first band. Many mark this moment as the beginning of Jazz even though the name *jazz* wouldn't be used for about 20 years. Buddy Bolden, born Charles Joseph Bolden, was jazz's earliest known star. He was able to bend notes on the horn with more facility than anyone had heard before and was known for *ragging* popular dance tunes, which means playing the tunes with some personal creativity. Bolden wouldn't allow anyone to touch his horn. It was said he could play so loud he could make rain stay up in the sky. By 1903 he was becoming known as King Bolden.

Then things went bad for Buddy. In the spring of 1906 after a beating, he began to suffer severe headaches and had major spells of depression. His behavior became more and more erratic, as did his playing. He was arrested for insanity, then released, but he never recovered. He was arrested again and this time was committed to an asylum. Mr. Bolden rarely ever talked coherently again. He died in 1931. No recordings exist of this player whose sound *went right through you, just like you were in church or something*, a fellow musician remembered. Buddy Bolden, the first jazz legend.

Joe "King" Oliver (1885-1938)

King Oliver was Louis Armstrong's idol and mentor. King Oliver was a New Orleans musician who eventually moved to Chicago to play music. From 1915 to 1923 he was known as jazz's best cornettist, succeeding Freddie Keppard. He was a master of special effects and could make his horn laugh, cry, howl and scream. He would often cover his hand with a cloth while playing so other players wouldn't know how he got those crazy sounds.

King Oliver died unknown and completely broke. On a tour of the South, Louis Armstrong ran into his old mentor selling fruit at a roadside fruit stand. Louis gave him all the money he had on him and King Oliver used some of the money to get his nice clothes back from the pawn shop.

Louis Armstrong (1901-1971)

Though he's best known as a trumpet player, Louis Armstrong got his start on cornet when he was allowed to play one (after much pleading) at the Colored Waif's Home in New Orleans. He had been sentenced to live in the home after a policeman caught him firing a gun in the air in celebration. He was only 12 years old. The act of giving young Louis a horn to play would shape the course of popular music to this day.

Louis was released form the Colored Waifs Home at age 14 and was befriended by Joe "King" Oliver who became Louis's idol and mentor. Armstrong began playing cornet with bands around New Orleans and at age 18 he landed a job playing with Fate Marable's band which played on paddlewheelers that ran up and down the Mississippi. Marable's band was like going to school.

A few years later, King Oliver had moved to Chicago and sent for Louis to come join him and his band, which Armstrong eagerly did. Things just got better and better for him. In 1925 he formed a recording band called the "Hot Fives" and recorded his famous *St. Louis Blues* with singer Bessie Smith.

The details of Armstrong's career are available in many places, so I won't go into much more detail here. Louis became a huge star and his gravelly voice, warmth, and genuine love of music were all part of his magic. His hits included *Mack the Knife*, *Hello, Dolly*, and *What a Wonderful World*.

In addition to being the pioneer of trumpet as a solo instrument in jazz, Louis was generous and thankful to all his fans, who came to hear his music, and also came to see him off as he got on the bus. He would pass through the crowd and as he shook hands and gave his thanks, he would often press money into the hands of those who needed it and tell them to take care of themselves.

Bix Beiderbecke (1903-1931)

A great natural musician, Bix Beiderbecke couldn't read music for much of his musical career and relied instead on his incredible ear and ability to improvise. He became one of the best jazz cornetists even though he died at 28 from alcoholism. Bix was born in 1903 and to his parents' horror, became caught up in the jazz world. It was all he cared about and that passion eventually led him to play with the Wolverines, Paul Whiteman's Orchestra, and Hoagy Carmichael. His beautiful tone and note choice earned him great respect. A saxophone player told Bix he was a note-miser and was too restrained. Bix replied, "The trouble with you is you play so many notes but they mean so little."

Roy Eldridge (1911-1989)

Known as "Little Jazz" Roy Eldridge was a small man with a big, fiery sound. He was known to visit a club where a rival trumpeter was working, take his horn out of its case outside the door and burst through the door blasting away a high C as he headed for the bandstand. He's a larger-than-life figure in the jazz trumpet lineage. Stylistically speaking he's the bridge between Louis Armstrong and Dizzy Gillespie.

Though his tour in the late 1940's with Benny Goodman was brief, it was significant because it was one of the first times a major musical group was integrated with both white and black performers. The tour was tough for Eldridge because of the unpleasant treatment he received because of his skin color. After a valiant struggle, the abuse was finally too much for him and he dropped out of the tour.

Mr. Eldridge took up residence in Paris in 1950 where he made some of his most successful recordings. After a 1951 return to New York, he worked with Coleman Hawkins, Benny Carter, Ella Fitzgerald, and Johnny Hodges. He made notable albums for Verve Records alongside Hawkins and continued freelancing and leading a house band at Jimmy Ryan's club in New York. In 1980 he suffered a stroke that ended his trumpet playing, but Mr. Eldridge continued to make music as a singer and pianist until his death in 1989.

Dizzy Gillespie (1917-1993)

The first time I became aware of Dizzy was his appearance on *The Muppet Show*. Mr. Gillespie told Kermit he liked frogs, "because they can do this..." and he puffed his cheeks out alarmingly. It freaked me out and entranced me at the same time. And then he played. Wow! Now that I'm more familiar with Dizzy, I realize that appearance was a perfect venue for his sense of humor and teaching nature.

Born John Birks Gillespie in South Carolina to a poor family, he was the ninth of nine children. He earned the nickname "Dizzy" early on due to his quick wit. Despite his humble beginnings,

Dizzy, with help from Charlie Parker and others, changed the shape of jazz. Dizzy was one of the originators of Bebop and probably its greatest proponent and early teacher. His musical hero and early influence was trumpeter Roy Eldridge.

Though he was a monster trumpet player, Dizzy was a good pianist too. On a recording session with Charlie Parker and a young Miles Davis, Gillespie played piano and then raced over to take the trumpet part that Miles couldn't handle. Dizzy's contribution to bebop can't be overstated. He was certainly one of its greatest Masters. He remains one of the most advanced trumpeter we've had yet.

Miles Davis (1926-1991)

Miles has always been different, always been out on the edge looking for a new thing. This musical curiosity coupled with the fearlessness of the explorer made Miles one of the most important figures in 20th century music. Davis' playing continued to evolve and change throughout his life, unlike other players who found their styles and simply refined them over time. Miles' main trumpet heroes were Clark Terry, Dizzy Gillespie, and Louis Armstrong.

Miles played bebop with the best of them, then he took his music in a different direction with what became known as "cool jazz" in 1948. About ten years later he began playing modal jazz which has since become widely used in jazz and other genres of music. He continued to push the envelope throughout his life, experimenting with fusion, rock, and used electronics to shape the sound of his horn.

Clifford Brown (1930-1956)

Clifford's life holds one of the most ironic tragedies of the jazz world. He started playing trumpet when he was 15 and by 18 he was playing regularly in Philadelphia. Fats Navarro, his main influence, encouraged Brown, as did Charlie Parker and Dizzy Gillespie. Brown was a virtuoso trumpet player who has influenced countless others, including Lee Morgan, Freddie Hubbard, and Woody Shaw.

Clifford only recorded for four years, and what a legacy those recordings are! In a time when some of the best players were using heroin or drinking themselves to death, Clifford Brown was a clean-living guy who didn't smoke, use drugs, and he rarely drank. All who knew him said he had a sweet disposition and gentle spirit. Though he didn't even drive a car, he died in a car accident at age 25.

Had he lived longer, Clifford Brown's influence today would be even more significant than it already is. Who knows what we missed.

Doc Cheatham (1905-1997)

Doc Cheatham is on this list because of his incredible stamina. He's the greatest 90-year-old player you'll probably ever hear. He's here to show you that you can play trumpet when you're over 70 years old, and play it well.

Cheatham always possessed admirable technique and was a master of the cup mute. He enjoyed small groups the most, though he played in many larger groups, including bands led by Chick Webb, Cab Calloway, Benny Carter, and Benny Goodman.

Cheatham did some of his best recordings late in his career, after his 70th birthday. In his later years, he sometimes added a rough edge to his tone which made his solos more exciting. There is nothing to stop you from continuing to learn and grow your entire life.

Maynard Ferguson (1928-2006)

In addition to being a phenomenal player who had stratoshpheric range, Maynard was also an instrument designer (see the Firebird, and Superbone, page 184), record producer, composer, educator/clinician, symphonic guest artist and film soundtrack artist, and a three-time Grammy nominee. He is perhaps best known for his ability to play very high, but in addition to that, Maynard can swing. His hits *MacArthur Park* and *Gonna Fly Now* (the theme from *Rocky*) made him a household name. He consistently won Downbeat and Playboy jazz polls.

"I'm only mad with people that leave my band if they are not successful afterwards," Maynard said. Some musicians who have passed through his band are Don Ellis, Chuck Mangione, Bill Chase, Wayne Shorter, Chick Corea, Bob James, Joe Zawinul, Slide Hampton, Greg Bissonnette, Willie Maiden and Peter Erskine.

Maynard always made time in his rigorous schedule to personally encourage young musicians, and he gave many clinics and workshops at high schools and colleges every year. "When I was young I listened to as many different trumpeters as possible and tried to learn from each of them," said Maynard in an interview with Scott Yanow. "If a student is a Maynard Ferguson freak, I immediately tell him to go out and buy some records by Dizzy, Miles, Freddie Hubbard, Wynton Marsalis, and Louis Armstrong. I try to teach them that one of the most fun rewards of playing music is when you start to sound like yourself."

Ingrid Jensen (1967-)

If you're a young woman playing trumpet and wonder where to find role models, look no further than Ingrid Jensen. Ingrid is one of the best jazz players around today. She's a hard-bop trumpeter influenced by Woody Shaw and Lee Morgan. She studied at Berklee College of Music in Boston, toured with Lionel Hampton, was a professor in Austria's Bruckner Conservatory at age 25, and in addition to playing with Hampton, has recorded with musicians like Enja and alto Virginia Mayhew as well as a whole slew of jazz masters past and present. She's been nominated several times for Canada's Juno Award (like the U.S. Grammy).

In 2003 she was nominated for the second time for a New York Jazz Journalist Association Award in and is seen yearly in the top five of the Downbeat Critic Polls in the *deserving wider recognition* category. Ingrid was featured on Gil Evans' Porgy and Bess at the San Francisco Jazz Festival, under the direction of Maria Schneider and was also a guest in the festival's "Tribute to Woody Shaw and Freddie Hubbard", alongside Terence Blanchard, Eddie Henderson, Bobby Hutcherson and Kenny Garrett. In addition to performing, she conducts master classes, clinics, and workshops around the world. Currently, she is an artist-in-residence on the trumpet faculty at the University of Michigan in Ann Arbor.

Wynton Marsalis (1961-)

Wynton Marsalis has done so much to revitalize jazz that even if he wasn't an incredible player, he deserves mention here. Through an exhaustive series of performances, lectures and music workshops Marsalis has rekindled widespread interest in an art form that had been almost abandoned. Some of the better known jazz musicians today have been students of Marsalis' workshops: James Carter, Christian McBride, Roy Hargrove, Harry Connick Jr., Nicholas Payton, Eric Reed and Eric Lewis to name a few.

At age 17 Wynton became the youngest musician ever to be admitted to Tanglewood's Berkshire Music Center. When Wynton moved to New York City to attend Juilliard in 1978 and began to pick up gigs around town, the buzz began. In 1980 at the age of 19 he earned the opportunity to join the

Jazz Messengers to study under the master jazz musician and drummer, band leader Art Blakey. In the years to follow Wynton performed with Sarah Vaughan, Dizzy Gillespie, Sweets Edison, Clark Terry, Sonny Rollins, and many other jazz legends.

In 1987 Wynton Marsalis co-founded a jazz program at Lincoln Center. The first season consisted of three concerts. Under Wynton's leadership the program has developed an international agenda with up to 400 events annually in 15 countries. Frederick P. Rose Hall, the new 100,000 square foot complex, has become Jazz at Lincoln Center's new home, and contains state-of-the-art performance, recording, broadcast, rehearsal and educational facilities as well as the world's first large venue built specifically for jazz.

In 1997 Wynton Marsalis became the first jazz musician ever to win the Pulitzer Prize for Music for his epic oratorio *Blood on the Fields*.

Wynton's greatest legacy, in my humble opinion, is his ability to inspire not only through his own performances and compositions, but also through his character and his willingness to teach. Here is a man who waited for a student in a dark, empty parking lot for an hour after a concert so the student could return home to get his trumpet for a lesson. He has been known to return calls to 4 year olds to talk to them about music. Marsalis personally funds scholarships for students attending the Tanglewood Music Center and the Eastern Music Festival. Wynton has selflessly donated his time and talent to non-profit organizations throughout the country.

Just a Few of the Best

The above players are simply a few of the best. I've included only those artists who have not only been great players, but also contributed to the greater good in some way. With a lot of hard work, almost anyone can become an excellent trumpet player. It takes something extra to be the kind of person who makes a difference in the world.

There are hundreds of other players out there, and I bet a few live close to you! Go find them and listen to them. Study with them if they are accepting students. You won't regret it.

Up Next

The next and final chapter covers one of the most ancient trumpets on the planet, and in my opinion it is one of the coolest sounding instruments, too. It sounds primal, eerie and ancient. It's the didjeridu, didgeridoo, or didj, an Australian Aboriginal instrument. Read on to learn more!

HOW DO YOU DIDGERIDOO?

We are the music makers, and we are the dreamers of the dream.

~ Arthur O'Shaunessey

In This Chapter

- What is a didgeridoo?
- Why play a didj?
- How to Play a Didj
- Circular Breathing

Terms to Know

circular breathing: A breathing technique which allows you to maintain a continuous sound without asphyxiating.

overtone toot: A higher note on the didgeridoo. Also called a trumpet toot. Often a P5 above the fundamental tone.

backpressure: The pressure created when blowing through a tube. The smaller the tube, the greater the backpressure

How Do You Do, Didgeridoo?

This is the oldest type of trumpet in continuous use in human culture. It's popularity is skyrocketing because it's such a cool instrument and is pretty easy to play. The true reason for its popularity is its sound. That powerful, hypnotic drone is mystifying and in the hands of a capable player, a didgeridoo can alter your consciousness. You've got to hear it to believe it.

If you'd like to hear samples of how a didgeridoo sounds, go to www.didjshop.com. Most of the didgeridoos available on the site have sound clips, and it's a great site. Though didj is pretty easy to play immediately, to play didj at a high level is like any instrument; it takes time, study and practice. The good news is that this chapter can help you with some of that.

Didgeridoos are sacred to many Australian aboriginal people and it is wise to respect this when approaching the didgeridoo. Also give consideration to the first Australians' role in the creation of the didj (their copyright, if you will). Don't buy a cheap didgeridoo made in India with indentured and low-wage labor. This disrespects the culture which is responsible for the didgeridoo, and is counter to the spirit of didgeridoo itself. Honor the Music and the musicians that created this instrument by being a responsible consumer. *Yidaki* is a name for a didgeridoo which has been made traditionally by first Australians using special tree harvesting and decoration methods. Didgeridoos have traditionally

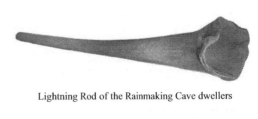

Lightning Rod of the Rainmaking Cave dwellers

Earthrise

been made from the eucalyptus tree, but can now be found in most types of wood, desert agave, PVC plumbing pipe, and even exhaust pipes. Any tube of the right length and back pressure will work.

Example 23.1 More didgeridoos, two of which have been painted in a semi-traditional style. The long winding line represents a journey (walkabout) and the circular designs represent a place of water. All didj pictures have been generously donated from www.laoutback.com

Motion Blue

Lost in the Humming Air (two mouthpieces!)

Outback Hot Rod

Play Didj to Enhance Your Trumpet Skills

Because you've been playing trumpet for a while, making a sound on didj will be pretty easy for you. You'll be happy to know that the buzz for didgeridoo is *much* looser than the one you use to play trumpet. This is one of the reasons playing didgeridoo is such a good thing to do after a particularly tough practice session or gig. Playing didj gets the blood flowing to your chops like nothing else and the slow, steady vibrations are a great lip massage. But wait, there's more!

In addition to loosening up the chops, playing didgeridoo helps you to breathe deeply, gets a lot of oxygenated blood to flow (especially to your loosely flapping lips), and playing didj is good for your sensation of tone and rhythm. It's great for the coordination of breath, lip, tongue, and even voice. Some of the multi-tonal skills (humming along w/ buzz) you'll learn in a moment can be converted to use with the trumpet.

As you learn to make cool sounds on this strange and wonderful instrument, don't be afraid to experiment with as many different sounds as you can come up with. Cries, screams, howls, hoots and hollers are all acceptable things do put through your didgeridoo.

How to Do Didgeridoo

Let's go through the steps to get you making a sound on this strange instrument. Remember to be persistent whenever you try something new. If one approach doesn't work, try another. Don't expect immediate success, though with an instrument like this, you should be able to get a pretty good sound after a few attempts.

The buzz for didgeridoo is a little different from the one used on your trumpet. The vibrations are much slower and because of this, they'll take more air to sustain than you may expect. When you need a breath, stop and take one. If you're prone to light-headedness, you may want to sit while doing this at first. If you do start feeling light-headed, stop until the feeling passes, then begin again.

Instead of the lips being taut as they are when you play trumpet, your lips should be slightly pursed to get a good sound on didgeridoo. Make a motorboat or old biplane sound instead of the fat bumblebee sound for the trumpet buzz.

Begin with the didgeridoo centered on your lips, just like the trumpet embouchure. Some play out of the corner of their mouth. I have been experimenting with this technique and have changed my embouchure as a result. I still come back to playing in the center of my chops to get the benefits for my trumpet embouchure. Your goal is a good sound, so don't let fear of mouthpiece placement stop you from experimenting with a different placement. Here are my three examples of mouth placement.

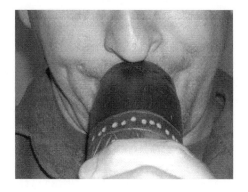 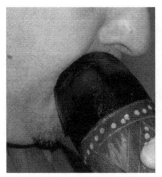 

The Fundamental Tone

Each didgeridoo has its own fundamental tone. This tone happens when the air column within the instrument vibrates. Didgeridoo fundamental tones are low and take a lot of air to produce and sustain, so the air you're pushing through the didj shouldn't be fast, but slow. Think of making your breath steam on a cold day, "haaaaahhhhh." That's the kind of air speed you want.

If you have trouble getting the fundamental tone on your didgeridoo, try relaxing your buzz even more; the fundamental tone may be lower than you expect. Keep trying. Once you find the fundamental tone for your didj, remember the pitch so you can produce it immediately the next time you play. For even more precision, play near a piano keyboard and when you have the fundamental tone, find the corresponding note on the piano. This will help you with singing chord tones later.

Overtone Toots

The didgeridoo adheres to the physics of blowing air through a tube, which is why it has overtones. When you speed up the air and the vibration of your lips, the instrument responds by playing a higher note in the overtone series. For more info on the overtone series (also known as the harmonic series), see "the harmonic series," "Around the middle of the 1700s holes were added at critical points in the tubing. These holes allowed the performer to tune out-of-tune notes. Trumpets without valves of some kind are limited to certain notes in the harmonic series, also known as the overtone series. The harmonic series is a naturally occurring phenomenon in music. The same ratios of the harmonic series can be seen in the physical world. It is another expression of the Golden Mean, a fascinating subject worthy of a book all its own. The harmonic series is a fairly complicated idea. All you need to know about the harmonic series for our purposes is that between low notes, there are big differences in pitch. For instance, the first two notes of the harmonic series are an octave (8 diatonic notes) apart. As you go higher in pitch in the harmonic series, the pitches are closer together. You can see this in the musical notation of the harmonic series above. See the big gap between the first two notes? A natural trumpet can't play the notes within the gaps at the low end of the harmonic series." on page 13.

A good didgeridoo will have two or even three overtone toots. Even a low quality didj will have overtone toots but they may be more difficult to produce. Your ability as a trumpet player will make these overtone toots seem like child's play compared to trying to play a first-leger-line A on trumpet.

To get a toot, simply blow faster and flex your lips like you would when playing higher on a trumpet. The didgeridoo will lock into one of the notes of the overtone series. Once you find the first overtone, try for others. See how many you can coax out of that hollow tube. As you become familiar with your didgeridoo, you'll know where those sweet spots are that get the best sound quality.

Circular Breathing

The great mystery of didgeridoo playing! The hypnotic drone of the didgeridoo needs to be continuous or its spell is broken. If you have to stop to take a breath, the silence created by the breath disrupts the feeling didj playing invokes in and evokes from listeners. Circular breathing allows you to continue the drone without asphyxiating and is an essential skill for high-level didj playing.

Not to worry. Circular breathing is a pretty easy with practice. Sound impossible? It's not. The musician performing circular breathing is filling her cheeks with air, then using that air in her cheeks to continue the sound while she breathes in through her nose, quickly refilling her lungs. It's a cool trick and there *is* a way to learn it.

First I'll throw a term at you. *Backpressure*. Backpressure is what helps you maintain a sound on a wind instrument. If you buzz into a room with just your lips, there is no backpressure. This is one of the reasons buzzing with lips alone is more difficult. A trumpet has much more backpressure than an open room because of the diameter of the trumpet tube. It's harder to push air through a smaller tube. That's backpressure at work.

A poorly made didgeridoo has slightly more backpressure than an open room and it will be difficult to master circular breathing with such an instrument. The good didgeridoos have decent backpressure, but still much less than trumpet. Didgeridoos come in a wide variety of back pressures. If you're learning, more backpressure will make circular breathing easier. You'll learn more about qualities to look for when searching for a didgeridoo in the section below on buying a didgeridoo.

Okay. On to the process of practicing circular breathing. This is not a really tough skill to master, but don't expect immediate results, either. You're practicing coordination of muscles which aren't normally used, so give your brain time to wrap itself around what you expect of it. If you really want to learn this skill, you must practice it daily until you get it. Write on your hand or pin up notes to yourself where you'll be reminded. Circular breathing can be practiced without an instrument, anywhere you are. Okay, here we go.

Step 1

Don't use an instrument for this part, and before you use air, try water. Fill your mouth and cheeks with water and push a stream of water out of your face by using your tongue and cheek muscles. Stay relaxed while you breathe in and out through your nose when your mouth is full of water. Do this a few times until you're comfortable with it.

Then do this same trick with air. Fill your cheeks with air and breathe through your nose. Simply fill your cheeks up until you look like a chipmunk or Dizzy Gillespie. Push the air through your lips and try to get a buzz. It will be a short buzz. When you're able to fill your cheeks with air easily and can get a little buzz as you force the air out, you're ready to try it with an instrument.

Play a drone on the didgeridoo or a low note on trumpet, 2nd line G or below. Once you've got a good solid tone, allow your cheeks to fill with air but at the same time, maintain a good steady tone. This will take a little practice. Just keep at it until you can do it.

Step 2

Use the air in your cheeks to power the vibration of your lips. Use your cheek muscles to force the air in your oral cavity through your buzzing lips, the didgeridoo, or your horn. Try it without the instrument first. Can you maintain a buzz with the air in your cheeks alone?

When you try this with an instrument, the trick is that you must maintain the pitch and sound quality. The speed at which you force air through your lips and the shape of the inside of your mouth will help you control pitch. Experiment until you can do it. It will take a little practice, so don't give up.

On didgeridoo, circular breathing can change your sound quality in an interesting way. This is often done on purpose to get a different sound. If you're trying this on a didgeridoo, don't worry if the quality of the sound changes. As long as the sound is continuous, you're doing it right. With trumpet, strive for steadiness of pitch and tone.

Step 3

This step is like patting your head and rubbing your stomach at the same time. As you force the air out with your cheeks, you must breathe in through your nose at the same time. This is a good thing to practice without an instrument on your face. Just sit there in your chair and fill your cheeks with air. As you push that air slowly out your embouchure, sniff in through your nose. I know, it's easy to say and not so easy to do. Keep practicing.

If you're having trouble, or even if you're not having trouble, find a drinking straw and fill a *large* glass with water. Pinch or bend the submerged end of the straw so that not much air comes out. This will give you more backpressure.

Time to make bubbles! As you make bubbles with the straw, fill your cheeks with air, then use the air in your cheeks to keep the bubbles going, and sniff in through your nose. For more backpressure use more water or maybe chocolate milk. Feel free to take a drink at any time and replace fluid as necessary.

Step 4

Practice.

Step 5

Practice.

Step 6

Once you've got the process automatic and can maintain a tone, take your skills to the next step by circular breathing on didgeridoo while keeping a rhythm going. You must incorporate the rhythm of the breath (and cheek-puffing, etcetera) with the rhythm you're playing. On the trumpet, try to change notes while you force the air through your cheeks and breathe in through your nose. Yeah, I know it's a lot easier to say than to do. Push yourself to do circular breathing with faster rhythms and, with trumpet, higher in the range.

Step 7

Practice.

Step 8

Get on out there to an open mic or to a drum circle and whip out your didgeridoo. If you have friends with rhythm, they can bang on a drum while you drone away on the didgeridoo. Better yet, take along a shaker and provide your own rhythm when you perform.

Harmonics

All sounds are made up of many harmonics and there are many different and wordy definitions of harmonics. For our purposes, it will be easier to experience and hear them than talk about them. First you must have a good fundamental tone on your didj.

Vocal and didjeridu harmonics are affected by the shape of the resonating chamber, which is your mouth. To change the upper harmonics you simply change the shape of the inside of your mouth. Sound confusing? It isn't. These are the same skills you use when you talk.

Try this. Sing a steady note and go through the vowel sounds A, E, I, O, and U (no, not Y). The change in sound is also a change in the upper harmonics. The most valuable of these vowels for didj playing is the O and the E which embody the greatest difference in tongue position. Say "O," and "Eee" to feel how your tongue changes for each sound.

Play a drone on your didj and change the shape of your mouth from O to E, slowly at first, then more rapidly. You should hear a buzzing in the upper register that also changes pitch as you change the inside of your mouth. This is harmonics. Any mouth shape you can devise will alter the sound of your didj. It's best to simply experiment and find what works best for you and what you like.

The word didjeridu is a great place to start with harmonics. As you play, use your mouth as though you were speaking the word *didjeridu* and notice what happens. Try *doo-wah-diddy-diddy-dum-diddy-doo*, or anything else you can think up that has a lot of vowel changes. Try to say your full name through the didj.

With practice, you can use this change in harmonics to sustain a rhythmic pulse.

Vocalizations

The fundamental drone and harmonics are just the beginning of the fun with this instrument. Once you have a good tone, start experimenting with other sounds in addition to the harmonics you just learned. You don't need to be able to circular breathe to do these sounds.

As you play the fundamental tone, use your voice at the same time. This may take some practice, but you should be able to sing, cry, scream, howl, hoot, bark and moan through your didj while buzzing. Masterful Australian aboriginal players imitate animals from Australia with the didj, like the kookaburra, frogs, and the bush pigeon. Try imitating a raven or a wolf howl. Experiment with low growls and high screams. Short bursts of sound like a barking big dog, or a yappy little dog are also very effective.

You can also sing through the didj, and this can be quite dramatic. Because the didj is pitched so low, the intervals I'll mention are often an octave or more above the fundamental; it depends on your vocal range. Intervals of unison (same note), perfect fifth, and an octave blend in very well with the fundamental tone. A cool effect is to sing any of these tones, get it perfect so the sounds are clean and clear, then slightly raise or lower your voice. You will hear *beats* in the sound that speed up the further you go from the fundamental. As you sing any of these tones (root, fifth, octave) you have to sing them perfectly in tune to avoid any of the *beats* in the sound. Keep practicing until you can.

An interval I particularly like is the major third above the fundamental (4 half steps). It has a rich, vibrant quality that sounds great and will really bring out the harmonics in your sound. Practice singing the root, third, fifth, and octave. You'll also be singing the tones of a major chord. When singing a chord tone you can really hear the changing in overtones when you use the vowel changes mentioned earlier

In addition to all the above, use changing volume levels of your vocalizations to add even more interest and musicality to your playing.

Inventing Rhythms

Rhythms on didj can be articulated many ways: with your tongue (t, d, k, g, j, l, n, z), your lips (p, b, m), and with a pulse of air. Double and triple tonguing, flutter tonguing, the growl, and any other tongue technique create interesting effects and rhythms. Try them all.

Inventing a rhythm to play through your didj is as easy as talking. Literally. The rhythms of speech are perfect for making up a rhythm. Try mouthing your full name as you drone away. Try "What are you doing," over and over again. Try a chant you may know. I particularly like a chant in the Oglala Sioux language, "Wakan Tanka tunkashila onshimala." Anything you can say, you can put through your didj. Tap your foot and keep the beat steady.

Or take a more *written music* approach. Tongue four quarter notes, or any combination of quarters and eighths. Add some sixteenth notes or triplets or other rhythmic figures. When you arrive at a rhythm that pleases you, write it down so you can recreate it later or share it with others.

As a way of punctuating your rhythms, add an overtone toot or a bark or scream on every third beat, or at the end of a two-measure rhythm. The rhythmic variations available are endless and are only limited by your imagination!

Finding a Didgeridoo

When you search for you own instrument, please don't succumb to your wallet and buy a cheap Indonesian or Indian knock-off. Though these instruments will play, they are generally produced

---

using cheap labor and do horrible ecological damage. This is completely contrary to the spirit of the instrument and does not honor either the instrument or the Australian Aborigines who gave us this wonderful musical voice.

If you can't afford an authentic didj, simply make your own out of PVC pipe. Use the 1 1/4" or 1 1/2" inch piece, ten feet of which is usually under five dollars. Ten feet of pipe will give you two nice didjeridus. Dip one end in beeswax for a mouthpiece and you're all set.

If you want to look for a didjeridu, doing it online is your best bet. Here are two of the best sites that honor the spirit of the instrument:

- www.laoutback.com: A fun site with an ever-changing array of didgeridoos, from concert quality to inexpensive versions for kids or beginners. Friendly folks.
- www.didjshop.com: at this site you can hear informative sound clips of the instruments. The monthly newsletter is usually a good read, too.

Sources for Further Study

Here are some of the sources for additional information on the magical didjeridu.

Book/Magazine/Video	Format	Author (available at)
The didgeridoo Phenomenon	book	Djalu Gurruwirri et al., (www.didjshop.com)
didgeridoo & Co. Magazine	magazine	(www.didjshop.com)
Playing the didgeridoo (vol. 1-5)	audio CD	(www.didjshop.com)
didgeridoo	video (30)min	Alan Harris (www.didjshop.com)
Learn How to Play an Australian Aboriginal Didgeridoo	video (60 min)	David Blanasi, Svargo Freitag

Up Next

That's it! Congratulations if you've gotten through the entire book. The last section of the book contains scales, practice aids, web sites, a musical terms glossary, book index, and the piano keyboard. All of these resources will help you become a better musician. Use them!

May you experience a lifetime of making music, and may you greet every challenge with a smile of confidence.

Sound the Trumpet: Codicil

Contained in the Codicil

- What to Look for When Buying a Trumpet
- Book Index
- Fingering Chart
- Piano Keyboard

Free Files At www.sol-ut.com

- Many Extras from the Book
- Trumpet Web Sites
- Forms to Track Progress
- Practice Journal
- Practice Record Sheet
- Scales
- Musical Terms Glossary

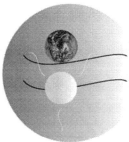

SolUt Press

Musician-friendly Resources.
www.Sol-Ut.com

How to Find a Trumpet for Your Very Own

Sell not virtue to purchase wealth, nor liberty to purchase power.

~ Benjamin Franklin

Consider Renting or Leasing

Most music stores will rent you an instrument, and many will put your rental fee towards the purchase of the instrument if you decide to stick with it. You can either rent a brand new instrument or, for a lesser fee, rent a used instrument. If you rent to own you may end up paying a little more than purchasing an instrument outright, but this is a good option if you're not sure you'll stick with this instrument or if you have limited savings to spend.

Where to Look

If you need a horn, start looking at the end of the current school year. This is often a time when instruments come available from those who have decided to discontinue their studies. Your local music store is also a good source of instruments for sale and information.

You don't have to buy a trumpet new from a music store. There are several alternatives available to you and with many of them you'll save some cash. Here's a list of some options along with pros and cons about the choice.

- Ask Around: Ask friends and relatives if anyone has a trumpet in an attic or basement that's not being used. Thousands and thousands of horns are bought every year and many of them go unused. They're out there, and someone you know might have one. If that someone is a good friend or a relative, you might get the trumpet for free or be able to borrow it.

- Garage Sales: **PRO:** the absolute cheapest way to find an instrument. **CON:** It's not often you'll find a trumpet at a garage sale, but try calling first if you have a number. Take a trumpet player with you. Be sure to test out any horn you find (more on this below). **TIP:** ask someone you know who visits garage sales regularly to keep an eye out for a trumpet for you. Be sure to offer less than the seller is asking unless what they're offering is too good to be true. If this is the case, be careful, it may be to good to be true.

- Classified Ads: **PRO:** this can be one of the least expensive options for finding a horn. It's easy as long as you can read and have a local paper. **CON:** Hit and miss. It's no guarantee you'll find a trumpet here (especially if you live in a small town), and if you do, you'll have to go find it and test it out. **TIP:** Take a trumpet player with you. Ask the seller to come down on the price, no matter what it is. Because they placed an ad, they're eager to sell and probably are asking more than they would actually take.

* Pawn Shop: **PRO**: also often an inexpensive option. A phone call can determine whether a pawn shop has a trumpet. **CON**: As above, no guarantees that a pawn shop will have a trumpet. It may be in poor condition (though this can be a benefit to you if it only needs minor repair or simple cleaning). If you find one, be sure to test it before you buy. **TIP**: Take a trumpet player with you. Ask the seller to come down on the price, no matter what it is. A pawn shop will ask more for a horn than they'll probably take. Beware that most pawn shop owners are very good at haggling.

* E-Bay (www.ebay.com): **PRO**: E-Bay always has many trumpets listed both from professional companies and individuals. Do your homework so you know what you want because you'll probably find it. The bidding system is often a good way to get an instrument a little cheaper, but this can also backfire and you could pay more than a horn is worth. Run a search on the horn you're interested in to find what prices are reasonable. **CON**: you can't try out the horn or be sure it is all the seller says it is. Though it's rare, some people have been ripped off by bogus offers. **TIP**: check the seller's rating to see if they have sold on E-Bay before (the more positive ratings the better, of course), and if possible, correspond with the seller via E-mail or phone and ask questions about the instrument. Ask the seller to play the horn over the phone. Don't pay the entire amount for the instrument up front. Pay half and send the other half when you receive (and check out) the horn. This may require an additional agreement with the seller.

Don't give up. Ask around and visit or call garage sales and you'll find a horn waiting for you eventually. It might be easiest at the music store, where you're sure to get a good horn, but where's the challenge in that?

What to Look For

There are many things to look at when considering a trumpet, some obvious and some not so obvious. If you're buying a used horn and you know what to look for you can spot potential problems. If it looks like you know what you're doing and can tell the seller why a trumpet may not be perfect, often this will allow you to get the horn for a lower price.

If at all possible, take an experienced player with you to help you determine whether a trumpet is worth buying. Someone who plays can try out the horn and give it a more accurate assessment than a non-player or less-experienced player. Be sure to give whoever helps a thank you coffee or soda or snack for going along.

The Obvious

A trumpet should have at least one mouthpiece with it, but there is no guarantee that it will, so you should take a mouthpiece with you. Borrow one if necessary. Without a mouthpiece you won't be able to try the horn out. Be sure to put one in your pocket before you walk out the door. In fact, you should carry one everywhere anyway so you can practice your buzz.

Look for major dents or dings. Appearance aside, large dents will affect the air flow of the horn and its intonation. Some dings are easily removed by an instrument repairman and others are impossible to fix without taking the horn apart. Any dents to the valve casings are usually fatal to a horn, so if a trumpet has this problem, look elsewhere.

If a trumpet hasn't been used, the slides and valves may be frozen and won't move. This isn't necessarily a bad thing because most of these problems are easily fixed. If you aren't getting your trumpet from a music store, take along some valve oil so you can oil the valves if they need it (see "Oiling The Valves" on page 152 for how to correctly oil valves).

The Not-So-Obvious

Pull the tuning slide (if you can). If you can't pull the slide see "Trouble-Shooting" on page 154. Once you get the slide out, look through the lead pipe. Digestion starts in your mouth with saliva, so saliva is pretty corrosive. The smoother the lead pipe the better. Older horns which have been played a lot may have pitting and scoring in the lead pipe and sometimes the pipe may be worn all the way through. When this happens the lead pipe needs to be replaced.

If you aren't taking an experienced player with you, oil the valves and finger them randomly. You'll get a good idea if they'll stick by doing this. Try as many different combinations as you can. Fan each valve (push it up and down really fast) individually, then try them in combinations. If they stick, drop some more oil into them and try it again. If they still stick, there may be a problem. If you're serious about buying the horn, clean the valve casings and the valves and try it again (see #4 under "The Monthly Overhaul" on page 154 to clean the valve casings). If the valves still stick after this, don't buy the horn.

As a beginner, you may not want a horn with a big diameter lead pipe (also called *bore*), because this will make it more difficult to play high and lessens endurance. The benefit to such an instrument is a fatter tone. If you have good air support and can get a good tone out of a larger bore instrument,

The Last Word

The best thing you could do when shopping for a trumpet is take along a trumpet player. The more experience that player has, the better, but anybody who knows more than you do would be an asset. This goes for not only the random trumpets at garage sales and pawn shops, but also the instruments in the music store, new or used. All trumpets are slightly different, even within a certain brand (Bach Stradivarius, for example), and a good player can tell the difference.

Keep looking if you don't find a horn immediately. Visit your local music store and sample a few horns to get an idea of what you might want and/or need.

Some folks have one horn and it's all they need. Others have vast collections. One of the most historic and interesting is the Utley collection. None of the instruments are for sale, but you can get an idea about what visiting garage sales in Europe will do to your closet space. Go to "http://orgs.usd.edu/nmm/UtleyPages/JoeUtley/Utley.html" for a gander at some of these rare old trumpets.

How to Find a Trumpet for Your Very Own

INDEX

Numerics

16th note 51
16th notes 49
8th note 109

A

Ab transposition 194
accent 189
accidental 102
air 34
air stream 92
Air Stream and Tongue 96
airstream 135
airstream vibrato 162
Akiyoshi, Toshiko 27
Al Hirt 233
alternate fingering 165
alternate fingering exercises 165
alternate fingerings 122
American Brass Quintet 21
ancient trumpets
   cornettos 13
   dung 12
   King Tut's trumpet 12
   natural trumpets 13
André, Maurice 232
aperture 31, 33
Arban, Jean Baptiste 230
Armstrong, Louis 21, 219, 233, 234
Art Blakey 236
Art Farmer 233
articulation 91
Au Claire de la Lune 108
Avec sourdine 175

B

backpressure 239, 242
Baker, Chet 25
Baldwin, James 143
bar line 113
Barbirolli 231
Basic Music Theory
   How to Read Write and Understand
      Written Music 120
   How to Read, Write and Understand
      Written Music 188
   How to Read, Write, and Understand
      Written Music 79
Basie, Count 27
beat 81
beats per minute (bpm) 211
Beiderbecke, Bix 234
Benny Carter 234, 235
Benny Goodman 234, 235
Berklee College of Music 236
Bernstein 231
Bessie Smith 234

Black Dyke 230
Blood on the Fields 237
Blood, Sweat, and Tears 28
Blue Mitchell 233
Bobby Hackett 233
Bolden, Buddy 233
book
   The Art of Trumpet Playing 53
Booker Little 233
Boss Dr. Beat 88 212
Boston Symphony Orchestra 231
bpm 211
breath 34
breath mark 53, 57, 107, 108
breathing
   3-stage breath 54
   breath mark 57
   exercises 56
   inhale 54
   NB 58
   no breath 58
   physiology 53
   too much air 58
   when to 57
breathing tube 53, 56
Brian Lynch 233
Brown, Clifford 22, 31, 235
bucket mute 179
bugle 186
busking 219, 226
buzz 32, 108
buzz instructions 33
buzz with mouthpiece 34
buzzing exercises 36
Buzz-Wow mute 180

C

C minor scale 114
C transposition 188
C transposition key 190
C trumpet 182
Cab Calloway 235
Canadian Brass 21
Capp, Al 49
Carnival 100
Caruso, Carmine 134
cases 216
   BAM Trekker Backpack Case 216
   Gator Lightweight Case 216
   Gig Backpack 217
   Reunion Blues Gig Bag 217
   The Torpedo Bag 216
   Wolfpack Quad Case 217
ceasura 164
cent 211
ceramic bugle 186
chamois cloth 156
changing notes 50, 86

Charles Mingus 211
Charles Schlueter Foundation, Inc. 231
Charlie Parker 235
Charlie Shavers 233
Chase 28
Chase, Bill 28
Cheatham, Doc 26
Chet Baker 233
Chiapanecas 109
Chick Webb 235
chops 31
Chops Builder 141
Chop-Sticks 134
chorus 217
Christian McBride 236
chromatic scale 38
circular breathing 239, 242
clam 50
Clark Terry 233, 235, 236
Clarke, Herbert L. 230
classical trumpet music
   solo trumpet
      André, Maurice 20
classical trumpet recordings 18
   brass ensemble
      American Brass Quintet 21
      Canadian Brass 21
   brass ensembles 21
   solo trumpet 20
      Andre, Maurice 20
      concertos 20
      contemporary 20
      Dokshizer, Timofei 20
      Hickman, David 20
classical trumpet soloists 232
Claudio Roditi 233
cleaning
   directions 155
   greasing slides 155
   monthly overhaul 154
   NO HOT WATER 155
   polishing 152
   reassembly 155
   routine cleaning 152
   stuck slides 154
   supplies 156
   tools 154
   valves 156
cleaning supplies 156
Cleveland Orchestra 189, 231
Clifford Brown 235
Coleman Hawkins 234
con sordino 175
concert pitch 118
Conte Candoli 233
cool jazz 235
corners 33
cornet 181
cornet masters 229

cornet players
  Arban, Jean Baptiste 230
  Armstrong, Louis 233
  Beiderbecke, Bix 234
  Clarke, Herbert L. 230
  James Shepherd 230
  Jean Baptiste Arban 230
  Joe "King" Oliver 233
  Marsalis, Wynton 230
  Shepherd, James 230
counting system 109
Craig Morris 230
crook 11, 13
cup mute 178

D

D transposition 193
dämpfers 175
Dave Douglas 233
Davis, Miles 23, 177, 223, 235
degree 143
degrees 145
derby mute 180
dexterity 49
diaphragm 53, 54
didgeridoo 186, 239
didj 244
difference tone 124
distortion 218
Dizzy Gillespie 234, 235, 236
Django Reinhardt 115
Doc Cheatham 235
Doc Severinsen 233
doit 161, 168
Don Cherry 233
double high C 129
double tonguing 95, 96
double-pedal tones 127
Douglas, Dave 29
duets 111
  recordings 87
dung 12

E

E transposition 194
Earth, Wind, and Fire 28
Eb Transposition 190
Eb/D trumpet 183
effects pedal 211
effects pedals 217
eighth note 93, 96, 109
Eldridge, Roy 234, 235
electronic effects 217
  chorus 217
  distortion 218
  flange 218
  phrase sampler 218
  reverb 217
  wah-wah pedal 218
Ella Fitzgerald 234
Ellis, Don 15, 29

embouchure 135
Embouchure Enhancement 141
embouchure muscles 31
Emerson, Ralph Waldo 43
endurance
  breath 148
  embouchure set 149
  exercise 145, 146, 149
  extending 148
  long tones 144
  resting 143
  schedule 144
  set 148
enharmonic notes 120
Enja 236
Eric Lewis 236
Eric Reed 236
euphonium 185
exercise
  mouthpiece buzz 38
exercises
  alternate fingering 165
  breathing 56
  buzzing 36
  double and triple tonguing 99
  double tonguing 96, 97
  eighth note 110
  embouchure set 149
  endurance 145, 146
  finger speed 51
  lip buzz 36
  lip failure 136
  lip slur 102, 103, 105
  pedal tones 126
  pencil 133
  pianissimo for range 138
  range 132
  tonguing 93, 94
  vibrato 163, 164
exericses
  chromatic scal buzz 38

F

F Transposition 192
fall 169
Fate Marable 233
Fats Navarro 235
Ferguson, Maynard 27, 236
fermata 79, 84
finger exercises 51
finger patterns 51–52
fingering chart 259
Firebird. 184
flange 218
flat 102, 107, 113
Flight of the Bumblebee 100
Flügelhorn 181
flügelhorn 182
Flumpet 182
flumpet 15
flutter tongue 170

foot tap 135
Frank Sinatra 231
Freddie Hubbard 233, 235
Freddie Keppard 233
French horn 185
Frere Jacques 112
fundamental 245
fundamental tone 241
fusion 235

G

garden hose trumpet 186
Gatsby mute 180
Gerard Schwarz 231
Gide, Andrew 161
Gilbert, W. S. 181
Gilbert, W.S. 181
Gillespie, Dizzy 223, 234
Glen Fischthal 230
glissando 161, 167
Go Tell Aunt Rhodie 108
Gonna Fly Now 236
grace note 172
Grand Pause 164
growl 170
Gunn, Russell 29

H

half note 81, 93, 96
half rest 81
half-valve 167
hand position 44
  left 44, 50
  right 44–45, 49
hand technique
  right 49
hand vibrato 162
Hargrove, Roy 27
Harmon mute 177, 218
harmonic series 13, 181
harmonics 244
Harry Connick Jr. 236
Harry Glantz 231
Harry James 233
Hello, Dolly 234
Helmholtz, Herman 121
heraldic trumpet 184
Herseth, Adolph "Bud" 230
high C 129
high range
  airstream 135
  Chop-Sticks 134
  exercises 132
  lip buzz 131
  lip failure 134
  lip failure exercise 136
  lip injury 130
  loose-lip flap 131
  pencil exercise 133
  pianissimo exercise 138
  pianissimo playing 136

progress 130
   special techniques 131
history of trumpet 12
horse whinny 169
Hot Cross Buns 110
Hot Fives 234
Hubbard, Freddie 25
Hume and Berg mutes 180
Hunt, Clyde 141
Huxley, Thomas Henry 129

I

Ingrid Jensen 236
International Women's Brass
 Conference 232
intonation 117
Irakere 28
Irons, Earl D. 106

J

James Carter 236
Jazz at Lincoln Center 236
Jazz Trumpet 21
   Big Band 27
   small combo 21
jazz trumpet
   solo trumpet 21
jazz trumpet masters 233
jazz trumpeters
   Louis Armstrong 233
Jazzology 115
Jensen, Ingrid 236
Jingle Bells 109
Johnny Hodges 234
Johnson, Keith 53
Johnson, Walt 141
Julliard School of Music 231
Jussli Bjoerling 231

K

kack 50
Kenny Dorham 233
keyboard info 83, 126
keyed bugle 14
keyed trumpet 11, 14
Knevitt 141
Korg MM-1 MetroGnome 212
Korg MM-2 212

L

lacquer 152
laquer 151
Learn How to Play Double High C in Ten
 Minutes 141
ledger line 79
ledger lines 80
Lee Morgan 233, 235
legato 91
leger lines 80

Lester Bowie 233
Lewis, Mel 27
Lightly Row 108
Lionel Hampton 236
lip slur 101
   ascending 104
   descending 102
   diagram 104
   exercises 102, 103, 105
   Irons, Earl D. 106
   large interval 105
   oral cavity 104
   tongue use 104
listening 17
listening tips 17
Little Jazz 234
long tones 48, 144
Louis Armstrong 233, 235
Louis Davidson 231
lungs 54
   diagram 54
   diaphragm 54

M

M. buccinator 32
MacArthur Park 236
Mack the Knife 234
Mahler
   Symphony V 19
major 114
Major pentatonic 148
Marsalis, Branford 170
Marsalis, Wynton 27, 100, 170, 230, 236
Marvin Stamm 233
Mary Had a Little Lamb 108
Maurice André 183
Maurice Andrè 231
Maynard Ferguson 184, 231, 233, 236
McClure, Barney 223
McLaughlin, Clint (Pops) 141
mellophone 185
metronome 49, 69, 211
   advice 50
mezzo forte (mf) 189
Michael Sachs 230
microphone
   adapters 215
   condenser 214
   cords 215
   dynamic 214
   stand 215
   Sure SM57 214
   Sure SM58 214
microphones 214
Miles Davis 235
minor 114
minor pentatonic 148
mit dämpfer 175
MM 211
modal jazz 235
Monarch Brass 232

Monette trumpets 14
Morgan, Lee 23, 165
Moussoursky 19
mouthpiece
   anatomy 40
   backbore 40
   cross-section 40
   cup 40
   information 40
   mouthpiece puller 43
   rim 40
   size comparison chart 42
   throat 40
   throat shoulder 40
   what to look for 41
mouthpiece brush 151, 152, 154
mouthpiece buzz 34
mouthpiece pressure 34
multi-track recorder
   Korg Pandora PXR4 216
muscles of the embouchure 31
Musical Calisthenics for Brass 134
mute 175
   insertion 176
   practice mute 176
   whisper mute 176
mute holder 180
mutes
   176
   bucket 179
   buzz-wow 180
   cork 177
   cup 178
   derby 180
   Gatsby mute 180
   Harmon 177
   holder 180
   plunger 178
   solotone 180
   straight 177
   wah-wah 177

N

natural 102, 107, 113
natural trumpet 11, 13, 186
NB 53
Neener Neener 111
Nicholas Payton 236
no breath (NB) 53, 58
Notes
   letter names 80
written music
   whole notes 81
   half 81
   quarter notes 81

O

ohne dämpfer 175
Oliver, Joe "King " 233
Oliver, Joe "King" 161

On the Sensations of Tone 121
open 79
open mic 187, 219
oral cavity 101, 104
oral cavity diagram 104
orchestral excerpts, recording 20
orchestral trumpet masters 230
order of sharps 191, 192
order or flats 191
ornament 161
ornaments 171
   alternate fingerings 165
   doit 168
   fall 169
   flutter tongue 170
   grace note 172
   growl 170
   horse whinny 169
   scoop 167
   trill 171
   turn 172
   vibrato 161
overtone series 13, 181, 242
overtone toot 239, 242
overtone toots 242

P

parameteric equalization 218
Paris Conservatory 232
Parker, Charlie 211, 235
partials 121
Paul Beniston 230
Payton, Nicholas 26
pedal tone 117, 125, 126, 129
pedal-pedal tone 127
pencil exercise 133
pendulum metronome 212
pentatonic scale 148
performance
   anxiety 220
   busking 226
   finding venues 226
   preparation 224
   stage craft 224
perseverance 143
Peter, Laurence, J. 151
phantom power 214
Philip Smith 230, 231
piano (p) 189
piccolo trumpet 183
piston valve 181
pitch bending 122
plunger 178, 218
pocket trumpet 183
polishing 152
posture 45
Practice
   beginning 63
   equipment 66
   how much to 62
   how to 66, 67

practice mute 176
pre-amp 217
pressure, mouthpiece 34
private teachers 62
Puente, Tito 28
Pulitzer Prize for Music 237
pulse 81

Q

quarter note 81, 93, 96
quarter rest 81
quarter-tone trumpet 15
Qwik-Time 212

R

ragging 233
range
   airstream 135
   Chop-Sticks 134
   exercises 132
   lip buzz 131
   lip failure 134
   lip failure exercise 136
   lip injury 130
   loose-lip flap 131
   pencil exercise 133
   pianissimo exercise 138
   pianissimo playing 136
   progress 130
   special techniques 131
recording devices
   215
   cassette recorder 215
   mini disc recorder 215
   Sony HI MD 215
recordings
   avant garde 28
      Davis, Miles 29
      Douglas, Dave 29
      Ellis, Don 29
   classical trumpet 18
      1812 Overture 19
      Also Sprach Zarathustra 19
      Ein Heldenleben 19
      orchestral excerpts 20
      Strauss 19
      Tchaik Sym. IV 19
      Tchaikovsky 19
      Tchaikovsky Capriccio Italien 19
   jazz trumpet 21
      Baker, Chet 25
      big band 27
      Brown, Clifford 22
      Cheatham, Doc 26
      Davis, Miles 23
      Ferfuson, Maynard 27
      Hargrove, Roy 27
      Hubbard, Freddie 25
      Louis Armstrong 21
      Marsalis, Wynton 27
      Morgan, Lee 23

      Payton, Nicholas 26
      Severinsen, Doc 27
      solo 21
   latin jazz trumpet 28
      Irakere 28
      Puente, Tito 28
      Sandoval, Arturo 28
   orchestral trumpet 18
   other trumpet music 28
   rock and roll trumpet 28
      Blood, Sweat and Tears 28
      Earth, Wind, and Fire 28
Reiner, Fritz 19
repeat sign 107
rest 81
reverb 217
Rhein horn 186
Ride of the Valkyries 192
Ride of the Valkyries 189
Rimsky-Korsakov 100
Roach, Max 22, 31
Roddy 141
Rodzinski 231
rotary valve 181
rotary valve trumpet 183
round 107, 111
Roy Eldridge 235
Roy Hargrove 233, 236
Ryan Kisor 233

S

Sail the 7 C's
   An Easier Way to Play Trumpet 141
Saint Louis Symphony Orchestra 232
Sandoval, Arturo 28
sans sourdine 175
Sarah Vaughan 236
Scheherezade 100
Schlueter, Charles 231
scoop 161, 167
senza sordino 175
set 129, 135, 143, 148
Severinsen, Doc 27
sharp 102, 107
Shepherd, James 230
Shew horn 15
Shew, Bobby 15
Sidewinder, The 165
sixteenth note 51
sixteenth notes 49
Skip to My Lou 111
Skwirl ii
Slaughter, Susan 232
Sleigh Ride 161
Sleigh Ride 169
slide 161
   stuck 154
slide grease 151, 157
slur 91
Smiley, Jeff 141
Smith, Phillip (principal tpt, NY phil.) 20

snake 151, 154, 157
solotone mute 180
Solti, George 19
Sonny Rollins 236
soprano trombone 185
sordino 175
Sound The Trumpet
  Exercises and Practice Routines 141
Sousa, John Philip 230
Sousaphone 185
space 80
spit valve 152
St. Louis Blues 234
staccato 91
staff 79, 80
staff lines 80
stage craft 224
staves 80
stem 177
stepwise 79, 86
Steven Hendrickson 230
Stokowski 231
straight mute 177
Stravinsky 231
stuck slide 154
Superbone 181, 185
Sweets Edison 236
Symphony IV (Tchaik) 100
Szell 231
Szell, George 189

T

Taktell mini 212
Tanglewood Music Center 231
Tchaikovsky
  1812 Overture 19
  Capriccio Italien 19
  Symphony IV 19
Tchaikovsky, P. 100
Terry, Clark 235
The Balanced Embouchure 141
The Muppet Show 234
The Truth About How to Play Double High C
On Trumpet 141
There is No Such Thing as a Wrong Note
  I was only trying something 223
Thich Nhat Han 60
third valve slide 120, 154
Tom Harrell 233
tonguing
  air stream use 92
  basic tonguing 91
  double 95
  exercise 94
  high notes 94
  jaw movement 92
  syllables 92
  tone quality 95
  tongue diagram 92
  triple 95
  warm-ups 93

track 211
tracks 216
transpose 186, 187
transposing
  Ab transposition 194
  Ab transposition key 194
  C transposition 188
  D transposition 193
  D transposition key 193
  E transposition 194
  E transposition key 195
  Eb 190
  Eb transposition key 191
  F transposition 192
treble clef 79
trill 48, 161, 165, 171
triple tonguing 95, 97
    97
  exercises 98
  listening examples 100
  technique 97
tritone 194
trumpet players
  Davis, Miles 223
  Gillespie, Dizzy 223
  Louis Armstrong 219
  Marsalis, Wynton 170
  Morgan, Lee 165
trumpet, decorated 15
trumpet, from a garden hose 15
trumpet, quarter-tone 15
trumpet, with bull kelp 15
trumpeters, classical
  Adolph "Bud" Herseth 230
  Charles Schlueter 231
  Craig Morris 230
  Glen Fischthal 230
  Michael Sach 230
  Paul Beniston 230
  Philip Smith 230
  Roger Voison 231
  Steven Hendrickson 230
  Susan Slaughter 232
  William Vacchiano 231
trumpeters, classical soloists
  Maurice André 232
trumpeters, jazz
  Al Hirt 233
  Art Farmer 233
  Bix Beiderbecke 234
  Blue Mitchell 233
  Bobby Hackett 233
  Booker Little 233
  Brian Lynch 233
  Buddy Bolden 233
  Charlie Shavers 233
  Chet Baker 233
  Clark Terry 233
  Claudio Roditi 233
  Clifford Brown 235
  Conte Candoli 233
  Dave Douglas 233

Dizzy Gillespie 234
Doc Cheatham 235
Doc Severinsen 233
Don Cherry 233
Fats Navarro 235
Freddie Hubbard 233
Harry James 233
Ingrid Jensen 236
Joe "King" Oliver 233
Kenny Dorham 233
Lee Morgan 233
Lester Bowie 233
Maynard Ferguson 236
Miles Davis 235
Nicholas Payton 236
Roy Hargrove 233
Roy, Eldridge 234
Ryan Kisor 233
Tom Harrell 233
Woody Shaw 233
Wynton Marsalis 236
trumpets
  bugle 186
  C trumpet 182
  ceramic bugle 186
  cornet 181
  didgeridoo 186
  Eb/D trumpet 183
  Firebird 185
  flügelhorn 182
  Flumpet 182
  garden hose trumpet 186
  heraldic trumpets 184
  natural trumpets 186
  piccolo trumpet 183
  pocket trumpet 183
  Rhein horn 186
  rotary valve 183
tuba 185
tuner 70
tuner use 118
tuners 213
  Arion UM-70 213
  Boss TU-80 213
  Korg CA-30 213
  Korg MT 9000 213
  V-SAM 213
tuning 117
  alternate fingerings 122
  basics 117
  by ear 122
  difference tone 124
  electronic tuners 118
  flat notes 121
  high pitches 119
  left hand use 119
  low pitches 119
  out of tune notes 120
  sharp notes 120
  slide use 120
  trigger 119, 121
  tuning slide 117, 118

turn 172
Twinkle, Twinkle, Little Star 109

U
upbeat 107, 109

V
Vacchiano, William 231
valve
  insertion 156
valve cap 154
valve casing 151
valve casing brush 154
valve oil 151, 156
valve, invention of 14
valves
  changing notes 50
  oiling 152
  stuck valve 153
Velimirovic, Nicholai 229
vibrato 161
  airstream 162
  exercise 163
  hand 162
Virginia Mayhew 236
vocalizations 245
Voisin, Roger 231

W
Wagner, Richard 189
wah wah pedal 218
warm-up 68
Weidinger, Anton 14
What a Wonderful World 234
whinny 169
whisper mute 176
whole note 81, 93
whole rest 81
Woody Shaw 233, 235
Wright, Steven 175
written music
  history of 79
Wynton Marsalis 231, 236

X
XLR 211, 215

Y
Yamaha Clickstation 212
Yidaki 239

Trumpet Fingering Chart

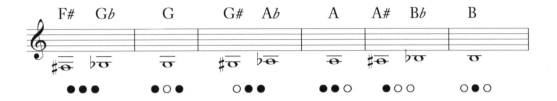

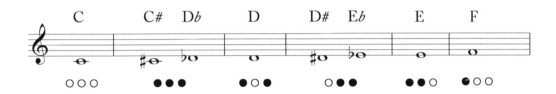

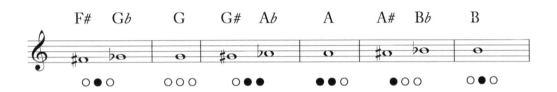

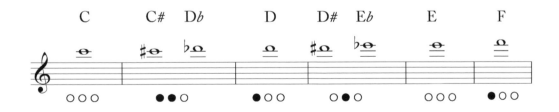

Alternate Fingering Chart

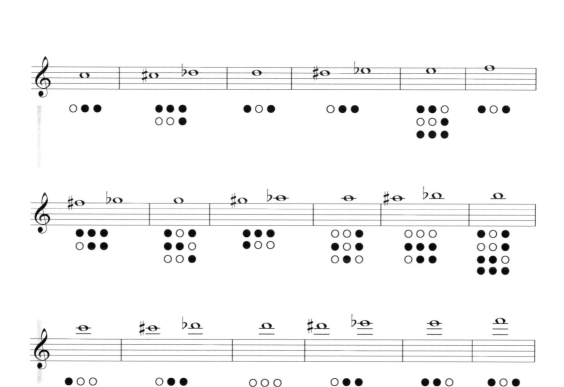

Cycle of Fourths/Fifths (Major)

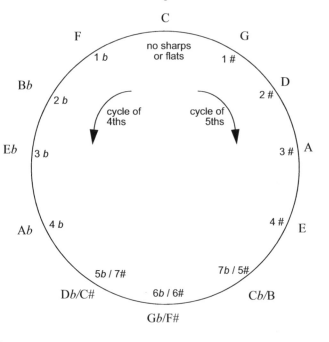

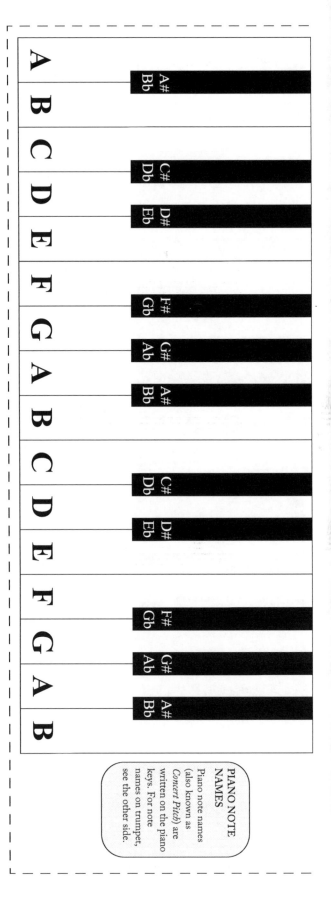

Important Terms

flat (b): lowers notes a half step.

sharp (#): raises notes a half step.

natural (♮): cancels the effect of a sharp or flat.

order of flats: BEADGCF

order of sharps: FCGDAEB

half step: the smallest interval in Western music. Two adjacent keys on a piano. Two adjacent frets on the same string for guitar.

whole step: two half steps.

natural half step: half steps without the use of accidentals. Occurs from E-F and B-C.

Note Lengths: 4/4

sixteenth note ♬ = 1/4 beat

eighth note ♪ = 1/2 beat

dotted eighth note ♪. = 3/4 beat

quarter note ♩ = 1 beat

dotted quarter note ♩. = 1 1/2 beats

half note ♩ = 2 beats

dotted half note ♩. = 3 beats

whole note 𝅝 = 4 beats

Transpositions

Concert Pitch or Key Signature	Trumpet Pitch or Key Signature	Concert Pitch or Key Signature	Trumpet Pitch or Key Signature
A	B	E♭/D#	F
B♭/A#	C	E	G♭/F#
B	D♭/C#	F	G
C	D	G♭/F#	G#/A♭
D♭/C#	E♭/D#	G	A
D	E	A♭/G#	B♭/A#

Note Lengths: 2/2

sixteenth note ♬ = 1/8 beat

eighth note ♪ = 1/4 beat

dotted eighth note ♪. = 3/8 beat

quarter note ♩ = 1/2 beat

dotted quarter note ♩. = 3/4 beats

half note ♩ = 1 beat

dotted half note ♩. = 1 1/2 beats

whole note 𝅝 = 2 beats

Tempi

Largo: mm = 40-60

Larghetto: mm = 60-66

Adagio: mm = 66-76

Andante: mm = 76-108

Moderato: mm = 108-12

Allegro: mm = 120-168

Presto: mm = 168-200

Prestissimo: mm = 200-2

Made in the USA
Lexington, KY
21 December 2013